ORGANIZATIONAL BEHAVIOUR AND PERFORMANCE
AN OPEN SYSTEMS APPROACH TO CHANGE

ALLAN WARMINGTON
TOM LUPTON
and
CECILY GRIBBIN

First published 1977 by
THE MACMILLAN PRESS LTD
London and Basingstoke
Associated companies in New York
Dublin Melbourne Johannesburg and Madras

ISBN 0 333 19917 0

Printed in Great Britain by
REDWOOD BURN LTD
Trowbridge and Esher

Contents

Preface

This book is the first major published outcome of five years of close collaboration between the authors and some members of a large manufacturing company. During this period much detailed research has been done in the firm, and the two groups have jointly worked out ways of making changes in the organisation and implementing them. We have learned much from each other that we would not otherwise have learned.

The task given to the team of managers was to make significant changes in the company. Our prime concern was to help define what kind of changes would be appropriate and how they might best be promoted. Equally important to both groups was the potentiality of using the programme of change as a vehicle for improving our general understanding of organisational processes.

This is a first report on these experiences. In it we explore the implications of the approach adopted towards change, and of the framework of analysis we have developed. At the end of the book we touch on an unresolved question: whether effectives changes can in fact be initiated from within an organisation by these methods.

We are particularly struck by three things about patterns of behaviour in large industrial organisations: the complexity of organisational processes; the frequent lack of appreciation of this complexity, both among those working in positions of formal responsibility in the organisation and among some of those who advise on or write about organisations; and the effect of controls and other formal elements in narrowing perspectives and discouraging people in responsible positions from taking account of many factors which are relevant to their problems. The three case studies we present in part II illustrate this clearly. Complexity has become a major and obtrusive theme of the book which in fact reflects much of this in its own structure. The complex nature of action research, the interplay of the various objectives we have for writing this book, and the complexity of organisational processes, have all affected the structure and style of the book. We make no excuse for this. In our view, to oversimplify the nature of organisational processes and to understate the difficulties of defining appropriate changes and making them effective, is to compound the felony of lack of understanding and narrowing of perspectives.

The very considerable body of literature on organisational change follows three main lines: (a) descriptions by researchers or consultants of successful (or very occasionally unsuccessful) cases of planned organisational change, often including discussions of their own role in the process;

(b) more or less prescriptive works by practitioners (albeit frequently from an academic base) written largely for other practitioners or for managers, and suggesting why change is needed, how best to establish and run change programmes of a particular conception, and how to achieve success in them; and (c) books which attempt to explain in theoretical terms the processes involved in organisational change or to account for the problems met when using certain methods of intervention.

Our interest in setting out to write this particular book was very much related to understanding and explanation of organisational behaviour under conditions of change. However, we have found it impossible to confine the book to analysis and description of theoretical developments. To put forward a theory of change (given that we chose to take a contingency approach to the study of organisations) means that we must use actual cases as the basis of exposition, as of research. Action-based research in 'real-world' situations means that to obtain access to our laboratory and to undertake experiments in it, we must have some procedures to offer: potentially successful change strategies, in the implementation of which we are able to observe the organisation in action. On the other hand, we cannot describe events in the organisation in abstraction from the effects of our own active role, its influence, purpose and justification.

So the methods, the purposes and the analytical framework for this research were integrated, and it would be invalid to treat any of them in isolation from the others or from the experiences and the lessons that have emerged in the course of the research.

The book is divided into five main parts. In part I we briefly outline the characteristics of the change programme as it was originally devised, and describe the elements of the approach we advocated. We then go on to examine in some depth the implications of this approach for us as individual researchers and the many implications about organisational behaviour that are involved in our use of the open socio-technical systems model as our main framework for analysis. Part II is devoted mainly to three rich and complex cases from the programme that illustrate clearly the approach, together with a brief introduction and comparison of the cases. Then in part III we use the framework to develop some structuring ideas about the nature of organisational processes, discuss the problem of defining organisational effectiveness, formulate some general rules for devising a strategy for departmental change, and discuss the consequences of our approach for evaluating and monitoring change. The ideas of part III are then put to some practical use in devising strategies for improvement in the three departments analysed in part II.

Part V comprises a concluding chapter in which the actual experiences are related and compared to the strategies suggested for each of the three cases. Some tentative conclusions are then drawn about the implications for methods of intervention, and some ideas introduced about the processes of planned organisational change.

PART I

Theme and Concepts

1 The Context of the Book: The Change Programme

This book has its origins and its stimulus in the authors' involvement in a programme of change that was being implemented in the early 'seventies' in a large industrial organisation in the United Kingdom. Yet it is not a book specifically about the change programme. Much less is it an analysis of the processes through which planned organisational change is likely to pass. Any large and effective organisational change programme has a complex pattern of existence and necessarily includes many messy and disorganised elements, and experiences many unpredictable turns and twists. It involves the use of techniques of persuasion, the promotion of attitude changes, political manœuvring and manipulation of the power structure, in order to get movement going, or to sustain it once started. It is accompanied by a constant search for legitimacy and by controversies among those involved in it about the criteria for effectiveness and about means of promoting it.

Yet the change programme must also incorporate some methods of analysis and some strategies must be evolved for it in relation to the defined goals of change. It must probably incorporate a monitoring procedure so that progress may be assessed. If these elements were absent, then it would be likely to lose any sense of direction. Activities on the programme would be reduced to processes of manœuvring, experimentation or confrontation, and its relation to any defined end might become rather obscure. The interventions by change agents into departmental activities or into methods of decision-making, or the group activities undertaken among middle managers, or the various forms of training for managerial groups, would be being held mainly for the sake of keeping some impetus going, giving some impression of effective action and perhaps maintaining the image of the change team as an active and enthusiastic group of people. Any effective attempt to change structures or decision-making processes, or to influence relationships between people, must be based on some clear idea of the purposes of change, and be related to performance criteria for the organisation. The consequences of particular interventions, or of particular changes in structure or relationships, must have been analysed in advance, and the means necessary to bring the changes about must have been discussed and agreed on.

Our main purpose in the book is therefore to describe and illustrate a method of detailed analysis of this kind, developed in the course of the programme of change, and to describe some techniques and tools developed from it in cooperation between university researchers and managers from the organisation—techniques used by management teams in improving departmental performance. We shall be concerned to demonstrate their theoretical validity, as well as to show their practical application, and we shall deal with them in the context of the overall change programme, while recognising all the time that they constitute only one aspect of the programme.

The central theme, then, is a particular approach to the understanding of organisational behaviour at the 'work face', and an illustration of this approach in the context of an ongoing change programme, together with some practical outcomes. This chapter briefly outlines the origins and theoretical ideas used when the programme was established. We shall leave to a subsequent work a description and critical assessment of the institution and development of the programme itself, the many complex processes through which it has gone, and how these are related to the problem of effecting planned organisational change. Here we are concerned mainly to put into context some of the analytical methods used on the programme.

THE CHANGE PROGRAMME

In 1969, the company concerned—a large and eminently successful one—was seeking to establish an internal inquiry into ways of improving its performance through better utilisation of personal talents and skills, more appropriate reward systems, and new personnel practices. Some internal strains were recognised. There had been a number of major changes in technology and in labour market conditions, hitherto unaccompanied by any changes in personnel management techniques or general management practice. A complex wage structure of long standing, based on widespread application of time-studied incentive schemes of various kinds, was becoming ever more difficult to operate and control. A job-evaluated salary grading scheme was creating some problems. Some parts of the organisation were experiencing serious difficulties in recruiting and retaining new employees, and people at senior levels had perceived a marked falling off in 'loyalty' and commitment among members of the organisation of all grades, reflected in lower stability, less acceptance of conditions of employment, more articulate criticism of overall company policies and philosophy, demands by various groups of employees (from operatives to senior staff and junior managers) for greater representation when decisions were made about their own conditions.

Changes were thus seen to be needed, particularly in reward systems and in the way the talents and skills of people were used in the organisation. Committees had already been set up to examine some aspects of the problem as it was then perceived, and after consultation between some managers closely involved in these committees, contacts were made with the academic world for advice on what more might be done. As a result of this activity, Tom Lupton was approached, and after discussion was asked if he would become involved. Further discussions took place during 1969, at the end of which the Board agreed to allow a programme of organisational improvement to be initiated which would incorporate a number of Lupton's suggestions. The final programme was thus considerably wider in scope than had originally been envisaged. Its aim was defined (in terms influenced by economic and political events of the late 'sixties') as to increase the productivity of [the company] in all its activities in order to achieve the most economical utilisation of its resources to enable it to improve its competitive position, and to use the benefits achieved for the good of the company, its employees and the consumer. Amplification made it clear that steps towards the overall aim were to include greater understanding of the needs of the company, its technology, its customers and its competitive environment, better use of the experience, knowledge and skill of employees, establishment of a fairer wage and salary structure, the encouragement of relationships, attitudes and procedures favourable to change, and development of greater trust.

As the programme was set out and conceptualised in its early days, it already had many facets. Its general structure and philosophy can be summarised as an attempt to provide mechanisms adequate to fulfil four needs

(1) *As a mechanism for change*, the establishment of a full-time team of company managers, coming from a number of disciplines, and drawn from areas such as production, engineering, management services, personnel and marketing, and working with one or two university research fellows, and with a chief consultant based at the university.

(2) *As a basis for intervention*, an assumption that improvement in performance could only take place if a programme of change were founded on the specific needs of particular operating areas, and if the programme managed to involve the people working in the area who best knew its problems.

(3) *As a general framework for diagnosis*, an open systems approach to organisational problems which would require an adequate framework to be developed in order to look at an area of the company in detail and examine it in relation to its 'product' markets (however defined), its 'resource' markets, its technology, organisational characteristics, control mechanisms, and social setting. The framework would, it was hoped, incorporate socio-technical concepts and techniques in investigating and as aids to understanding events and behaviour.

(4) *As a means of future development*, an assumption that if the process of investigation, strategy formulation and implementation of change in defined operating areas was successful, various mechanisms could be called into play (by a process we shall explain, and which we termed 'cell

division') to effect the spread of the process over wider and wider areas of the company.

Thus the programme incorporated from the start a full-time team of company managers, who were to become specialists in methods of investigation, analysis of facts in the light of an unfamiliar systems framework, bringing the facts together into a model of the area concerned and later acting as change agents by involving others concerned in understanding the model and introducing improvements. It was also to include part-time groups of managers from individual works and office situations, who would work together in project teams with one or more of the full-time team members and become involved in specific investigations and experiments in implementation. It included academic consultant-researchers, whose role was to put forward to the company and to the full-time change-promoting team some principles and ideas for the programme and some of the concepts they thought should be taken into account if effective change was to be produced; to work out with the team the methods of investigation, analysis, strategy formulation and implementation, which would be needed if the conceptual framework were to be adopted consistently; and informally to monitor the whole process of organisational change and its characteristics, and to learn from this in such a way that concepts could be advanced and methods could be adapted as circumstances changed and as greater understanding became available.

COOPERATION BETWEEN MANAGERS AND RESEARCHERS

We are concerned here with the formal structure and expected roles of participants. The formulation of strategies and tactics for the programme was to be (at least in the early stages while the programme was being established and joint learning was taking place) a cooperative effort between managers and researchers. In practice, as we have already suggested, the whole process of joint involvement and participation in a change programme of this kind is much more complex than any formal statement implies, or than could have been seen at the outset. Roles were 'emergent', and the development both of roles and of role expectations depended a great deal on how they were developed by their occupants.[1] To live through and participate in this development was a fascinating and frequently disturbing experience for all concerned, and it will be necessary in another work to expand on the interactions which occurred between the different parties and between the planned programme of change itself and the strategies and tactics actually adopted. Here we shall only mention one broad aspect of role specialisation which provides a context for this book.

One important and effective role of the academics is continually to relate the methods of the programme to the theoretical and methodological needs which they believe to be essential for success, given the developing understanding of the change process as it has emerged on the programme. The members of the management team on the other hand have an enormous fund of knowledge about the technology and market environment and about company culture and behaviour, the power structure and political system in the company hierarchy, and how these can best be manipulated in order to maintain legitimacy within the company for the activities of the change programme in the short and medium terms. A point which seems to have been confirmed by experience is that if either of these two perspectives is neglected, and either party fails to monitor its own area of special knowledge, then the effectiveness of the change process is greatly reduced. If the academic specialists cease to be effective in convincing the management team of the theoretical and methodological needs, the tendency could be for the cultural and political constraints on the operation of the programme (the search for legitimacy and acceptability) to be overemphasised, and for these to a large extent to dictate the programme's activities to the detriment of effective change. If on the other hand, the management team failed to promote strongly the 'credibility' needs of the team within the existing culture, the wherewithal to apply the new methods could be withheld by those with authority or power in the company, and there would be no opportunity to use them effectively. Both must play their proper part, but in doing so the programme became characterised by (to say the least) a certain tension, and only slowly did the importance of role specialisation and the legitimacy of the parts being played by each of the participants become accepted and made effective in practice.

THE PROGRAMME AS A PROJECT IN ACTION RESEARCH

This book is written by, and so largely from the point of view of, the university-based researcher-consultants in the programme, and for them it has been (among many other things) a large project in action research. Now, the term 'action research' has been used in a number of contexts, and more recently the emphasis has been on involvement of the researcher in action, and his willingness to work within the value system of those with whom he is involved, who have themselves defined the frame of reference for the research. The research aspect of the process has been assumed to arise from the understanding that comes from involvement. Our definition would be rather different. For us, effective action research occurs where the researcher, having a definite theoretical framework and point of view about the problems into which he is researching, enters an organisation, not solely with the object of studying it, but fully aware that his presence in the organisation, the activities he undertakes, and the framework he is adopting for research will all influence the modes of behaviour which take place in the organisation; and therefore a research design must be chosen that takes full advantage of these influences. The research methodology takes carefully into account the dynamics of the research process. It is not confined to observation, experimentation and generalisation of under-standing, but may include an explicit and conscious effort, in collaboration with members of the organisation, towards influencing behaviour and activities in the organisation being studied. Thus the researcher is attempting to use the changes his presence creates, or that he is consciously involved in, as means of observing the dynamics of organisational change. He can take advantage of those dynamics and use them as means of increasing understanding. Action research on this definition (so long as it can be made effective) is obviously suited to studying the processes of change and the dynamics of organisational behaviour.[2]

However, real problems arise from this close involvement with members of an organisation, and with a programme devised mainly by members of the organisation in accordance with their perception of organisational needs. For example, the defined objectives of the programme may appear clear and unambiguous at the beginning, and generally acceptable to the researcher, yet when the change team begins to analyse a particular situation it may well discover some objectives to be in conflict with others, or the needs of that situation to be in conflict with the formal statement of objectives. The researcher from outside the organisation then has to be concerned with values, both for himself and for organisational members, if he is to be usefully involved in the situation. Choices have to be made and judgments formed about which ends should be given precedence, and what compromises between objectives are acceptable.[3] This kind of difficulty, which is less evident for the action researcher who has decided not to question the value systems of those he is working among, is discussed in more detail in chapter 2. To some extent it is the combination of an open systems framework of analysis for examining change, with the decision to become openly involved in the implementation of change, that has made this problem particularly evident to these authors.

There are of course some similarities—in method and superficially in some results—between action research as we define it here, and con-sultancy; but the differences are great. One object of research is to discover new, generalisable truths about, in this case, the nature of organisational change. It is not merely to improve the organisation in question, though attempts at 'improvement' may be a most important, and, indeed essential step in the research process. Action research so defined also takes a step forward into the management process which consultants take but rarely. As well as observing, advising and hopefully understanding the motives and the problems of those with whom they are working, the researchers become closely involved in the formulation of the problems which are jointly worked out with management, take some responsibility with them for the process of implementation and the way it is monitored, and finally for the adaptations which are made to the proposals as a result of learning during the implementation process; for it is from this last step that the most understanding comes.

The researchers' role therefore had the characteristics of: observation; advice on methods of investigation, analysis and model building; assistance with these processes; consequent conscious interference with existing organisational functions; involvement with and shared responsibility with those who subsequently make decisions on change and implement it; monitoring of the changes; a process of joint learning as a result of the experiences gained during implementation; and attempts to generalise from this learning.

THE APPROACH TO CHANGE

In the remainder of this chapter we shall outline the nature of our approach to organisational analysis and summarise our theoretical position. In chapter 2 we shall examine this position more critically and make some claims for its validity in the context of recent advances in organisation theory. By putting the approach into context it may be possible to examine both its provenance and the validity of the techniques which have arisen from it, and which are described in parts II, III and IV.

In fact, the framework in which the research design was initiated was largely eclectic. It used a number of related concepts drawn from a range of sources, but used in such a way as to constitute a consistent whole: to provide the elements of a fairly sophisticated model which incorporates both a philosophical and a methodological approach to organisational problems. This we claim is of considerable practical potential.

Let us, then, outline the way we have approached the problems. *Organisational change* is not a simple concept. Change is rarely needed for its own sake and rarely takes place in the absence of some compelling need. A change in structure or relationships may occur as a consequence of people within the organisation recognising a changing situation, either externally—a change in product or resource markets, a change in the technology being employed by competitors, etc.—or internally—the existence of high levels of stress or perceived inefficiencies, etc; or attempts may be made by policy makers to induce some changes, with the idea that change will lead to improved performance, or is necessary because of expected external developments the organisation will have to cope with, or that it is expected by some organisational participants.

Change can take the form of an apparently straightforward introduction of a new product, process or production technique, accompanied by the unplanned adaptations which follow from any more or less radical innovation; or it can be intended as a carefully planned and internally stimulated change in structure, technical arrangements or management style introduced for reasons which may not be directly or immediately related to external changes or labour market or competitive conditions. It can be brought about as a consequence of legislation affecting the organisation—for example, to do with safety, pollution control, labour legislation or economic contingencies. It can result from wide-ranging changes in economic and market conditions such as were experienced by some industries with British adherence to the Treaty of Rome, or with fluctuating world commodity prices or with a revision of world tariff rates.

Any of these forms of change has its own distinctive features. But all change tends to have in common the fact that it brings in its train many interrelated consequences, not all of which are as a rule foreseen, and some of which probably cannot easily be predicted even after sophisticated analysis.

Moreover, the reactions which occur in an organisation under conditions likely to stimulate change will be distinctive to that organisation. The behaviour which results will depend on structural features of the organisation, value systems of people within it, the way control systems are operated, and many other factors. If an organisation has had a history of stability and environmental benignity, it is probable that these features will have been developed in such a way as to produce some lack of sensitivity to environmental change, and to establish change-resistant mechanisms by which success is sustained in stable conditions: mechanisms which are effective in preventing small oscillations, or newly fashionable techniques and ideas, or changes in senior personnel, from diverting energies away from the tasks which lead to success, or 'pushing the organisation off course'. Experience of a changing or uncertain environment, on the other hand, is more likely to have resulted in modes of relationship, organisational structures, functional specialisms and other mechanisms for detecting and fairly quickly adapting to change.

In the research being described, change was to be induced into a successful, technologically orientated company from within in order to help those in whose hands the decisions would lie to meet future challenges which they saw coming from society, from changing market conditions and from the effects of advancing technology. An attempt was to be made to deflect members of the organisation away from a predominantly technical orientation in decision-making, towards other habits of thought and action which took into account as a matter of course a whole range of organisational and social factors, market reactions and so on.

Thus while the programme was one of planned change in much the sense written about by Leavitt (1964), Bennis (1966), Beckhard (1969), Dalton (1970), Greiner (1967), and others,[4] it was change for a series of fairly well-defined purposes and it was an attempt to change an extensive but fairly well-defined range of decision criteria and structural characteristics in the organisation, rather than a concern with either improving personal and social skills for their own sake, or making specific technical innovations.

Contingency Approach

In broaching this idea of organisational change, we eschewed any overriding preconceptions about the effectiveness of given processes of change, or about the best way of inducing it. We had no package of techniques to effect improvements. We did however have one strong set of preconceptions. These were that circumstances, environmental conditions, past history and present modes of behaviour, the existing, rather complex sets of expectations about what was legitimate in that organisation, and many other characteristics, would have to be examined and their significance understood before changes could be induced. If this understanding were neglected, such changes as were made would be likely to produce adverse reactions either in the form of rejection by some important groups, or of serious unforeseen complications. The consequences of particular innovations would depend on circumstances and could only be predicted on the strength of an adequate analysis of the features of the organisation.

Lawrence and Lorsch (1969) were the first to use the term 'contingency theory' as a convenient way of expressing this empirical view of organisational behaviour and structure, although the usefulness and validity of the approach had been demonstrated earlier, in the work of writers like Burns and Stalker (1961), Woodward (1965) and others.[5] Further, Lawrence and Lorsch show that not only does each organisation have its own needs, but that large complex organisations tend to be composed of differentiated units (departments, divisions, functions) and that the needs of these units may well differ markedly one from the other. The twin concepts of differentiation and consequent integration, as developed by these writers, were useful ones to be borne in mind in our explanations of, and predictions about, events occurring as change affected the wider, complex, organisation. It is however the idea that any industrial organisation, or a part of an organisation, has its own requirements determined by characteristics such as its history, social and administrative structure, technology and market environment which is of most relevance to our own approach.

There are a number of possible implications of this contingency approach for theory and method. One possible consequence, suggested for example by Thompson (1967), is that the investigator hoping to advance our understanding of organisational needs and behaviour must look for patterned variations among the common elements found in organisations. Thus, according to Thompson, ' . . . the design, structure or behaviour of organisations will vary systematically with differences in technologies. If our understanding of organisations is to grow, we must compare organisations with different technologies; but to do so we must learn to categorise technologies with some precision'.[6] Again, ' . . . the design, structure and behaviour of organisations will reflect variations in task environments; . . . we must learn to make systematic comparisons of organisations in terms of their task environment'.[7]

This concept of patterned variations rests on a particular assumption: that a science which assumes that everything is particular or unique is not a science at all, while a theory which is unversalistic, in the sense of postulating universal principles of design or structure for organisations in general, does not adequately match with or explain or meet the needs of, real situations. Therefore, it is proposed, the scientific method appropriate to the analysis of organisation must be one which proceeds by classification, categorisation and taxonomy, grouping phenomena together in classes in much the same way as in botany and zoology. Only by devising and refining relevant taxonomies can progress be made. This idea also seems to be the basis of a considerable number of typologies devised during the 'sixties' and using a variety of factors (technology, size, structure, environment, mode of compliance, etc) as a basis.[8]

There is however another possible way of resolving the dilemma created by our recognition of the contingent nature of organisational problems, and it is this alternative approach which we have found most profitable. With it we decide to forego the taxonomy and to assume that every organisation, whether large and complex or small and partial, is in fact unique, but that we can bring to it a common framework of analysis, a consistent logic and a single agreed strategy of investigation. This analytical framework is universal (in a different sense from our use of the word in the last paragraph), but it is a framework which allows us to examine and to treat the organisation in all its uniqueness and complexity. In other words, we assume that what is common to organisations is the conceptual framework and the analytical approach which we ourselves bring to it and into which in a sense we constrain it, as a basis for our investigation of it; and that what is of greatest interest and practical importance is the unique set of interrelations that exist in that organisation or that small unit within the organisation.

There still remains the problem of choosing the analytical framework, and the main criterion for choice has to be one of relevance. The framework of analysis used should be one well suited to the examination of those relationships in the organisation that are most relevant to the overall purposes of the inquiry. Now, our objectives in this study are: to increase our understanding of, and to promote, organisational change, with a view to improving overall performance. Therefore we seek a framework of analysis that enables us to examine and where possible to explain, the influences on organisational behaviour as they exist at any moment in time, and the consequences brought about by changes in technological, social and environmental factors such as might result from managerial decisions, from changes in the product or labour markets, or from interventions we ourselves might make.

The framework of analysis we have chosen to use is one we call for the sake of convenience *the open socio-technical systems approach*.[9] In brief we may set out the main features of this approach as follows. There is an assumption that in examining organisational design and behaviour some variables are more likely to be useful in the analysis and in helping the investigator towards an understanding than others. The variables likely to be of value in studying change in an industrial organisation will include such things as characteristics of the product market, including the product mix; the state of competition and short-term and long-term trends in the market; characteristics of the internal and external labour markets and other resource markets; major elements of technology including the design and layout of plant, capacities of and flexibility of various pieces of equipment, and the designed skill levels, training procedures, work allocation procedures etc. which follow from the technical design; such elements of the organisational control system as management and supervisory structure, wage payment systems and other systems of reward, selection procedures and other aspects of personnel policy, production scheduling, purchasing and warehousing policies, engineering mainten-ance policies, and so on. They include those consequences of the above which are usually seen as partial indicators of performance like the make-up of unit costs, level of rejects or wastage rates, rates of breakdown or idle time, turnover and absence of employees, levels of output per man, actual earnings and actual manning levels; and some other variables like the level of motivation or morale, the expectations which exist about proper relationships between effort and reward, or about one's own or others' proper behaviour, the attitudes which exist towards the task, working hours, and various parts of the control system, and actual role behaviour as distinct from prescribed behaviour.

In any given industrial organisation and any given investigation, the approach suggests, these variables will have varying degrees of relevance to the needs of the investigator. The importance of any particular variable to the enquiry will depend on the characteristics of the organisation and the purpose of the research. However, we can say with some confidence that it is less likely that other variables (like the personalities of members of the Board of Directors, or the way financial accounts are presented, or the political views or affiliations of members of middle management, or the style of its public relations literature, or even its capital structure or the methods used to raise finance) will be found to be of crucial importance to an inquiry which has the kind of objectives we have outlined.

More important than the kind of variable to be examined and included in a systems model of the organisation is the philosophy of causation: that the variables will be related to each other in a rather complex, interactive, way, and that it is the relations between the variables which are of most significance in generating the processes through which the characteristics and the recurrent patterns of behaviour in a particular organisation emerge. The systems framework thus provides a method for investigating and for formulating explanations about, the organisation, in such a way that the relationships between the relevant variables *in that particular organisation* is assumed to be of most interest and value to the investigator and to provide the greatest understanding for him about the processes that occur in that organisation. What gives it its characteristic culture and mode of behaviour is the network of causal relationships particular to that organisation.

In chapter 3 we shall set out what were for us the essential elements of the open socio-technical systems approach, and in the four chapters of part III we show the way we have adapted it to these inquiries. The cases reported in chapters 4, 5 and 6 may throw further light on this rather complex explanation. There are in fact two allied, but at the same time distinct, elements in the approach as a whole: the open systems view of organisations and the concept of a productive organisation as a socio-technical system. Both are models of the same type in that they incorporate elements and relationships abstracted (as described above) from all the myriad possible elements of an organisation, on the assumption that these are the significant ones for the purpose of the investigation being attempted.

The foundations of the open systems approach have been described in some detail by a number of writers, and the application of this approach to industrial organisations has been made, perhaps most notably by Rice (1958, 1963) Emery and Trist (1960) Katz and Kahn (1966), and Miller and Rice (1967). The sophistication into which the open systems approach can go need not concern us at this stage. What we are particularly interested in is its logic, which enables us to look at almost any organisation as having a few essential characteristics. It may be seen as a transformation process, from which a number of dominant activities can be identified, some of them focal to the apparent primary purposes of the organisation and some secondary activities whose main function is to support and facilitate the focal activities.[10] The organisation can also be seen to interact with an environment from which it takes a number of inputs (which may be physical or in the form of services or energies, knowledge, skills or information) and to satisfy which it produces a number of outputs. The whole of the environment in which it exists will exert constraints on the activities of the organisation and will help to determine the criteria for survival, development and growth as an organisation.

The systems approach also enables us to regard the boundary which separates the organisation from its environment as being a somewhat arbitrary one, and one which we can define largely from the standpoint of convenience. We can also look at a subordinate part of the organisation, as we can the organisational entity, as a system in itself.

We have used this open systems approach as a philosophical paradigm—a tentative perspective—in our approach to organisational analysis and understanding and we have combined with it the various concepts associated with socio-technical systems. It is from the combination of the two that our more important tools have been developed. The socio-technical view suggests that the various focal and support activities which comprise the transformation process of an organisation, and the activities which mediate between the organisation and parts of its environment, are carried on by groups of people whose behaviour is constrained by, though not wholly determined by, the formal job requirements of the organisation as defined by its technology, control systems, management structure and other features. Patterns of behaviour

In the first and last chapters a number of references are made to a sequel, in which we shall hope to take forward many of the arguments touched on or hinted at in this final chapter. That sequel will perforce again have complexity as one of its principal themes.

We have many debts to acknowledge in the writing of this book: first and foremost to the members of the company concerned, and particularly those with whom we have collaborated most closely as members of the company change team (who must for the moment remain anonymous). We gladly acknowledge the help of members of individual project teams and all those who have in one way or another tolerated the activities of outsiders in the organisation, whether by agreeing to submit themselves to questioning, advice and cajoling, or by suffering interference with operational routines. The names appearing on the title-page happen to be those of university-based social scientists involved in the overall change programme. However, necessarily those mainly responsible for the progress of this programme were our colleagues from the central company change team; this book owes an enormous amount to the collaboration, controversy, conflict and constructive discussion that has been a remarkable and continuous feature of this whole programme. It is impossible for us to guess at the origin of many of the ideas and developments that we report, many of which have their origins in particular problems discussed and jointly solved in the course of the programme. Ample illustration of this will, we hope, appear in a subsequent work, in which the company-based participants will be able to contribute in full measure to an outline of many of the themes that arise in the course of investigation and implementation.

We must also acknowledge the amount this book owes to our colleagues at Manchester Business School, with many of whom particular ideas and difficulties have been discussed from time to time. Names which appear on the title page of a work like this are to some extent arbitrary, and we must acknowledge the contribution of Alan Gillespie, who was directly involved in the programme for several periods, who made a considerable contribution to the original Finishing Shop Report, and whose keen-edged criticisms were crucial in formulating some of the ideas introduced in part III. The pervasive influence of Dan Gowler's thinking, both directly through discussion and indirectly through his writings will, we hope, be obvious to readers, particularly in the three case studies.

The transformation of a series of illegible and inaudible drafts into beautifully clear typescripts has been effected successively by Mrs Joyce Young, and by Mrs Muriel Wood and the staff of the Central Secretarial Services of MBS.

For all the shortcomings of this book, and for the personal orientations and slants put on to it, the authors of course take full responsibility.

Manchester 1976   ALLAN WARMINGTON
                                                     TOM LUPTON
                                                     CECILY GRIBBIN

in the organisation are, it is assumed, influenced by and to some extent constrained by a highly complex series of interactions between groups of people, and between people on one hand and designed features of the organisation on the other, and it is largely these complex interactions, the attitudes, values and conflicts they generate and the effects of these which define the uniqueness of a particular organisation.[11] The techniques of socio-technical analysis, which we have to some extent developed in the course of this investigation, are important elements in our common framework, and examples of their application are given in part II.

THE APPLICATION OF THE OPEN SOCIOTECHNICAL SYSTEMS APPROACH

As it stands, the open socio-technical systems approach has a number of implications. Its main advantage is that it gives the investigator an insight into the complexities of the organisational relationships in which he is interested. But in essence it is a static form of analysis. It provides an instantaneous picture, a model of those relationships as they exist in a more or less stable situation or at a given point in a changing situation. The historical processes which have helped to determine the relationships may have been considered, and may be important elements in the model, but the effects of any rapid changes now taking place, or likely to occur in the immediate future, cannot easily be dealt with. How these changes will be perceived by members of the organisation, what meanings will be given to them and therefore how they will change existing values and modes of behaviour are all problematic.[12]

However, because of its flexibility and also because of its relative absence of bias as between different strata of authority or power groupings, the open socio-technical approach provides a framework which we consider more adequate than other developed approaches to organisational analysis and more adequate also for advancing our understanding of the dynamic processes—understanding organisations in action.

We have in the course of this change programme been able to develop the open socio-technical framework so as to analyse and predict how change would be likely to affect behaviour and the effects it would have on performance, and in parts III and IV we examine some of these developments. Firstly we discuss the general nature of organisations as seen in open socio-technical systems terms; that is, we look closely at the general structure which we are imposing upon the unique organisation by our universal framework of analysis. Secondly we suggest a means of using this structure, and the model of the organisation in question which is derived from it (using the word 'model' in the sense outlined earlier but applied to the particular circumstances of particular organisations) as a basis from which to plan a sequence of changes, predict the consequences of these changes and monitor the actual consequences against the predictions so as both to evaluate success and to test and verify the original model.

It is to this second development that we attach more importance. We believe it is possible to plan a series of moves in a defined industrial organisation or a subunit of an organisation, taking into account the needs of, and the nature of, the whole complex system, and moving it as a whole towards an improved situation, while avoiding many of the unforeseen difficulties and reactions from within the system which so often interfere with the success of management-initiated innovations. To do this successfully one must engage in processes of model building, identification of the criteria for assessing improvement, formulation of a strategy based on some socio-technical and systems principles, step-by-step moves towards implementation of the strategy, and continuous monitoring of the system's reactions to change, so as to verify the model, test the predictions and modify both the model and the later steps in the strategy when some predictions are not borne out. Part III is largely devoted to a description of these ideas about implementation strategy, and the application of them to three separate cases is discussed in part IV.

THE RELATION BETWEEN THE INVESTIGATING PROCEDURES AND ORGANISATIONAL CHANGE

It will be clear that socio-technical analysis and the developments in procedure arising from it are not by any means the whole of the change programme. But because of our preconception that overall change, if it is to be effective and lead to improvement, must be based on the needs of individual units, and that effective improvements in the larger organisation must entail improvement in unit performance, we necessarily give considerable importance to the understanding of, and the implementation of, change at the operating level. For this we believe our framework of analysis and our techniques are appropriate, and the developments are worthy of treatment in themselves. Specific changes, and techniques designed to promote specific changes, must however be set in the context of the whole programme of organisational change and improvement.

There are some important aspects of the change programme as a whole which we do not emphasise in the present work. The first, the significance of which becomes greater as the processes of change develop, is what may be called organisational design—the principles by which the identified needs of separate units, and the improvements proposed in individual factories or departments or functional areas may be coordinated, so that performance in the organisation as a whole is optimised.[13] Overall organisational improvement can be much more, or much less, than the sum of improvements in individual areas, and whether it is one or the other will depend partly on the success of the coordination processes and the way sub-systems match with each other—in fact the effectiveness of organisation design. This is in a sense another well-defined problem requiring a theoretical basis and techniques of skilled analysis comparable to those described in parts II to IV.

A second aspect, and perhaps the most difficult part of the programme, is the need for those trying to promote change to have a thorough grasp of the history, culture and political structure of the organisation and to use this understanding to devise means of inducing those with important decision-making roles in the organisation to accept, support and use the new ideas and the new skills available to the organisation. An open socio-technical systems analysis may lead to a clear understanding of the needs of a production unit, and to an adequate strategy for change in that unit; or a study of information flows, or of the integration needs of a large division, may lead to proposals for an improved organisational design; but unless those in positions of authority or power, or with control over important resources or holding strategic positions, are willing to allow change to occur, or are prepared to provide the necessary resources or lend moral support to those involved in making the improvements,[14] the ideas will remain stillborn or will quickly wither and die. Newly acquired skills will not result in changed behaviour. This problem we shall comment on in more detail in the final chapter.

The third aspect of the programme is a related one, and again concerns techniques, in this case techniques of transferring ideas to colleagues and getting them made manifest in behaviour. There is a need to use the specific technical, economic and structural improvements, whether in individual units or in the overall organisation, as means—albeit essential and important means—towards more general objectives: improved management understanding, skill and motivation, greater satisfaction of organisational members in general, changed authority relationships, more supportive behaviour between individuals and groups working towards agreed organisational objectives, and better mechanisms for monitoring the environment and for discovering and supplying the needs of the workplace and those closely involved with it. These require that individuals acquire and use new skills and sources of understanding, and they entail a change in the overall culture and modes of relationship in the organisation. Usually the one cannot change without the other.

We began by proposing that managers and decision-makers must employ the kind of understanding that arises from open socio-technical systems approaches and techniques. Thus it follows that we must find the means to transmit the principles of our approach, the understanding of organisational behaviour and the lessons for the management of change which result, to company managers, for on them the success of the change programme relies. There has to be a philosophy of, and machinery for, disseminating new ideas and new practices, and there has to be a theory of learning implicit in the programme. Both of these must be consistent with our overall approach to change.

The mechanisms we advocated for spreading the understanding and for implementing the wider purposes of the programme we have already referred to as a process of 'cell division'. As a result of the initial investigation a small cell of able and committed people from different areas of the company would be established, would have worked on the inquiries, and as a result of their involvement in the process and the discussions on possible strategies arising from it, would have begun to understand and apply new principles of design and behaviour in limited areas, and to see their implications for company performance. These people would then, we thought, be available to be used in several ways to spread the new skills. Some could be kept together as a group, and could continue to work, through involvement with groups of line and specialist managers, on specific investigations and projects in limited areas of the company. In this way they would gradually involve more and more managers in new ideas and different understanding of processes, so that methods would gradually spread. Or individuals from the original cell might be made the nuclei of further cells—the expert consultant members of further investigating teams—and members of these teams in their turn could become change-agents in yet further cells. Or some team members might be given new management responsibilities in which they had opportunities to apply new methods and train a group of able subordinates. Moreover, the success of specific strategies for change within particular areas might increase the interest and approval shown by superior levels of the organisation in the whole programme, might help to reward and reinforce the change teams, and make the rest of the organisation more receptive to the philosophy of the programme, the methods it was using and the conclusions coming from it.[15] There are a number of ways in which we believed the 'leaven' might work to bring about a general change.

That was to be the mechanism for implementation and spread of the principles of the programme. There is a theory of learning implicit in these ideas and we must outline this very briefly. The concepts needed for success of our approach had to be transmitted to members of teams in such a way that the learning became effective in behaviour, and moreover in behaviour that was not specific to the particular context in which the learning took place, but was a generalised, self-sustaining change, continuing to be manifested as new situations arose. This kind of learning we believed would take place best in guided problem-solving groups working on real problems in areas with which they were concerned. The areas chosen for investigation and improvement on the programme were to constitute these problem-solving situations. A group of people collaborating together as a project team would bring to the situation a wide range of skills and techniques from many different disciplines and, provided they recognised it as a learning situation, they would learn from each other and from the situation, and each member would find his own skill and understanding increased as a result of his experience and would naturally begin to put these skills into operation. However, in order to ensure that this form of 'learning by insight' took place, the group would also need some kind of guidance to point out when opportunities occurred for generalisation of the learning, and to allow new concepts to be introduced as appropriate.[16] This would be provided by the university researchers in cooperation with experienced and expert members of the original team, and the vehicles would include discussions about techniques such as are described in parts III and IV. Individuals would learn by achieving new insights in the course of problem-solving, and by being involved in the action necessary to improve the situation they would get reinforcement of these insights. Success in implementation would, we hoped, not only act as a reinforcement of learning about a specific situation, but would act as an incentive towards generalising the learning to new situations team members would have to deal with in later roles.

The learning process was then to be an essential part of the change programme, in company with the various processes of 'cell division'. It is necessary to create conditions in which highly committed members of the programme are able first to gain expertise and then to use their knowledge and their commitment to begin to spread the new ideas throughout the organisation.

These were the initial ideas with which the programme began. It will be obvious before the end of this book that there were inadequacies in the framework of ideas we began with on the programme. In fact many modifications occurred, in methods, and also in the concepts used, from the early stages of the programme. The way the programme developed as a consequence will be examined in detail in a subsequent work, where much additional light can be shed on actual problems and processes.

Let us summarise the import of this chapter. Whether or not a programme of this kind is successful depends on three things in particular

(1) the relevance and soundness of its theoretical and conceptual framework;

(2) the design of the methods of implementation, the structure of the learning process and the effectiveness of the mechanisms used for extension of the programme throughout the organisation;

(3) the quality of the people involved in it, the relevance of their previous training and experience, and the mix of skills, abilities and experiences present among the various implementation teams working with the programme.

In this book we concentrate mainly on the framework and on some techniques derived during prolonged work with it on a large number of cases. Later work will describe in more detail our thinking about the second condition, and particularly recount the experiences encountered in the practice of implementation and the greater understanding both of the management of change and of the behaviour of organisations which has been acquired as a result of these experiences. It is to that subsequent work that the reader must look for any kind of account of the change programme, in the form of analysis of historical data.

NOTES TO CHAPTER I

1. For a description of some aspects of emergent roles in a fairly comparable context see Goldner (1967). A theoretical statement in terms of role strain is given by Goode (1960).

2. For the United Kingdom the Tavistock Institute has been the centre of many of the developments in action research. Two somewhat different definitions and some historical perspectives are given by Rapoport (1970) and Foster (1972). Argyris's (1968) arguments also favour their approach.

3. Analyses of some of the value problems are available in Rapoport (1970) and Walton and Warwick (1973).

4. The literature on aspects of planned organisational change and organisational development is voluminous and deserves a separate commentary, supplementing Trist's earlier (1968) enlightening review, and the comments by Kahn (1974). By contrast the number of field studies of organisations subject to unplanned changes is rather limited. The well-known examples include Gouldner (1954), Blau (1955), Burns and Stalker (1961), Guest (1962), Trist *et al.* (1963).

5. See also the Harvard Business Review article by Leavitt (1962). For some history of the contingency concept, see Lawrence and Lorsch (1969) chapter 8, and Lupton (1971a). Lupton (1971b) has also briefly discussed its application to planned change.

6. op. cit., page 161.

7. idem.

8. See for example Woodward (1958, 1965), Etzioni (1961), Blau and Scott (1963) chapter 2, Pugh *et al.* (1963, 1969), and Perrow (1967). For some discussion of the purpose and nature of typologies, see also Udy (1965), Katz and Kahn (1966) chapter 5, and Burns (1967).

9. The term 'open socio-technical systems' seems to have been used first by Emery and Trist (1960). Our usage is much the same. In fact two separate concepts with different ancestry are involved: the socio-technical systems concept and the idea of organisations as open systems.

10. Rice (1958, 1963), Trist *et al.* (1963), and Miller and Rice (1967) used the term 'primary task' to denote the task the enterprise must perform in order to survive. We neglect the idea of task and prefer to work in terms of activities. Focal activities are those pursued within the organisation that appear to be related directly to satisfaction of (and to survival and development in) its present environment. The idea is elaborated further in part III, especially in chapter 9.

11. The socio-technical concept developed out of the work of the Tavistock Institute during the fifties and stems particularly from the important paper by Trist and Bamforth (1951)—a paper that incorporates all the essential elements entering into the concept, though not actually using the term. This seems to have been used first in a published document by Rice (1958). For some history of its origins and development, see Trist *et al.* (1963) chapter 1, and the introduction to Davis and Taylor (1972).

12. The best discussion of this problem occurs in Silverman (1970) chapters 6 and 7.

13. See especially Lorsch and Allen (1973). Earlier work includes Miller and Rice (1967) chapter 4, Argyris (1967), Galbraith (1969, 1971), Lawrence

and Lorsch (1969) chapter 9, Lorsch and Lawrence (1970), Dalton, Lawrence and Lorsch (1970), Schumacher (1971).

14. The importance of this has been emphasised only recently, notably by Pettigrew (1975a, 1975b); but see also Burns (1961), Chin and Benne (1969), and Greiner (1967) for papers that recognise the problem.

15. A rather fuller description of this mechanism was given in Lupton and Warmington (1973).

16. These ideas are based on some theories of learning put forward by Gagné (1965), and they are attempts to procure conditions to stimulate the learning of principles and learning by problem-solving.

2 Plurality and Change: Problems of Value, Method and Analytical Approach

This chapter is largely a digression away from the themes of the rest of the book. It has been written, and much of the thinking in it has developed, subsequent to and as a consequence of the work described in later chapters. It constitutes an attempt (which will not be relevant to the needs of all readers) to examine the legitimacy of our role as academic social scientists involved in a programme of industrial change, as well as to test the analytical framework we have used, and to discuss concepts such as 'performance' and 'improvement' that are elaborated in part III.

In selecting our framework of analysis we have been particularly concerned with applicability to the real problems of the organisation and with the processes of change in real situations. So a high degree of generalisation has not seemed very relevant to us. The analytical framework and the methodological apparatus must attempt to match the complexity of the real situation. This raises some difficulties. We are conscious of many existing gaps between the approach of the practising change agent or the prescriptive adviser on one hand, and the broader positive theories of organisation on the other. One of our concerns has been to begin to close the gaps between those whose main concern is with general explanations of organisational behaviour and those concerned more with the problems of specific industrial situations, a gap that is frequently widened by differences of orientation between those from different academic disciplines.[1]

To set the arguments of this chapter in context, we may mention two distinctions in academic approaches to organisations that have been outlined by earlier writers. The first was noted by Gouldner (1959), who described the many contrasting features of two prevalent views of organisations. One he termed the 'rational' approach, where

> the organisation is conceived as an "instrument"—that is a rationally conceived means to the realization of expressly announced group goals. . . . The rational model assumes that decisions are made on the basis of

a rational survey of the situation, utilizing certified knowledge, with a deliberate orientation to an expressly codified legal apparatus.[2]

The other he called the 'natural systems' approach, which

regards the organisation as a 'natural whole' or system. . . . Its component structures are seen as emergent institutions, which can be understood only in relation to the diverse needs of the total system.[3]

Gouldner pointed out that the defects of the latter include its neglect or underemphasis of rational structures, patterns of planned adaptation and use of professional and technical expertise to further rational goals. Members of organisations do in fact plan and structure and specialise and use energy and enthusiasm in order to promote purposive organisational ends, often through technical means. Our approach predisposes us towards the natural systems view of events. Explanations in terms of behaviour, or of decision-making processes directed specifically towards satisfaction of 'rational' organisational purposes do not appear sufficient to explain more than a small part of the activities taking place in an organisation. However, Gouldner's point is valid and some of our explanations must be made in terms of actions which have been conceived with rational purposes in view. This has to be reconciled with the more complex patterns of causation that stem from the individual and social needs, attitudes and relationships existing (and indeed being generated) within actual organisations.

The other distinction, discussed notably by Strother (1963) is to the effect that some models of organisation confine themselves largely to explanation and understanding of events, whether these be social, behavioural and 'organic' on the one hand, or performance-orientated, technical and 'rational' on the other hand: they are concerned mainly with understanding *why* in the event things happen in the way they do. They tend to be divorced from judgements about efficiency, and certainly are unconcerned about what *ought* to happen. Other models, by contrast—both natural systems models and rational models—make assumptions about performance and efficiency, at least to the extent of defining what is better and what is worse. They may thus encourage the student to infer prescriptions for improvement. Some of the best-known rational models of the classical and scientific management schools, and the natural systems (or in some cases the mixed) models of the modern behavioural scientists are normative, in the sense of being concerned, if not with the definition of efficiency and high performance, at least with ways of improving or optimising it.[4]

This book is more concerned with the process of explanation and understanding of organisational behaviour, than with fairly simple judgements as to better or worse, or with straightforward ways of maintaining efficiency or promoting improvement. However, we have been involved in action research in an industrial change programme; so, in describing, analysing and explaining various organisational processes, we must also have in view the possibility of change away from the existing situation, towards some 'better' situation. To advocate change in a particular direction is to imply that the change will bring improvement, and already some judgement has been made about what would constitute improvement. Further, if the judgement is to be accepted and action on it contemplated it probably has to be related to rationally conceived organisational purposes. So we have of necessity to get involved in definition of 'performance' and 'efficiency'.

Many of the problems we are concerned with in this chapter bear on this fact. There is a compensation, but this has its dangers. By being forced by the action research mode into proposing change, defining performance and eventually monitoring reactions when the proposals are implemented we gain feedback from inside the organisation. The feedback in turn helps increase our understanding, firstly of the value systems existing in some segments of the organisation at least, and secondly of the working of the whole system undergoing change. As a result of our involvement, therefore, our understanding of the organisation and our skills at prediction may be extended. This is the rationale behind the action research approach, and it approximates to what von Bertalanffy (1968) has termed the development of a sociological (or in this case organisational) technology.[5]

This process however raises some problems, which are the main themes of this chapter and which have remained with us throughout the programme.

AREAS OF DOUBT IN OUR INVOLVEMENT IN CHANGE

We have identified eleven different questions about our involvement in industrial change, about this approach to a change programme, and about the open socio-technical systems approach to organisational analysis in general. There are, for instance, a number of controversies in modern organisation theory that impinge on our research and invite us to take a stand, and to demonstrate that our approach has allowed us to deal adequately with them. Criticisms have also been levelled at the open socio-technical systems model in particular. These have tended to focus on a number of closely related areas where it is claimed the model provides a poor analogy with actual organisations. Systems models have been said to be both inadequate and misleading as explanations of behaviour, especially under conditions of change.

There are also a number of closely related problems to do with bias and objectivity (in the sense of an analysis that is not coloured by some value or belief brought in by the observer). Problems of values are generic to investigations in the social and behavioural sciences. They are of particular concern to us because of our explicit involvement in action as well as in observation and understanding.

We shall now look at these various controversies and areas of doubt, and show how we have met the criticisms they appear to evoke. It is, as we have said, the fact of change and of our involvement in change, that bring these sets of doubts together and make them particularly pressing for us. They cannot be separated, and although the first few areas we shall discuss are mainly concerned with values, and the last few mainly with criticisms of the usefulness of the systems model, none of these sources of criticism can be answered satisfactorily without reference to the others.

The difficulties are

(1) The danger of looking at organisations in managers' own terms and accepting managerial ideologies as an acceptable framework for investigation, analysis, and particularly, evaluation.

(2) The danger that the prejudices and orientations of the investigators will affect the research design, and the interpretations they put on their findings, to the extent that they do not take properly into account all the factors involved in the situation.

(3) The danger of assuming that because a 'respectable' analytical framework has been chosen for the investigation, selected by some process of scientific logic, there are therefore no hidden value positions present in the framework itself, or in the paradigm derived from it.

(4) The recognition of the plurality of interests in any industrial organisation and the difficulty or impossibility of striking a balance between them when it comes to examining changes that will affect them differentially.

(5) The question of organisational and personal goals and purposes and the usefulness of examining organisations in the light of them.

(6) The difficulty of examining or explaining the decision-making processes in organisations, and how these can be interpreted within an open systems framework.

(7) The need to recognise that organisational participants are individually motivated human beings whose behaviour is not perceived by them to be structurally determined and some of whom will see themselves as the determinants.

(8) The difficulty of dealing with the meanings attached to features of the organisation by its participants, as distinct from the meanings attributed to activities by an observer.

(9) The many problems raised by the dynamics of change within an organisation, and whether the open systems approach can accommodate these.

(10) The tendency of systems models (in common with some others) to 'reify' the organisation.

(11) Problems to do with identification of the state of performance or efficiency of the organisation given our recognition of some of these earlier questions.

The rest of this chapter is devoted to a discussion of our involvement in this research and our framework of analysis, in relation to these closely related challenges. In the course of the discussion the implications for our general treatment of the concept of organisation and for our choice of a measure of performance will become clearer. Because the points raised are fairly fundamental ones it is necessary to answer them carefully and the discussion has to be lengthy.

DETAILED DISCUSSION

(1) The first possible reproach is that we may have fallen into the trap of looking at organisations *in managers' own terms*, and have become the slaves of an existing management ideology. If this were so, our approach might have led us simply to provide prescriptive techniques by which managers of an existing industrial organisation could improve the methods they were using at present, and improve what they conceived to be the overall performance of their organisation, without in any way opening to consideration, much less radically challenging, the value systems inherent in the way the organisation was at present directed, and in their own criteria of effectiveness.[6]

However, our main concern is not with prescription, but with understanding the nature of organisational behaviour; and organisations as they exist today and with today's values and ideologies provide our laboratory for this. The advancement of understanding we have seen both as a goal in itself, and as an essential prerequisite to effective change, whether this be change and improvement within an existing ideology, or effective change in the ideologies themselves. It is true that we may be exposed through our present contacts and past experiences to greater influence from managers than from other segments of the organisation or of society, and that our selection of areas of interest within the organisation may show this influence. However, if we choose an appropriate framework of analysis, independently of these influences, and apply this framework carefully in the course of our enquiries, some of the dangers can be corrected.

It is true also that we describe techniques, and we do nothing to discourage managers in existing organisations taking up these techniques and applying them. However, the development of techniques and procedures, as described in later chapters, has seemed to us to be an effective means of further developing our understanding of behaviour: by attempting to apply new procedures, and observing the reactions from inside the organisation to the processes of implementation, greater understanding becomes possible. And since we are working in an ongoing organisation with the cooperation of members of that organisation, it behoves us to ensure that the new proposals or procedures in whose formulation we are involved, and the new relationships which result, are ones which satisfy the needs of those members for the time being. We are then able both to justify our place in the organisation in the short term and to use our involvement to gain the insight needed for wider and longer term purposes. That this position involves some dangers we are well aware. We discuss some of them later in the chapter.

Thus, while this question of management orientation is a potentially serious one, we would contend that we have from the beginning of the research been aware of the different levels on which we must operate and of the place of each. Short-term prescriptions and practical proposals for change are to be seen at least in part as steps to greater understanding, and the formulation of more adequate organisational concepts. Eventually, if that is desired, this understanding may be used to induce some more fundamental change, which could include a change in the whole balance of ideology and values in an industrial organisation. The desire to do this however itself brings in the question of the values lying behind the research and the researchers' motivation to participate in the change.

(2) So we are led on to a second criticism which is rather more difficult to answer. It questions what we mean by greater understanding. In carrying out our analysis of organisational problems, have we taken up an initial *point of view about the nature of the organisation* that is open to question? What assumptions have been in the minds of the investigators in formulating their research design, in defining what is meant by 'organisation', or organisational purpose or structure or in defining the areas on which to concentrate during the research? The point here is that the investigators may have gone into the organisation (and almost certainly have gone into the organisation) with prejudices and orientations which have affected their ability to take properly into account all of the interests involved and all of the interactions taking place in it. If this fact is not appreciated the steps taken towards improving understanding will themselves be partial, and the understanding will be biased.

This is unavoidable. Firstly, the selection of the matters that interest the investigators and of the activities they wish to understand is necessarily partial because as individuals the investigators have orientations which they cannot avoid bringing into the study, and of which they are often unaware. These may lead them to reject some events or some group interests as insignificant or unimportant that might have considerable importance for those with other value systems. What is more, as well as bringing elements of bias into the analysis, the investigators may unconsciously have brought in some normative judgments about the situation revealed. So bias may be implicit both in the analysis, and in the meanings placed upon the findings.[7] Both may influence the practical proposals resulting from the analysis.

There is probably no real solution to the problem of personal bias. For the action researcher there are additional dangers, for he may be subject to a range of pressures during his research that discourage self-criticism—pressures that include the time constraints placed on him during investigation, his need for role legitimacy within the organisation and other sources of personal stress. In any case the researcher finds it difficult to examine or to recognise the sources of bias he himself brings into the investigation. Probably all he can do is: (a) examine as closely as is possible for him the values and orientations he starts off with and those he begins to develop under stress; (b) try to make these explicit in his communications to colleagues in the organisation and to users of the research findings; and (c) choose a framework for analysis that helps bring to light some value positions that might otherwise be hidden.

A formal, well-chosen and consistently applied, analytical framework may help to control the sources of bias in analysis, but it cannot do much to overcome the further problem of imputing a set of values (of the investigator, the managers or some others) into the interpretation of the situation *after* the analysis is complete. So it is necessary both for the researcher and for those to whom the research is later communicated always to bear in mind the likelihood of partiality in the judgements made about the situation, and to attempt to discover the values that lie at the root of these assessments. No more, we believe, can be done by people involved in social investigation.[8] Some of the consequent dilemmas are discussed below.

(3) *No analytical framework* provides a perfect representation of the situation being studied that *is free from selection or avoids imposing a structure* on the situation. Faced with a complex pattern of organisational behaviour, the investigator must select, structure, analyse and explain the situation in terms of a model of his own choice. Choice of the model would normally be in terms of its relevance to the purposes of the enquiry or its usefulness for that investigation. In any case it necessarily involves assumptions as to what factors are relevant and what not to the analysis and to the explanation—relevant, that is, according to his initial perception of the situation and subsequently according to some rules of scientific evidence, incorporated in or related to the structure and status of the model.

So in choosing an open socio-technical systems model (and its corollary in a contingency approach to organisational phenomena) we have become committed to particular ways of structuring the data and particular sets of rules for selecting the variables concerned and determining what is relevant to an understanding of them. Further, the open socio-technical systems approach incorporates a view of organisations as above all interactive. Considerable attention is directed towards the interactions between the particular organisation and various segments of its environment, and among the most important means to understanding the organisation is to be a study of the interactions that take place within it, and the conflicts, values, attitudes and relationships that these generate, and how the latter influence patterns of behaviour.

The approach therefore involves a very specific view of the nature of the organisation and of the way patterns of behaviour there evolve. There are equally specific implications about the kind of phenomenon that is relevant to the analysis and the explanation being made. Moreover there are not only implications about the nature of the organisation, but some inferences can be drawn about satisfaction of organisational 'needs'. Ideas of 'satisfaction' and of 'fit' are imputed to the organisation by the use of the open systems approach. They are concepts we find it useful to employ when considering possible criteria of performance or effectiveness that could be more relevant to our needs than some perhaps more orthodox criteria. The fact that we do find advantages in these concepts, and that we have related them to a particular definition of performance is itself an indication of a position we have chosen to adopt, and of which we are fully conscious. Some difficulties and some advantages it brings for us are discussed in succeeding sections.

(4) Burns (1967) has referred to *the plurality of needs* that exist within organisations. In any large organisation there are many groups with distinctive roles and specialisms, distinctive sets of activities, distinctive perspectives from which they view the organisation and distinctive views of what is better or worse for it, of what its objectives should be and what the organisation should provide to satisfy their own needs from it.[9]

One characteristic of the open socio-technical systems framework is that so long as the investigation proceeds at the level of description, analysis and understanding, it more or less forces the investigator to recognise and take into account the existence of individuals and groups who demonstrate to him the plurality of needs and the variety of perspectives that exist, and to some extent to examine the origins of these. What analysis cannot do however is to show which of the various perceptions are to be given most weight in making judgments about the situation, especially where needs and objectives of different groups are incompatible or conflicting.

This fact is relevant to the problems we discuss later of defining organisational performance and effectiveness without falling too inescapably into the trap of reification. We shall suggest that it is not possible to find any such definition that is free from values drawn from outside social science. The temptation that many pieces of research have succumbed to is to assume either

(a) that there is one group or coalition of groups in the organisation whose needs or decisions or perspectives are the relevant ones to be considered, and that the goals which that coalition defines, either implicitly or explicitly, also are to have most weight in defining the criteria of performance or of improvement; or

(b) that the state of performance for the organisation can be defined objectively independently of the goals of any of these groups through some technical or economic criteria such as cost efficiency or profitability, or some systems criterion like environmental satisfaction, organisational survival or growth.

Either of these assumptions (or any other that might be made) brings in some ideology or some value position. So long as the investigator is acting *qua* social scientist, he has no criterion given him from within a scientific discipline which will enable him to choose between any of the perspectives he has discovered. He may possibly show the implications of a particular change for any one group or any one set of goals. He cannot judge between the values held by different groups or decide that organisational needs require particular sets of values to be satisfied and others overriden.

As will become evident in part II, we bear this fact of plural needs and perspectives in mind in our analysis and model-building exercise, and it has helped both in guiding the investigation and in forming a useful perspective from which to report our findings. It also provides a context for the development of some of the later arguments in this chapter—arguments about the identification of goals, ideas about decision processes, etc. Recognition of the pluralistic nature of the organisation, however, makes clearer the dilemmas associated with intervention and participation in change directed towards a defined end; and it does not help us with the problem of developing an acceptable definition of organisational effectiveness, or in defining what is meant by improvement in performance. These problems we have to consider carefully at the end.

(5) Much discussion has taken place in the literature on the question of *organisational goals*. A common contention is that organisations are differentiated from other social units mainly by the fact that they are purposive, and that they have identifiable tasks leading to goals in terms of which success can be assessed.[10] However, an open systems approach throws some doubt on the usefulness of the whole concept of organisational goals. If organisations do have goals, it may be asked, how are they defined, and how relevant are they to the actual behaviour which occurs in the organisation?

It may be agreed that organisations are purposive in the sense that they are created in the first place by some individual, group or coalition of groups which had a purpose in mind at the time of creation. But organisational purpose as defined by the founder does not imply specific organisational goals so much as a general direction of operation, or a 'mission' in the terminology used by Selznick (1957). Moreover, in the course of time the purposes for which the organisation was created may cease to operate, present-day purposes may have become very vague or may have been subtly changed.[11] Once having established a stable existence within a given environment, organisational existence tends to acquire a certain inertia. New purposes arise, or existence for its own sake becomes an accepted end, or groups and individuals continue more and more explicitly to pursue their own goals, using the organisation as a convenient means for this. If this is so, then current organisational goals and purposes can only be inferred from the behaviour taking place at the present time within it.[12]

One way the problem of goals has been dealt with in the literature is to try to distinguish between the goals of the organisation and the goals of its members, and then to examine how these two relate to each other. This is the position taken by Cyert and March (1963) and Simon (1964). It led the first pair of authors directly into a fruitful discussion of how decisions are actually arrived at in organisations through the working of coalitions, the identification of organisational goals with the negotiated goals of coalitions and the concepts of unresolved conflicts and organisational slack. For Simon however it produces further problems. In order to escape from the danger of reification Simon differentiates between an individual's personal interests (which by implication are irrelevant) and the goals implicit in the performance of his occupational roles. For the performance of roles members of the organisation are provided with inducements and are subjected to constraints as a result of decisions made elsewhere (typically in specialist units of the organisation and apparently on 'rational' grounds). The goals of the organisation thus emerge as a result of the operation of these inducements and constraints on individuals' role performance.

There are doubts about the logical consistency of this argument. Moreover, the differentiation made by Simon (and also by Gross, 1970) between personal interests (or what the individual desires for himself) and the motivation to carry out certain occupational roles does not seem a valid or useful one.[13] In our earlier comment about rational models and natural systems models we suggested that much of the behaviour taking place in an organisation is directly concerned with the satisfaction of social and psychological needs of members, in groups or as individuals, while other activities (to the outside observer) apparently comprise the use of energies or specialist expertise in pursuit of some identified rational need. However, it is dangerous for an observer to try to distinguish between the two, or having apparently distinguished, to be able to relate either form of activity to defined organisational goals, or to be able to impute motives or classes of satisfaction from observation of manifest behaviour. We shall revert to this point in later sections.

For this kind of reason we have neglected the concept of organisational goals, considering that its usefulness for us, and its relevance to any criteria of organisational performance we need, are very limited.[14] We have, however, brought in from time to time an examination of the requirements of the organisation for survival and development in the environment in which, for whatever reason, it is at present operating. A definition of performance in terms of current environmental needs for survival and growth appears more satisfactory for our purposes than the imputation of goals to the organisation from either the behaviour of, or the stated desires of, the people within it. Again, however, we recognise that it is essential to identify the standpoint we are adopting in choosing to use this definition. The point will be developed in a later section.

(6) The main stress of open systems theory has traditionally been on structures and on interactions of the system with an environment, and its tendency has been to ignore (or at least to abstract from) individual characteristics, and to deal with people, whether as individuals or groups,

only in so far as their behaviour is influenced by the structure of the situation. The processes of *decision-making* within the organisation are thus not usually dealt with in detail within this framework. However, we do not believe this is inevitable. There is considerable current interest in the processes of organisational decision-making, and none of the commonly discussed explanations has received general acceptance, or appears wholly satisfactory. In the next few paragraphs we put forward some hypotheses about the processes of organisational decision-making that appear compatible with our own observations, within the framework of analysis we have described. Analysis of these processes may be capable of further development as systems are examined that are further removed from the technically constraining production line.

As we have implied earlier, many needs, objectives and interests (only some of which are 'rational' in formal organisational terms) have to be taken note of and understood if a complete explanation of behaviour, events and activities in an organisation is to be made. Now, the total organisation is made up of the individuals who have these needs, goals and interests (often acting as members of groups and coalitions) and of their interactions together and with the technical artifacts, tasks and processes, the status and authority structures, the sources of political power, the accepted ideas as to what is and is not legitimate, and the formal rules and procedures, with which the organisation has, in some sense, been endowed. It is the sum of these complex structures and processes that goes to make up the organisation. When the 'organisation' acts coercively to constrain the actions of its members, or when it appears to act as an entity in itself, in taking some new direction, or acting in accordance with some new policy decision, or when it undergoes some unpredicted change, in reaction to external stimulus, then this view of organisations would indicate that it was the result of some concerted decisions or some individual actions or some initiatives on the part of some groups and coalitions, and of the interactions these generated.

However, this process is not a random one. In almost any organisation there are certain groups and coalitions which have particular influence over decisions about the overall direction of the organisation—groups which control sources of significant power.[15] Members of such coalitions spend some of their time looking outward (outside the organisation or at least outside their own group or coalition), and in the course of time acquire some skill in monitoring and interpreting the environment in terms of the pressures it is putting on that group or coalition to change in particular directions, and also in terms of the ability of the coalition, its allies and its other sources of influence, to neutralise or change or respond to these pressures. The environmental changes and pressures which concern such a coalition may be those it identifies in the external market environment or in the social or political environment of the organisation; or they may consist of shifts of power or changes in attitudes or behaviour in other parts of the organisation, including what is happening in rival coalitions, and including the effects of any technical innovations or structural alterations which have taken place.

In the same way, the members of the coalition hold or accept tacitly some perceptions about 'what is best for the organisation' as they define it, or as it has been negotiated among its members. Any group or coalition is likely to have developed a particular perspective from which its members set out to define what is needed for the good of what they identify as the whole organisation, but which may well give considerable weight to the interests of their own coalition. The perceptions about what is happening in the environment (however environment is defined by the coalition) and the concept of what is best for the organisation, or for the coalition, will be subjective. However, the fact that its members hold certain perceptions may induce the coalition to act, or to come to an agreed decision, as a consequence of these perceptions.

Now in most large organisations there are rival, or neighbouring, or perhaps overlapping coalitions, each having significant ability to influence events, and each constraining the kind of decisions other coalitions can effectively make. The perceptions of some of these groups are probably in conflict with others. This being so, a rather subtle process of negotiation[16] is likely to take place between influential groups (though it is unlikely to be recognised in these terms by group members), and the final, widely accepted definition of 'what is the best course for the organisation' may emerge as a compromise between the views of influential rival coalitions and may frequently reflect political and power relations between them.

Of course the decisions arrived at will be constrained to varying degrees by, for instance, technical factors (including in these the structure of formally designed tasks), environmental factors and the formal structure of authority and systems of control[17] as well as by established ideas about legitimacy, which may be derived from historical and cultural influences, some of them brought in from outside. These constraints are likely to be tightest in 'total institutions' especially coercive organisations like prisons and mental hospitals, and least in evidence in institutions like universities, political parties or cabinets. Within industrial organisations the influence of these constraints on decision-making is likely to vary directly with the dominance or lack of tolerance available in the technical process, and inversely with the degree of control the organisation is able to exercise over its environment.[18]

In any case movement towards the state perceived to be desirable at the end of the negotiating process is then seen by the outside observer as a response by, or a piece of behaviour by, the organisation as a whole, often divorced from the stated goals or observed needs of its important members and sometimes even at odds with decisions which have been formally taken at Board level, the Board being only one of the coalitions, and not necessarily the one whose members are the most highly involved or the most influential when it comes to actual behaviour in response to perceived pressures. Changes in the organisation are the observable consequences of a complex process of negotiation, compromise, decision-taking, decision modification, and finally effective implementation. They are the outcome of a long series of constrained but vaguely defined strategies negotiated between various groups and coalitions with frequently conflicting interests and outlooks.

In this process of coalition formation, monitoring of some (internal or external) environment, negotiation with rival groups and so on, the personal needs of individual participants must play some part. Because of the constraints imposed by the formal structure, the technology and task structure and the political structure of the organisation, its members have not a great deal of discretion as individuals and are likely to see their personal needs best met for the time being via membership of coalitions and groups (or their occupational roles encourage group membership). In the effective decisions taken, and the movements which take place as a result, observable personal needs may appear to have only a peripheral place just because individuals are constrained to act according to group goals.

Thus slowly and apparently inefficiently the values of the organisation emerge and the organisation itself appears to act in such a way as to be independent of identifiable social and psychological needs of either individuals or groups, and of the immediate goals of the members as individuals.[19] As Barth (1966, page 2) says, the values that emerge 'are the cumulative result of a number of separate choices and decisions made by people acting *vis-à-vis* one another . . . and in their form they reflect the constraints and incentives under which people act'. Thus there is a constant interplay between processes of choice and decision-making through which individuals attempt to achieve their goals, and an emergent structure that acts as a constraint on these processes.

This long statement constitutes an untested proposition about some of the processes that go into decision-making and decision implementation in complex organisations, but it is one that nevertheless seems compatible with much observed behaviour. In fact we believe that this statement is an oversimplification of the process, and that detailed research at any level of organisational decision-making and implementation shows complexities at that one level which bear most of these characteristics.

It now becomes possible to understand better organisational behaviour in a changing situation. Behaviour tends to change because the changing situation changes the perceptions of members of the participating coalitions, alters power relationships both within and between coalitions and alters the constraints under which they act. It induces new decisions to be made as a result of the new perspectives, new power structure and changed constraints and opportunities. Radical changes, leading to major discontinuities, will, when they have been monitored and recognised by organisational participants, tend to result in major changes in the distribution of power in the organisation, completely altered sets of relationships between groups, perhaps a change in the structure of coalitions and a new political system. Such major changes may in extreme cases result in quite different characteristic forms of organisational behaviour.

The difficulty of analysing and explaining behaviour in organisations during periods of rapid change remains. The difficulty is due to the complexity of this process of structural and political change rather than to any defect in the systems framework of analysis.

If these statements do bear some relation to actual organisational processes, it is interesting to examine how they affect the achievement of particular states of performance or efficiency. Obviously, these processes do not fit any 'rational' model, and in relation to concepts of rational organisational goals, tasks, needs or environmental satisfaction, they would give poor results. Compared with an imported systems view of effectiveness, related to environmental satisfaction, or to some concept of defined goal achievement even with 'bounded rationality', the 'natural' organisational processes are likely to be inferior in rational terms, but at the same time more subtle, and much more likely to reflect the existing power structure and the needs and goals of influential groups, and possibly be more acceptable to organisational participants given the culture as it exists.

We take the comparison of these processes further in a later section.

(7) A related point to be considered is that members of organisations are clearly not automatons, prisoners of a system whose structure determines their behaviour and the kind of relationships they form, but *individually motivated human beings*, each with his own temperament and personality, past background and present needs, and some measure of freedom of will. Now an assumption of the socio-technical approach is that structure, interdependency of relationships, interactions between individuals within groups, between groups and between people and technology generate tensions, conflicts, dissatisfactions, values and opportunities that can to some extent be predicted, and that these factors act as constraints on the way people respond to the pressures on them, so that patterns of behaviour are also predictable, within certain limits.

It is necessary to reconcile the idea that patterns of behaviour are predictable from the structure of the situation, with the existence of individual personalities with individual characters, temperaments, impulses, domestic, family and social environments, and expectations. Indeed, two questions arise: why should individuals conform to the social norms and the patterns of interaction which sociologists identify as arising from the structural aspects of the organisation; and why should they comply with the rules and organisational norms laid down by the upper levels of the formally constituted hierarchy of authority?

The usual explanation of the latter, at least for lower participants in an industrial organisation, is that individuals enter an organisation voluntarily on a contractual basis in which they implicitly agree to conform to the rules of behaviour laid down for the organisation, and the controls imposed within it, in return for the rewards provided by it.[20] This explanation goes some way to account for self-selection of particular groups of people, or of people who typically possess certain behavioural characteristics, into an organisation; but as a general explanation of compliance it appears somewhat off the point if our earlier analysis is accepted. New members on first entering the organisation do not comprehend all of the formal requirements the organisation expects of them, and certainly do not see the full implications of them in terms of the tensions, dissatisfactions or positive values they create. These come to light in a process of trial and error, probing and pushing at the constraints. Indeed, the formal requirements as initially designed usually become considerably modified in the process of testing, and even these modified requirements are not wholly conformed to. There is tacit resistance to and manipulation of formal rules, controls and regulations to the extent that they are made tolerable to and consistent with the expectations of participants and the satisfaction of individual and social needs, while at the same time allowing the tasks of the organisation to be carried out.[21] As we suggested earlier, formal requirements are but one element in the whole structure of constraints, rewards and modes of interaction that influence patterns of overt behaviour.

The process of tacit modification and manipulation of the formal controls gives us a clue as to how the paradox of predictable behaviour patterns and individually motivated people can be explained. The social structure (or the socio-technical system) is not an inflexible, mechanistic structure in which the individual finds himself placed, which wholly constrains his behaviour, and in the face of which he is powerless. Indeed, every individual entering the organisation has a large number of choices, both as to his patterns of behaviour and as to the range of satisfactions which he will try to meet through the organisation. By his choice of behaviour, by his adherence to or separation from group membership, and in the final event by his decision whether to stay in or leave the organisation, he is at the same time influencing the structure, and portraying by his own actions within the constraints imposed by that structure, some of the predictable behaviour patterns.[22]

Thus at all levels of the organisation individual participants are determining the characteristic patterns of organisational behaviour. This they do in the first place by processes of self-selection: who decides to enter, who to stay in and who to leave the organisation. Secondly, those who stay do it largely, but not exclusively, through the formation of groups and coalitions whose members influence each other and whose members tend to possess similar interests and to exhibit appropriate patterns of behaviour to further them and whose members are subject to similar constraints. Within any one group, members tend to act together, and to some extent accept and conform to the norms of that group, and undertake activities which are to that extent predictable. They do this, not because they are in any way slaves of a social system, but because they choose to pursue their own goals in this way. Many of the activities of individual participants will be directed to the 'rational' ends of the organisation, given its present-day purposes. This is done partly because of the constraints constituted by the expectations of groups and individuals controlling superior sources of power, and partly so as to produce the material rewards which form an important part of the satisfactions to be obtained from organisational membership. But cooperation in purposeful activities for 'rational' objectives can also be an important way of obtaining social and psychological satisfaction from participation.

The relative importance of formal controls laid down by a formally constituted authority, the extent to which these controls are modifiable and the extent to which they are manipulated, depend on the power and influence structure of different elements in the organisation. Power in turn is partly determined by the processes of group attachment and cooperation and partly by the influence of technology, market environment, resource procurement, etc., and the processes by which control over these is exercised.[23]

Thus to say that behaviour patterns are predictable does not imply determinism, nor does it assume that individuals are unable to exercise personal initiative, though we do suggest that the organisational structure places constraints on the responses it is possible to make, and it is because of these constraints that these responses are open to analysis and to a limited degree to prediction.

(8) There is a difference between facts and perceptions. When we start to consider *the meanings attached to features of the organisation by its participants* a considerable number of complications arise. People behave within the organisation not just in response to the objective facts of the situation, but to the meanings they attribute to those facts.[24] We have frequently referred in the last few pages to the perceptions of various organisational members and the perspectives of the members of different groups and coalitions. Our recognition of the importance of these forces us to consider this point seriously.

We have said earlier that the search for completely value-free organisational analysis has eluded us. One reason for this is that the observer finds it difficult to distinguish between objective facts (if such there be), the meanings that he himself gives to those facts, and, particularly, the way he structures them in his analysis. But he has another, possibly greater difficulty: to discover what are the meanings that organisational participants give to these same facts. An analytical structure whose basis is limited to observable facts may not be wholly relevant to causation within the organisation; an analysis which incorporates members' own perspectives and perceptions is needed, but that can never be wholly verified, except perhaps *post hoc* through a process of monitoring and feedback such as we describe in chapter 11.

This is not to say that we need to ignore, nor that we have ignored, meanings and perceptions, when using the open socio-technical systems framework to develop models of parts of the organisation. Indeed, as the case studies in part II show, the interactions between observed perceptions of different groups frequently emerged in this programme as important influences on behaviour. However, we suggest that the reliance that can be placed on interview and questionnaire studies, even with the aid of sophisticated techniques of interpretation, is limited, and in the absence of supporting evidence they are subject to considerable doubt. We are saying that the aspects of our models relating to perceptions can never be wholly verified so long as they rely on observation and verbal responses to questions.

We have suggested that an observer, seeing a variety of patterns of behaviour in the organisation, and classifying them into those that appear to serve 'rational' ends and processes and those which apparently satisfy social and psychological needs, would still be unable to recognise, purely from an analysis of the behaviour, what significance the activities had for the participants, and how participants related them to organisational purpose or goal. Even quite obvious 'rational' activities entailing the exercise of skills, or purely muscular effort, may offer psychological rewards because some unobservable meanings are given to those activity patterns. And it may not be seen as legitimate for the participants to articulate these meanings or these satisfactions to an outsider.

Again, we have suggested that members of powerful coalitions and groups influence organisational behaviour as the result of a variety of perceptions and from a number of perspectives; and individual participants modify their activities and group attachments and themselves influence the character of the socio-technical system for reasons that may be inaccessible to the observer. Much of the difficulty about perceptions and about the inaccessibility to outsiders of the meanings given by actors to their own situation, is commonplace in the literature of industrial psychology and of industrial relations. Not only the outside observer, but the members of a different group within the organisation, may be unable to appreciate the meanings given to a situation by participants in a different sector. It is clear in the case studies in chapters 4 and 5 that the meanings given to the work situation by groups of shopfloor workers was hidden from even departmental management, some supervisors and cooperating peer groups.

(9) Obviously more systematic examination is still needed of the problems associated with meanings and perceptions, and as a consequence there are still problems in dealing with *the dynamics of change* within the organisation. Use of the socio-technical systems framework gives us what is essentially a detailed successional picture of a part of the organisation at given instants in time. Socio-technical analysis is to a large extent static. Yet we are engaged in a programme of change and we need to observe and explain the changing situation and hopefully make some predictions about it.

One inherent problem of change is that, even though knowledge were obtained of the present-day perceptions of all the many segments of an organisation, it would be impossible to predict how each of those segments in turn would perceive the changes with which they were faced. The attachment of meanings to a new situation is perhaps a far more fickle and unpredictable process than the development of fairly persistent meanings attached to relatively stable situations.

There are a number of levels at which we should be able to undertake the analysis of change, and it is only at the microlevel of the small socio-technical system that we feel confident about the techniques so far developed. In dealing with small socio-technical systems such as the shopfloor departments described in our case studies, the structured framework we have adopted allows us to make some analysis of the processes that occur during change, and hence make some predictions about changes in behaviour. However, predictions must make assumptions about the meanings which the individuals and groups concerned (including groups outside the particular system who are aware of and to some extent affected by the changes) attach to those changes.

The suggestions we make in part III about the way a strategy for improvement should be formulated attempt to deal with this problem. For if those who are helping to influence the situation can be persuaded to introduce changes progressively in relatively simple steps, and predict the total effects of each step before it is made, then these predictions can be continuously monitored against actual events. The models being used, and the predictions about the way perceptions will change, can be tested, verified, or falsified and corrected, as the changes proceed. Further, if it becomes possible to involve those most closely affected in the processes leading up to the change, then they will be able to throw some light on the meanings they attach to the changes and how they affect them; and the meanings themselves may be altered as a consequence of the involvement. Thus, whether by monitoring or by involvement, change itself is being used as a vehicle towards greater understanding of the dynamics of behaviour in that organisation.

At the level of the wider organisation our understanding that decision-making processes are taking place continuously through the interactions within and between coalitions gives us no more than an overview of the complex dynamics of shifting centres of power and shifting alliances between groups. One would have to be closely involved in the decision-making processes, probably as an active member of the organisation, to be able to monitor the processes by which organisational behaviour changes, or to explain the effects produced by external stimulus to change.

In the case of a specific technological innovation affecting the wider organisation, it may be possible to make some predictions about the effect the innovation will have on the way individuals and groups interact with each other, on the sources of power in the organisation, and hence on some of the likely overall reactions. However, with many other changes, particularly those emanating from the market environment, it will be difficult if not impossible to predict how the changes will be perceived and monitored by various groups of people in the organisation, what meanings will be attached to them, and therefore what kind of decisions will result and what kind of effects they will have on the social and political structure. This of course has lessons for the success of the overall programme of change in which we have been involved.

(10) One problem that has for long dogged writers on organisation has been the danger of *reification*—that is to say treating the complex of relationships, attitudes and behavioural patterns, the many human participants and the physical artifacts and processes that go to make up the organisation as though together they constituted a physical entity with an independent existence and perhaps even with the adaptive, creative and motivational characteristics of a living organism. It is a danger to which systems models are said to be particularly open.

Our recognition of the diversity of interests, needs and goals in an organisation, and our conclusions as to the complex decision-making processes in it lead us to consider this question and to justify our treatment of the concept of the organisation in parts II and III. We do so as follows. Any investigator attempting to examine and observe activities and events within an organisation is limited as to the time and resources he has available; no practicable piece of research can possibly examine in detail all the complex and dynamic processes of coalition formation, patterns of conflict, operation of constraints, shifting negotiating systems and so on if its aim is to analyse some aspect of the organisation to which these were only indirectly relevant. Given the normal constraints of time and resources the investigator has to choose the level at which to undertake his analysis. Whatever choice is made, a great deal has to be taken for granted, and some form of words has to be devised which subsumes the many processes that are taken as given. The research model at a particular level of analysis must abstract from some of the complexities of behaviour at levels with which he is not directly concerned.

Now for most situations the level at which we worked during this study took the organisation structure as a constraining influence on performance at the departmental or microlevel. Therefore if we say that the organisation imposes constraints on individual members or groups, we are simply considering them as emergent properties of the organisational structure (defined in relation to the environment in which for the moment the organisation exists). We still recognise that complex processes are continuously taking place and that the participants acting as individuals help to generate these constraints, though within an existing structure of authority, status and influence, given technological constraints, and power structure, and probably exerting influence through groups and shifting coalitions.

Some understanding about the way organisational behaviour is determined must lie at the base of any explanation that is made at any level of analysis. However, once the understanding has been established, it may be legitimate to use a form of words such as that 'the organisation has developed mechanisms which enable it to adapt effectively to changes in its market environment' which to the critic give an appearance of reification. This form of words, we suggest, is a means of abstracting from the complexities of actual behaviour when the details of that behaviour are not relevant to the purposes of the inquiry or the level of analysis selected for it.

We believe it is necessary to make this point because in this programme we were dealing with change and with the reactions of an organisation to a change situation, and it is said to be especially difficult to explain and deal with the problems of change and the organisation's total reactions to change, within a systems framework, without in some sense objectifying the organisation itself. Much of the argument in part III of this book could appear to come close to reification. Discussion in the last few pages will make our own position and its underlying assumptions clearer.

(11) Our involvement in action research and in promoting change has also brought us up against the question of *evaluation of organisational performance* and much of the earlier discussion has made reference to this. In the course of our close collaboration with the management of an industrial organisation we are necessarily under pressure (and probably under an obligation) to advise on how the outcome of change is to be evaluated for the organisation. The question of evaluation forces us to consider the choice of the criteria for evaluation. Since one of the explicit purposes of the programme was to assist an ongoing organisation to improve the way it was meeting the demands imposed by its environment, it was impossible to stop short of evaluating how far these improvements were taking place. Yet, as will have become obvious, there are many dilemmas in trying to define the criteria for evaluating change.

The investigators' initial temptation may be to accept management's criteria, and by accepting them implicitly accept management's value system for that purpose at least. This we were prevented from doing if for no other reason than that culture change, and value changes among managers, were likely to be essential for the success of the programme. For the investigators to accept evaluation on the basis of existing perceptions and value positions would therefore have inhibited success.

Alternatively, the investigators could claim simply to help provide data for a management-initiated evaluation without accepting either the values of management or the evaluation that was being made. They could claim to be neutral about the evaluation process in the short term, while working on changing management perceptions and understanding over the longer period. For the time being they could claim they would allow their managerial colleagues to evaluate. However, this way out is blocked so long as some of the changes brought about are the result of proposals which the investigators have helped to formulate. The proposals for change must have been chosen with some evaluation criteria in mind, and therefore those involved in making the proposals cannot evade responsibility for the evaluation.[25]

As we shall show in part III the definition of performance and effectiveness we have chosen to use on this programme arises from considerations of relevance to the needs of the research. It is a consequence too of our choice of the open systems approach as the appropriate framework for the research. It is concerned mainly with the 'fit' of the organisation (over a number of dimensions) with its environment, and with the 'fit' between a number of different processes within the organisation. We outline this definition and argue for it in chapter 9. If we have to justify the choice we do so on grounds of its usefulness in the context of this programme and given the level at which it was appropriate to make the analysis.

We recognise (a) that choice implies certain values; (b) that using this definition as a basis for action evades to some extent the problems connected with action when a plurality of interests are involved. It is probably not enough to claim that our whole analytical framework recognises and takes account of many of these conflicting needs and values if we then by implication ignore or underweight them in our assessment of the state of performance; and (c) that the usefulness of this definition is contingent upon a demonstration that the open systems approach is itself a useful one.

The usefulness of our analytical framework has been demonstrated clearly in the course of this chapter. The open socio-technical systems model provides a framework allowing us to draw boundaries within which the explanations made are still basically compatible with the existence in the wider organisation of a set of complex processes influencing behaviour in the ways described earlier. At a particular level of analysis the concepts of 'fit', 'environmental satisfaction', 'task' and 'need' can be used as properties of the organisational structure while still recognising the existence of these processes.

There remains, however, the basic dilemma, which is not one of definition, but one created by our involvement in action: that to intervene and stimulate change, and then to monitor the change, both involve a disturbance of existing relations that will be experienced differently by different people. Nevertheless, action will always occur. Our criteria for evaluating it stress the organisation's survival and development rather than, for example, maximisation of returns or optimisation of resource use. If the tasks necessary for survival are not fulfilled, then, unless a new structure emerges, the *raison d'etre* for members' participation in the organisation is likely to disappear. It seems likely that pursuit of simple maximisation would be more destructive of existing values among lower participants than ours. Nevertheless the dilemma of involvement in action remains.

We have referred earlier to the difference between a rational definition of performance, such as we have selected, and the implicit definition of performance that is a result of 'natural' organisational decision-making processes. The latter, we have suggested, will be less effective in either optimising resource utilisation or satisfying existing environmental demands, and it will certainly be less intellectually satisfying. However, our definition is based on an imported point of view about the purpose of the organisation, and on an outside observer's perceptions of the characteristics of a rather simple environment. It is probably far less subtle than the position arrived at by the natural group decision-making processes. It is less likely to satisfy the needs of influential groups, and it will be more difficult to gain (*post hoc*) acceptance for it.

In our definition of an improved situation, and particularly in the strategy required to move towards it, many influence factors (technical, social and political) are taken into consideration, so far as is possible for the outside observer who has his own rather blinkered perceptions and perspectives. Whereas the definition we suggest separates (conceptually at least) the nature of the improved situation from the processes required to get there, the actual processes tend to treat both as a matter for simultaneous negotiation and compromise. Our model of improvement has the advantage of logical consistency, limited by simplification of the issues and doubts about perspectives; the natural behaviour may exhibit a more realistic picture of the complexities of the organisational power system, but the 'satisficing' changes which result may be inferior in rational terms to those we propose—so far as rationality is in any way important.

SUMMARY AND CONCLUSIONS

It is difficult to summarise this long discussion. We have suggested that action research, as an effective way of gaining deeper understanding, involves us in a number of problems: working within an organisation at the invitation of members of the organisation and with the aim of promoting agreed changes in it, we have to make continual reference to the instrumental activities and purposes of the organisation; and we have to try and define what we mean by performance and improvement. These considerations create difficulties for us, and they have led us to make our position clear on a number of points which may constitute possible lines of attack on our approach. We will conclude by summarising the answers we have given to these points.

(1) The danger that by providing techniques we may be supporting an existing management ideology without fundamentally challenging its values, is a real one. However, we see the use of techniques as means of generating greater understanding (ours and members of the organisation) about organisations in change. Wider understanding may in time help change managerial orientations and values if that is desired.

(2) There are problems of selectivity and bias in any approach to

organisational analysis. As individuals we can never avoid imposing constructs of our own on to the facts we discover. The only way we know of dealing with this danger is through making as explicit as possible the values and limitations we have brought in.

(3) By our choice of a systems model we have imposed a certain structure on the situation, and put some constraints on the kind of understanding we shall achieve and the kind of implications we shall draw from it. We make this choice on the grounds of its particular usefulness to the needs of the research on which we were engaged.

(4) Every organisation incorporates a large number of different groups, each with their own interests and needs and perspectives. There is no criterion from within a scientific discipline that would allow us to decide that some of these perspectives are more valid than others, or that any interest (say 'rational' interests as opposed to 'social' interests) or the needs of any group, should take precedence over others. This we have recognised and our approach enables us to take note of different perspectives in analysis.

(5) The concept of 'organisational goals' as necessary attributes of organisations does not seem a useful one in this research. We do not think it adds to our ability to explain behaviour or to assess performance, to impute 'goals' from observation of existing behaviour patterns. Although we identify certain dimensions of 'fit' with environmental needs, and have elected to assess performance in those terms, this is in itself a matter of somewhat arbitrary choice, made on grounds of relevance to our purpose, given the level of analysis appropriate to our research.

(6) We suggest that patterns of behaviour in organisations, and changes in patterns of behaviour, emerge slowly and somewhat inefficiently, as a result of decisions made during some subtle processes of negotiation between competing groups and coalitions and within the constraints imposed by technology, formal structure, authority systems and ideas of legitimacy. Individuals elect to join these shifting coalitions because they see them as the best means of satisfying personal goals within the organisation. Fundamental structural and cultural change in the organisation is likely to occur when for some reason the membership of coalitions or their power structure changes radically. It may not be appropriate to seek too hard for 'rationality' in the behaviour manifest in organisations, since the processes by which decisions are arrived at and later implemented are not themselves rational in this sense.

(7) The members of an organisation have many choices open to them. It is in their exercise of these choices (whether acting as individuals or as members of groups) that the structure and values of the organisation and its characteristic culture and modes of behaviour emerge. The interactions between organisational participants and the decisions they make are at the same time constrained by the structural features of the organisation and help this structure to emerge. Our analytical model enables us to examine closely at the microlevel the operation of choices and the patterns of

interaction and motivated behaviour, while treating the emergent structure at other levels as a constraint on these choices.

(8) However, what causes individuals to act in particular directions is the way they perceive the situation; the meanings they attach to it. A practical, very real problem for an investigator is the inaccessibility of the meanings people place on events, or of the perceptions they have of their part of the organisation, or even the satisfactions they achieve from participation. He is even less able to predict what meanings they will give to a new situation created as the result of some change process. We have paid close attention in all our case studies to meanings, perceptions, attitudes and relationships, but there must be some uncertainty about the accuracy of these so long as we have to rely on interview data or inferences made on the basis of observed behaviour. This fundamental inaccessibility of meanings is not a defect of the socio-technical systems approach as such. It is something inherent in social investigation, and perhaps more easily resolved by some of the techniques we suggest later.

(9) The problem of dealing with change is considerable, especially predicting what meanings will be attached to changes occurring in the wider organisation and what reactions will result. Working at the level of smaller units change becomes less of a problem so long as implementation of change is accompanied by a monitoring process that allows predictions to be verified or falsified, and the systems model modified as steps in the change strategy proceed. The techniques we describe later in the book rely very much on this dialogue between prediction and actual outcome.

(10) Although we consider it invalid to treat the organisation as though it had an existence of its own independent of the behaviour of individual members, it can be valid to abstract from many of the complexities of the decision-making processes and use the term 'organisation' to represent the emerging structure that can be regarded as constraining the patterns of behaviour under examination, given the level of analysis appropriate to that particular investigation. However, we should have a clear understanding of the processes that are actually occurring and ensure our model is compatible with them.

(11) Criteria of organisational performance, or means of evaluating performance, must be chosen on the basis of some external system of values. Our criteria are derived from the open systems model and we recognise the fact that this incorporates a certain value position that needs to be made explicit. The choice is made on grounds of relevance to this programme of research and change promotion.

There is a further, related, question that concerns the authors as individuals: that of the values and motives we started out with on this programme and of the effects actually produced, or even potentially produced, as a result of our involvement. The purpose of the programme, as seen by the sponsors, was to induce changes into the organisation, to make it more effective (as effectiveness was perceived by those who made the decision that our involvement should be permitted). We therefore became associated with a programme to promote change—change that was to be based on criteria we had accepted, or helped to select, or could defend on logical grounds, but which would inevitably change the structure of values, and the relative degrees of satisfaction obtained by different organisational participants. The argument we have put forward, that our involvement would lead to greater understanding of the many influences on behaviour, and that therefore it would eventually result in higher overall satisfaction, genuinely expresses our motives for getting involved. It may however evade an important issue. It is not by any means certain that the long-term effect would come about. We are not in control of the way better understanding might be used, and the argument ignores the differential effects in the short run on the satisfactions experienced by the people who at present hold membership in the organisation. This is a dilemma of the action researcher about which we remain concerned: by what right do we become involved in change of this kind? The answer will have to await a full assessment of the consequences of this programme.

NOTES TO CHAPTER 2

1. For some critical comments on the orientations of much literature on organisational change programmes, see Trist's (1968) review, and some later contributions in support by Glueck (1969), Raia (1972), Greiner (1972), Weisbord (1974), and Kahn (1974). Countering these criticisms it is possible to assert that some authorities concerned with general principles of organisation have not grounded their theories sufficiently in empirical findings, and so middle range theories are not of great relevance to the needs of practitioners.

2. Gouldner, op. cit., page 404. The rationality concept has been frequently discussed, but its usage has tended to vary considerably between writers. See for example'Argyris (1962), Burns (1966), and Thompson (1967, chapter 2).

3. ibid., p. 405.

4. The distinction is not always so clearcut in the literature. Nevertheless it is a distinction that needs to be considered in action research. The role of an action researcher contains many sources of conflict: among other things it has to combine positive analysis with judgement and with proposals for action based on some normative view.

5. op. cit., page 51. Other examples where feedback is advocated as a useful tool towards understanding are in Greiner (1967), and Mann (1957). See also Scott (1965), pages 266–283.

6. See for example some sharp comments on the hidden assumptions of some more orthodox programmes of organisation development by Ross (1971), Bier (1972), and Brimm (1972). Rapoport (1970) also touches on the problem.

7. This distinction is similar to the one Kaplan (1964) makes between act meanings and action meanings, and also to Myrdal's (1969) distinction between beliefs and values. We are suggesting that (using Myrdal's terms)

our beliefs can be kept fairly successfully in check by use of a well-chosen analytical model, but our values must be made explicit if their effect is to be controlled.

8. This is not the place to make a detailed examination of the problem of values in investigation. The position we have adopted is close to that of Myrdal (1958, 1969) but we do not consider the problem is overcome by careful choice and articulation of value premises. Rather, the intractability of the problems is made explicit.

9. See also Cyert and March (1963), pages 26–30, Fox (1966), and Yuchtman and Seashore (1967). Although the idea that organisations include many groups with diverse interests is an old one, the distinctive standpoint of these four papers is that the perspectives of any of these groups is probably as valid as any other. This view we respect.

10. For example Blau and Scott (1963) chapter 1, Simon (1964), Etzioni (1964) chapter 2, Parsons (1960) chapter 1, and Gross (1970).

11. See for example Selznick's (1949) study, developing the concepts of recalcitrance and unanticipated consequences, Blau's (1955) study of the effects of social cohesion among professional employees, Sills (1958) analysis of the succession of goals among voluntary organisations, Etzioni's (1964) discussion of displacement of organisational goals, and especially Thompson and McEwen's (1958) interesting arguments about methods of goal setting in response to different forms of environmental pressure.

12. Perrow (1961) makes a strong case that the relevant goals for organisational analysis are not the goals officially set for the organisation, but the operative goals. Largely he contends these are the sum of daily decisions made in the organisation. Etzioni (1960), however, shows clearly some pitfalls in this kind of position, not the least of which may be the practical identification of the outside observer with one segment of organisational participants whose values and experiences he shares or with goals of which he approves.

13. This point is made strongly by Burns (1966), in whose view both Cyert and March, and Simon, are proposing rational models of organisations and ignoring the involvement of members in many overlapping social systems, of which the formal system of the organisation is only one.

14. The view of organisational goals that seems most compatible with our conception of organisational processes is that of Thompson (1967) who defined them as 'the future domains intended by those in the dominant coalition'. However, if this is so, we consider the concept is not essential either to understanding of overall patterns of behaviour, or the definition of efficiency.

15. The basis of power in organisations is a matter of current interest; despite some uncertainty about its precise nature and an occasional suspicion that we revert to its use when we are unable to explain some organisational processes in other terms (March, 1966). Mechanic (1962) and Perrow (1970b) relate power to dependence and equate it with control over essential resources or (for Mechanic) access to persons, information and instrumentalities. Goldner (1970) seems to relate the power of a subunit to the ability to exploit others' perceptions that it was in possession of specialist information, to uncertainty and to occupation of a boundary maintenance function giving wide access to many key groups inside and outside the organisation. Hickson *et al.* (1971) and Hinings *et al.* (1974) see power based in control over strategic

contingencies that arise through the existence of uncertainty, avoidance of substitutability and centrality to the main processes of the system. Certainly the source of power seems to be control over some resource desired by and necessary to others.

16. This statement seems compatible with the detailed hypotheses put forward by Carter (1971) based on empirical studies to test the Cyert and March model. See also Burns (1961), Burns and Stalker (1961), pages 141–148, Pondy (1968), pages 312–320.

17. The perspective of most studies has been that decisions would be expected to be made at the formally appointed levels in the hierarchy of authority and with rational objectives particularly in view, perhaps after advice from lower levels and specialist departments. The studies have then suggested that this process becomes distorted by such defects as bounded rationality or political manœuvring or recalcitrance. There seem to be advantages in treating the decision-making process essentially as a political one, but constrained by ideas of legitimacy, formal authority relations, technological requirements, the environment and other needs for organisational survival. The new perspective may be more useful as an explanatory device.

18. See the analysis of influences on decision-making in Thompson and McEwen (1958). Also Emery and Trist (1965), and Terreberry (1967).

19. Blau (1964), Kapferer (1972), pages 6–8. See also the discussion of this position in Buckley (1967) chapter 5.

20. A new development from this argument was made by Mumford (1972) in setting out five implicit contracts between firm and employee over which a fit is required. This has been elaborated and criticised by Gowler (1974).

21. Examples occur in Roy (1952, 1955), Dubin (1958), chapter 4, Lupton (1963) chapter 10 and *passim*; and Jones (1969).

22. See Blau (1964), and Barth (1966).

23. Or so we assume. See note 15 above.

24. Perhaps the clearest statement of this as a problem occurs in Silverman (1970) chapter 6.

25. Further comments on this are made by Burgoyne and Cooper (1975). This position raises some problems of collaboration with managerial colleagues. How far are managers to be induced to use the criteria selected by researchers? If they are, must not the full reasons for selecting the criteria be made explicit? Ought managers then to be aware of all the value implications they entail, or does this involve either a perceived digression away from the essential tasks of the change programme, or a level of ethical and sociological sophistication too great for much progress to be made? These considerations must be considered in another work.

PART II

Applications of the Open Socio-technical Systems Approach

3 The Socio-technical Framework

We have said a good deal in part I about the theoretical respectability or lack of respectability of the approach we have described. In this part we begin looking at some detailed investigations made during the programme in more practical terms, as illustrations of the general approach.

To recapitulate, the purposes of the overall programme of which these detailed investigations were a part were to bring about changes in the company that would improve and maintain the organisation's capacity to survive and develop in increasingly difficult technical, economic and product market conditions. Essentially, it was hoped to increase the capacity of people generally who worked in the organisation to improve their own effectiveness. This would be done by increasing their understanding of the way organisational behaviour and organisational performance were determined, and encouraging them to apply this understanding in their day-to-day work. To this end members of the change team would work with local managers looking in detail at the needs of specific small operating areas and so they would jointly bring to light new facts about the influences on behaviour and discover more about the causes and consequences of organisational adaptation within that area. This investigation would probably lead to proposals for improvement in the area concerned, though, as we have made clear in the last chapter, the definition of improvement would itself be a matter for investigation.

Most of the individuals who had been involved in an area study would then, it was hoped, be given opportunities and encouragement to apply the new understanding either in the management situations for which they were responsible or would be responsible in future, or as the nuclei of further groups studying new areas, the members of which would in turn become familiar with new ideas and new ways of dealing with production situations. The aim was to create a self-sustaining increase in motivation as well as to develop new skills in organisational diagnosis. If managers could be encouraged to understand and use the new approach in their normal activities the perception by higher levels of authority that there was a continual need for formal direction and control might lessen, and superiors could take on a more supportive coordinating role, responding to the needs of subordinate departments with resources and encouragement so far as environmental constraints permitted, rather than monitoring them through tight and often inappropriate controls.[1] At the same time senior management would have more time for creative planning for the future, and if they could be guided into developing and using the skills appropriate to this a gradual change in the characteristic style of the organisation might occur.

At the base of this approach there had to be the development of a technique of analysis and model building for use in specific operating areas. In this chapter we describe what at the beginning of the programme we defined as open socio-technical systems modelling. In the rest of part II case studies from the programme will provide examples of how the techniques were applied, and in parts III and IV we develop further some of the implications from these studies.

As a first step in the formulation of a method for investigation and diagnosis the following rather simple construct was put forward and discussed by the team. A manufacturing department or service area may be usefully conceived of as requiring a *technical organisation* including typically, equipment, machinery and machine controls, process layout and workforce administration; and a *social organisation* to carry out the work. The social organisation comprises the participating human beings, their perceptions and motivations and the relationships they form with each other. The nature of the social organisation is constrained (but not wholly determined) by the technical organisation. It has some properties of its own, independent of the technology. There is a relationship of *mutual dependence* between the two, and this may be thought of as a source of efficiency or inefficiency, satisfaction or dissatisfaction.[2] It is the interdependence between the technical and the social that is crucial, and not just each of these taken separately. This interdependence constitutes the basis of the socio-technical system.

At the same time, manufacturing systems are open systems, organised to procure inputs—for example raw materials, technical knowhow, human skills and commitments—and to dispose of outputs, in such a way as to create a surplus which can be used to procure the fresh inputs the system requires if it is to survive and develop.[3] Thus the relationships between the work organisation and the technical organisation will be influenced by some parts of the environment, while the system must continue to satisfy certain obvious economic criteria in order to survive.

This basic open socio-technical systems model was to provide a simple conceptual framework for the investigation. The use of socio-technical systems techniques involves skills and specific methods of investigation. Firstly, it is necessary to have a fairly well-grounded conception of the kind of variable which will enter into the model and the kind of relationship which are being sought. Some discussion of these has already been made in chapter 1. Secondly, in order to collect and deal adequately with all the relevant information, skills may be required from a number of specialisms like work study, industrial engineering, ergonomics, statistics, accountancy and so on. It will also be necessary to involve members of the organisation including line and specialist managers, maintenance en gineers, foremen and shopfloor workers, who alone may know how a job is done in practice and what the implications of it are both for social relationships and for departmental efficiency.

The third need is for a technique of analysis that can be applied to the information so as to identify and map out the interconnections between the elements of the complex system, and the transactions which the system carries out with different segments of its environment; and to set out the consequences of things being as they are at a particular point in time.

Thought may then be given to possible ways of redesigning the system, the likely consequences of the redesign and some strategies by which the elements of an organisation might be amended without running into seriously adverse consequences.

What we have said in the last few paragraphs constitutes the elements of the approach we suggested might be used by an investigating team, and the kind of concepts they were invited to use when looking at each area. By adopting this fairly loose and general framework, and supplementing the concepts which were new to members of the team by the results of their own past experience, specialist knowledge and skills, they could then collect the data needed to fit into the framework and as a result they would be free to confirm or to reject the usefulness of these ideas.

We stress throughout that it is the interactions that take place in a system that are the most significant in formulating an explanatory model. When examining these interactions there are some elements which will almost certainly have to be included in the model if a satisfying explanation of behaviour and performance is to be obtained. These elements will include the inputs into the organisation in the form of materials, knowledge, skills and energies; the outputs going to a 'product market' of some kind which can be identified; and other elements of the environment which could constrain or influence the operation of the system. The elements within the system will usually include a technology, various control systems (including the hierarchies of authority, status and power, reward systems, budgetary controls and so on) and the social structure, the values held by and attitudes expressed by individuals and groups, which are generated in part by the formal elements of the organisation.

The open socio-technical systems approach thus provides a framework within which the investigating team may work. It allows for a considerable amount of discretion in the way an investigation is tackled. Indeed, since production systems vary so much in their characteristics, this discretion is almost essential and a great deal must be left to the knowledge and experience of the investigating team in their inquiries.

Further, how the findings are structured and reported is also a matter for the judgement of those involved in the investigation. The skill in socio-technical analysis is not that of carrying out a routine step-by-step technical procedure through to a final solution. It is rather that of devising some means by which relevant data may be identified, obtained and structured in the particular circumstances of that system, so that the workings of the system are fairly well understood. Thus the three cases reported in the following chapters do not follow any highly structured reporting system. They are individual reports on three very different production departments, and it is evident that the way in which the three investigations have been done shows considerable variations. The methods have been selected quite explicitly to suit the circumstances of each department and the structure of its investigating team. Nevertheless, in each case the framework of open socio-technical systems analysis is implicit in the way the investigation was undertaken, and in the report given of it. The amount of discretion which this technique allows lets us examine the particular circumstances of an individual system within the limits of the common framework we impose on it.

We suggest that the use of the open socio-technical systems approach in any given application can be justified only if it is demonstrated to be adequate for that application. We use the technique here for four separate but related purposes: as a means of analysis and explanation of behaviour and events in the areas under consideration; as a means of using the consequent understanding to outline the dimensions of performance for that area; to formulate a strategy for improvement of the situation; and as a means of implementing those improvements and monitoring the implementation. For the first purpose—analysis—some confidence can be placed in its use if in a whole range of different situations it can be shown to give explanations of behaviour more appropriate to the purposes of the analysis than some alternative approaches. We shall aim to demonstrate that this is so in this part of the book. Our attempt to carry the technique over into definition of performance, strategy formulation, implementation and monitoring are demonstrated in later parts; and it could be that different conclusions about its usefulness are to be derived from that experience.

The approach therefore is not put forward as a new orthodoxy to be used uncritically; it has continually to be tested against specific situations and against alternative approaches which might suggest themselves for any given situation and any given purpose. There must always be attempts to improve and to modify the approach on the basis of experience gained in each new situation to which it is applied. In the cases outlined in this part we suggest that it provides a powerful tool of analysis. The models of behaviour derived from it appear more satisfying as complete explanations of some of the features of those cases than explanations produced by alternative techniques. To demonstrate this is one of the purposes of this part.

We shall return in parts III, IV and V to the other applications we have made of sociotechnical systems analysis—to assess the state of performance to make proposals for overall improvement, to implement the change and to monitor it. Meanwhile in chapter 7 we shall explore further the nature and the value of open sociotechnical systems analysis as a means of explanation in a more detailed comparison of the findings from each of the three cases.

NOTES TO CHAPTER 3

1. On this concept of management, see for example the conclusions of Emery and Trist (1960), Lawrence and Lorsch (1967) chapter 9, and Lupton (1971b). What this approach would stress is the fit of senior management role—its appropriateness to the specific requirements of operating departments. Frequently it will be found that changes in style and methods of control in the direction favoured by, for example, McGregor (1960), Argyris (1962), and Likert (1961, 1967) are appropriate, but this needs testing in context and the needs fully understood before a change in role can be made effective.

2. Compare the statements of Trist and Bamforth (1951) page 37, and Rice (1958).

3. Katz and Kahn (1966), page 20 ff.

4 The Finishing Shop

The first case concerns a department which we will call the Finishing Shop. For this study the work of the management members of the change team whose project this was is combined with what the authors have supplied to the case: namely information obtained from those working in the shop about the attitudes, values and relationships which seemed to exist there and the integration of all the data into a socio-technical systems model. The study of this case was in every way a collaborative undertaking.

The Finishing Shop undertook the final surface treatment of a range of products manufactured in another part of the same works. The main manufacturing plant had a capacity considerably in excess of either current market demand for this range or the maximum capacity of the Finishing Shop. The components were manufactured for a period of several months, and put into an intermediate warehouse stock from which they were drawn as required. The main plant then turned to manufacturing other products that did not require finishing in this way. The Finishing Shop itself was kept going over the whole year, drawing all its components from the intermediate stock which therefore fluctuated considerably from one period to another, reaching a peak towards the end of each manufacturing cycle, when large stocks of every variety in the range would be held.

There were approximately thirty different sizes, types and shapes in the range processed in the shop, although about 80 per cent of the output consisted of eight types. Essentially the department, working to a schedule determined by current customer needs, carried out the following set of operations to each component

(1) semi-skilled work of manually grinding the surface of the component, the time taken to grind one piece varying from three to five minutes;
(2) polishing the surface in a semi-automatic hand-loaded polishing machine with a nominal cycle time of from eleven to seventeen seconds for each component;
(3) an automatic washing and drying process;
(4) visual inspection of the finished products which were then wrapped,

palletised and transported to the finished product warehouse for eventual despatch.

There are a number of alternative finishing techniques, some of which were being used by competitors. Others had been used in the past. The methods now being used were instituted about eight years before the investigation, after study of the market requirements and the techniques available at that time. Consequently, a considerable amount of capital was sunk into the process, and there were some constraints on a radical change.

Stocks of finished products were kept at a level much lower than intermediate stocks. The week's finishing programme was based on advance information given to the company by one dominant customer as to his likely call-off over the next few weeks. The works management had reduced finished stocks to the lowest convenient level which would enable it to meet short-term fluctuations in call-off, and for a long time the production programme had been matched very closely to the current call-off pattern. So the length of product run was relatively short, there were considerable fluctuations from month to month in the output from the shop and a quite marked seasonal pattern in production, in addition to fairly large random fluctuations in output with fluctuations in final consumer demand (often associated with government restrictions on credit). These were all superimposed on a slow long-term decline in the product market. Within the next few years little more than a replacement demand was forecast for the products and they were expected to be gradually phased out over the next decade. A feature of the product market over the previous fifteen years had been a marked change in product mix and particularly an increase in the average size and complexity of the components.

PROCEDURES IN THE SHOP IN DETAIL

The shop employed from 60 to 90 semi-skilled and unskilled men, working a five-day week on shifts, the shift system alternating from time to time according to demand between two shifts with considerable overtime and three shifts with regular opportunity for some voluntary overtime on Sundays. Five separate occupational categories were identified in the shop. For instance, there would typically be two conveyor men (loaders), from ten to eighteen hand-grinders, two polisher machine operators, three inspectors, and two or three final packers on each shift. Usually two different types were being finished simultaneously, and the grinders divided themselves, or were divided by their chargehands, into two groups, each specialising on one type. Normally one conveyor man and one polishing machine operator specialised on each type of product.

The general layout of the shop is illustrated in the plan (figure 4.1). Pallets of unfinished components previously brought in by fork-lift truck were pulled by a conveyor man to a position convenient to his unwrapping

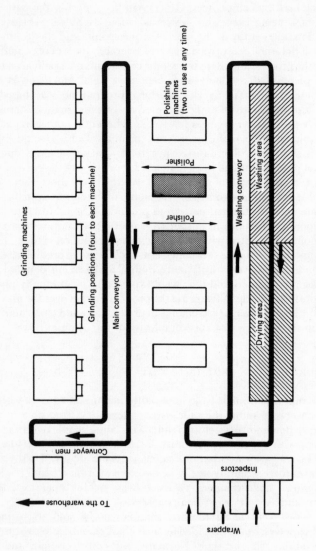

FIGURE 4.1   The finishing Shop layout

table. He unwrapped the components one by one and placed them on an assigned level on the conveyor, on which they travelled past the line of grinders. Each conveyor man used a different conveyor level, so that the types were separated. The grinders took the components off as they travelled past, ground the surface until they were satisfied with the finish obtained, and put the finished components on yet another level of the conveyor, whence they travelled on past the polishing machines.

The polishing machine operator removed the components one by one from the conveyor to the polishing machine, and after each short polishing cycle, he took the polished product out of the machine and carried it over to a second conveyor, on which it travelled through the automatic washer and dryer and on past the inspection position. The inspectors took the components, inspected them under strong lights, and graded them into three categories. If they were acceptable, the inspectors passed them on to the packers for rewrapping and stacking on pallets for despatch to the final warehouse. If the quality was unacceptable, but could in the inspector's opinion be corrected by regrinding or repolishing, the component was put aside for recirculation through the process. If not obviously correctable, it would be put aside to go to a reclaim shop or finally to the reject bins.

The packers wrapped up the products after they had been passed, stacked them onto pallets and removed the pallets to a despatch area ready for transport to the finished product warehouse. They also loaded the products marked for recirculation (usually known as 'regrinds') onto trolleys and wheeled them to the conveyor man, whose job it was to place them back on the conveyor, from where the identifying chalk mark signalled to the original grinder the fact that one of his components was unsatisfactory, and he had the responsibility of correcting the fault.

Much thought had been given to this system by the plant engineers who had originally designed it, and the work-study and time-study engineers and skills analysts who had devised the occupational structure, payment system and training schemes, and a complex series of rules and procedures had been devised. For example, ratios had been laid down, determining the proportions of men in any occupation who would be working at any one time. So, according to the number of grinders being used on any shift, specific numbers of conveyor men, polishing machine operators, inspectors and packers would be employed.

Further, a complicated payment system had been devised which reflected general company policy over methods of pay, namely that there should be a job-evaluated basic rate for each occupation, plus a large bonus based on the work content of the output actually achieved. This policy had resulted in different pay rules for different occupations. For example, the grinders (in 1969) were paid a basic wage of just under £16 a week, plus a group incentive based on the number of components passed at the end of the shift. Each size and type of component had, in theory, been work-studied separately, and the grinders' bonus would be based on the number of good components produced multiplied by the appropriate work value for that type and divided by the number of grinders actually working. However, above the conventional average of 80 pay units per hour production was rewarded less favourably than production up to 80 units, and an absolute maximum to permitted earnings was set at 109.5 pay units per hour.

The polishing machine operators had a job-evaluated basic rate of about 50p per week less than the grinders, and in addition a direct incentive bonus based on the total number of polishing operations they performed. The basic rate of the conveyor men was about 20p per week less than the polishing machine operators, and their bonus was based on the number of grinders who were present on any shift. For instance, when between ten and twelve grinders were at work, each conveyor man was credited with 78 units per hour bonus, for thirteen grinders he was given 79 units and for fourteen grinders 80 units.

The job-evaluated rate of the inspectors was very close to that of the grinders, and their bonus was based on the total number of components they examined. Each type and size of component was again given a different value, and in this case there was a different rate of bonus according to whether the components were passed as good, were allocated for recirculation, or were rejected. Finally, the wrappers had a job-evaluated basic rate similar to that of the conveyor men, but their bonus was based on the number of components they actually handled, and they were given an allowance for the handling of regrinds.

On each shift were two shift chargehands, responsible for training and for the progress of work up to the end of the washing and drying machine. A day foreman was responsible for overseeing this same part of the process, and he answered to a junior manager who was in charge both of this shop and of a newly developed finishing process elsewhere. The inspectors and packers, although working within this area and relying on the same conveyor system, were not part of this authority system, but were treated as part of the warehouse and made responsible to foreman inspectors in a neighbouring part of the factory.

THE APPROACH TO THE INVESTIGATION

There were two strands to the methods of investigation. On the one hand, data were collected on, for example, the costs of the operation, utilisation of plant, incidence of down-time and breakdowns, the percentage rejects of components and materials before, during and after processing, incidence and nature of customer complaints, labour productivity, labour turnover and the patterns of absence, the distribution and make-up of earnings and similar information over a wide field.

The second source of data was interviews with all those directly concerned in the shop, including managers, supervisors and shopfloor employees, partly to identify the varying perceptions which were held by different levels and different occupational groups, and partly to find out about employment histories, and the backgrounds of the individuals who worked in the shop. The interviews with managers and supervisors were largely unstructured, but with shopfloor employees they were more highly structured.

An explanatory model was then constructed showing the links between the engineering design, workflow, company rules, control procedures, supervisory and management structures, the perceptions held by various occupational groups, social structure and relationships, and the different aspects of behaviour which went to determine the performance of the Finishing Shop. A significant feature of this particular study was that data of all kinds were collected before any attempt was made to formulate detailed explanatory hypotheses about causes of behaviour or about the state of performance.

CONVENTIONAL INDICES OF PERFORMANCE

Despite the sophisticated design and controls, the local managers were very concerned about low efficiency, and expressed considerable dissatisfaction with the performance of the Finishing Shop as a whole. There were low output per man, apparently excessive machine down-time, earnings which in terms of skill, working conditions and application appeared to be out of line with the rest of the factory, fairly high rates of loss of components during processing and rejects of finished products, high rates of absence, and very high rates of labour turnover among conveyor men and polishing machine operators.

The work-study engineers were convinced that the average rate of grinder output was only about 75 per cent of what they considered reasonable. In fact, the grinders almost always achieved a nominal work rate of about 120 units an hour, which, given the gearing in the bonus scheme, gave them their maximum permitted bonus; and they usually achieved this about an hour before the end of the official working day. There was evidence in addition of slack time and of extended meal and tea breaks. The explanation given for this situation was that work values had become 'slack' over the course of time and that nominal performances bore little relation to actual work content. Gradual improvements both in manufacturing standards and in average grinder skill, meant that the effort involved in grinding a typical component had gradually been reduced. The grinders and their representatives were said to have resisted proposals to restudy and revise the rates, and had used agreements between the company and the trade union to support their case. Moreover, as new types were introduced, grinders insisted on taking the rates on existing types as the payment standard, rather than present-day time-studied work content. More and more of the piece rates in the shop were based on 'synthetic' values rather than up-to-date time-studied values.

Holding the company to the terms of the agreement, the grinders' representatives spurned any revision of piece rates except on condition of removing both the gearing and the ceiling to their earnings potential.

Managers were also concerned about apparently excessive recirculation of components returned for reprocessing by the inspectors. The 'average' component was said to circulate 1.6 times round the system, whereas only about one in five of the components at the most should need to be returned for regrinding or repolishing.

TABLE 4.1

Average Earnings Over Thirteen Weeks for Different Occupations
(1969)

	Basic wage[a] (£)	Incentive Bonus (£)	Total earnings within shift cycle[a] (£)	Overtime (£)	Total[a] (£)	Average·pay performance (u.p.h.)
Grinder	15·72	8·98	24·70	5·40	30·10	107
Conveyor man	15·14	3·42	18·56	7·18	25·74	80
Polishing machine operator	15·33	4·04	19·37	4·55	23·92	99
Inspector	15·75	11·50	27·25	2·60	29·85	115
Packer	15·20	10·28	25·48	2·71	28·19	113

[a]These figures do not correspond exactly with the rates given in the text. Being departmental averages, they reflect also differential rates of absence and overtime working as between occupations. Absence rates were high.

An analysis of earnings in the shop showed some curious features. Some of these are illustrated in table 4.1. For instance, although the differential between the grinders' and conveyor-men's basic rate was only about 70p for a forty-hour week, the differential in total earnings for forty hours was over £6. Although conveyor men and packers were on approximately the same basic rate, the packers regularly earned between £5 and £6 more than conveyor men in the course of a forty-hour week. Polisher machine operators received very low bonuses compared with grinders, inspectors or packers. Further analysis brought out that although the grinders' bonus earnings remained fairly stable from day to day and week to week, the bonus earnings of the other four occupations tended to fluctuate somewhat at random. Bonus was based nominally on the amount of work a man in a particular occupation did on the particular type of component he was handling. However the polishers and inspectors were entirely dependent on the grinders for the amount of work available to them and the grinders, by controlling their own output, determined the amount of bonus earned by polishers, inspectors and packers. Because there was no consistent ratio between the amount of work done on components of different sizes by different occupational groups (table 4.2) the effect of the grinders stabilising their own incomes was to build random fluctuations into the incomes of other groups.

TABLE 4.2

Comparison of Work Values per Component for Different
Occupations and Component Sizes
(values expressed in units per hour)

Occupation	Basis for pay	Type of component				
		A	B	C	D	E
Grinder	Units per component passed by inspectors (grade B values)	3·05	4·40	4·95	6·25	7·90
Polishing Machine Operator	Units per component going through polishing machine	0·380	0·395	0·395	0·510	0·565
Inspector	Units per component inspected and passed as good	1·40	1·60	1·60	1·95	1·70
Inspector	Units per component inspected and sent for regrind	1·00	1·20	1·20	1·45	1·20
Inspector	Units per component inspected and rejected	0·95	1·05	1·05	1·25	1·05

The marked seasonal fluctuations in production had traditionally been met by redeploying grinders to other work, and although redeployed men frequently left the company, little difficulty was experienced in recruiting the same men back at the time of re-expansion. Recruitment to the grinders' job was in theory from polishing machine operator, and the polishing machine job was usually filled from the conveyor man, but very high rates of labour turnover were experienced among conveyor men and recruitment of the right type of man was thought to be difficult. Turnover among polishing machine operators was also high.

About three per cent of the components entering the shop were wasted. There seemed to be three separate causes of wastage: losses during processing or rejects at the end of it due to equipment faults or lack of skill, defects which were present in the raw components entering the shop and which had not been detected by previous inspection processes, and rejects due to inappropriate inspection criteria in the shop. Most attention had been given to wastage caused by operator practices within the Finishing

Shop, and there was no information as to how much was due either to faulty incoming components or inadequately defined quality standards. Wastage through all causes added between £20000 and £30000 per year to the costs incurred in the shop.

TABLE 4.3
Absence and Labour Turnover

	Annual rates of turnover (%)	Absence rates (%) (including sickness absence)
Grinder	38	14·2
Conveyor man	220	21·7
Polishing machine Operator	180	17·0
Inspectors	5	7·6
Packers	32	12·8

Finally, there was considerable under-utilisation of machinery due to stoppages caused by mechanical breakdown, absence among the grinders (leading to unoccupied grinding positions) and excess capacity on the polishing machines. The incidence of breakdowns was very high. The factory generally tended to give low priority to the maintenance needs of small areas like the Finishing Shop and the declining market had induced managers to cut maintenance costs. However, the shop relied on its continuous conveyor systems and a breakdown in one small part of a conveyor could bring the whole work of the shop to a standstill. Because of the excess capacity, breakdowns in a polishing machine or on one grinding position were not serious. Nevertheless, lost time, as illustrated in table 4.4, was high.

TABLE 4.4
Mechanical Breakdown

Hours during which machines were inoperable in one recent year due to breakdown

Main conveyor	31 hours
Grinding machines	65 hours[a]
Polishing machines	1100 hours[b]
Washing conveyor	48 hours

[a] In the case of grinding machines, breakdown of one machine is generally followed by immediate substitution of a standby.

[b] There are five polishing machines, of which only two are usually in use at one time. Not all are fully substitutable, but a standby can usually be set up, and if on average one of the five is out of action of fifteen to twenty per cent of the total time, the effect on production may not be serious.

THE DIFFERENT PERCEPTIONS OF THE FINISHING SHOP

Orthodox measures of departmental performance are usually interpreted within a particular perspective: that of those who designed and laid down the policy for the department, and particularly that of engineering efficiency. They do not constitute a complete or objective description of the department. Further, the interviews showed that interpretations of these data were affected by many subjective views, and these views differed very considerably according to the perspective of the interviewee. It was possible to identify at least eight different perspectives among those closely associated with the shop, and the more important views of these groups about the nature of the shop as a system will now be summarised.

Senior Management
The senior management in the works had a fairly clear view. The Finishing Shop was a labour-intensive area and consequently there was much scope for restrictive practices and much potential for improvement. Technical problems had been met in the past and in solving these, earlier departmental managers had made mistakes which had resulted in loss of management control in the shop. Piece-work values had become extremely slack, but because of this history the grinders were in a position of considerable bargaining strength and able to bargain more and more concessions from managers. Grinders' earnings were greatly inflated and yet time-wasting, and extended meal breaks were blatantly practised. They did not deny their low productivity, but refused to renogotiate any job values, and used their bargaining strength to resist any reasonable values for new types of component. Because of this history the only practical solution appeared to be to replace the whole Finishing Shop by another more capital intensive process used for finishing other, more technically advanced products. Without analysing costs in detail it seemed obvious to senior management that if the same components could be finished on this new process with only twenty-five or thirty per cent of the labour force, efficiency would be increased and many of the present problems would be solved.

Departmental Manager
The departmental manager saw the shop in rather greater detail. Again, the main problems appeared to be the slackness in the work-studied values, low productivity of the grinders and their resistance to any change in the situation. He recognised that the grinders would not move on re-negotiation of their bonuses without a removal or modification of the gearing and of the absolute ceiling to their earnings, but concessions on this were prevented by his superiors, who feared that the effect on earnings differentials with other departments might cause disruption there. The departmental manager felt himself under considerable pressure from senior management to reduce costs of all kinds and increase his pro-

ductivity, and saw no cooperation forthcoming from his subordinates in helping him meet these strong pressures. He had become convinced that their 'mentality' was hostile and they were incapable of seeing reason, and he felt himself in a situation of continual bargaining with the grinders' representatives over the smallest matter, while they knew he could not concede any fundamental point to them.[1]

Disputes were continually occurring about quality variations in raw components. The grinders made unreasonable time-wasting demands for compensation for poor quality, and the manufacturing department appeared not to appreciate or to care that avoidable variability caused problems for the Finishing Shop management.

The departmental manager saw the pay system as being one of the main problems, particularly because of the effective differentials it produced between occupations. However, he could do nothing to change the pay system as a whole until the grinders had agreed to renegotiation of their own bonus rates. Labour turnover among conveyor men and polisher machine operators he recognised to be connected with the pay structure, but it appeared unreasonable to him that men would suddenly leave, just as they were becoming proficient in their own jobs, simply because there were no short-term prospects of promotion or transfer.

The manager resented his lack of control over the inspectors and packers, whose conditions of work and pay seemed out of line with the rest of the shop. In particular, the packers worked less hard than the conveyor men at a job which was of comparable skill, and yet could earn £5 a week more than them. He felt that comparability between the high standards of discipline he attempted to impose on the department, and rather slacker discipline on the inspection and packing side also caused difficulties for him.

The recirculation of components for reprocessing created additional costs in power and materials and created bottlenecks on the conveyors and polishing machines. Recirculation was mainly due, he thought, to grinders skimping their job, sending the components on round the system without inspecting their own work and using the final inspectors to do the job for them. There was also a suspicion that recirculation was practised by the inspectors as a means of creating double handling in order to raise their own pay.

Finally, the manager criticised the quality of the shift chargehands. Of the two chargehands on each shift, one was instructed to concentrate on the training of new grinders and on increasing grinder skills generally, while the other supervised the flow of work. The manager believed that neither chargehand on any shift carried out these duties efficiently. They acted rather as servants and assistants of the grinders, polishers and inspectors, working through every break period both on the polishing machines and on the final conveyor, polishing half-finished components left on the main conveyor by the grinders, and then emptying the final conveyor at the inspection position. This practice the department manager saw as encouraging subordinates in their slack approach to work. There was no noticeable improvement in the skill standards of the grinders since a chargehand trainer had been appointed.

One thing he admitted the chargehands could not avoid was the minor maintenance work they did to the polishing machines and other equipment. The manager was particularly concerned about the poor standards of maintenance in the shop and the consequent frequency of breakdowns. This he felt unable to influence, especially since he was under pressure actually to reduce current costs. He recognised that if the work of the shop were not to be wholly disrupted, then his chargehands must do some of the maintenance and emergency repairs. However, this was another distraction from their proper job.

Chargehands and Foreman

The chargehands and foreman held fairly strong and rather different views. The main problem as they saw it was the pay structure, especially the effective differentials, which necessarily reduced the motivation of conveyor men and polishers. Another important problem which they felt management did not appreciate, was the layout of the plant and the way work flowed round the conveyor system, which was liable to keep the grinders at the far end of the conveyor starved of components. There was a tendency for the longer service and more skilled grinders to have gravitated towards the near end of the conveyor, where not only did they get a plentiful supply of raw components, but were able to some extent to pick and choose between them and to select those which required least work. Those at the far end tended to be less skilled, to be less accessible to supervision and help from the chargehands, and to have a poorer selection of components to work at, for which they might sometimes have to wait. One consequence, the chargehands felt, was that those at the far end of the conveyor tended to rush and skimp the job to keep up.

Supervisors also believed that the conveyor forced the polishing machine operator into a number of difficult situations; on the one hand, if he did not work very fast at the time grinders were at their maximum output, the main conveyor became congested with half-finished components, with consequences on grinder behaviour; on the other hand, if the final conveyor, or the washer and dryer, were giving trouble, that conveyor could also become congested, causing the polisher to slow down. It was because of this crucial balance around the polishing machines that the shift chargehands were forced to work during their breaks clearing both conveyors for the beginning of the next spell of work, in order to avoid the tense situation likely to arise through continued congestion.

The conveyor problem was exacerbated by the frequency of mechanical breakdowns of the conveyors and the polishing machines. Breakdowns which caused loss of production had an immediate effect on grinders' pay, and the chargehands and foreman recognised the importance of repairing breakdowns and getting the system in operation again as soon as possible.

These circumstances made heavy calls on shift chargehands' time and although they recognised the importance of grinder training, they had found it impossible to supervise new starters or to implement the skills analysis training scheme, and had found the only effective way of training recruits was to revert to the practice of allowing them to work alongside a skilled man and occasionally to give them a helping hand. They saw the whole situation as most unsatisfactory, but did not believe the manager appreciated the problem.

The men actually operating the equipment tended to present rather narrower and more particular perceptions of the department, centred on their own occupations rather than the overall performance of the department. The structured interviews tended to direct respondents' attention to their own circumstances, and to look at other people mainly in relation to the effect on themselves.

Grinders

Grinders saw their job as fairly satisfying but incorporating frustrating elements, centring particularly around the conveyor system, variable quality of raw components, breakdowns and poor maintenance, and the general layout and working conditions. Recirculation of faulty components was seen as causing extra work and difficulties in achieving production targets.

The satisfactions in the job seemed to be due largely to the perception of considerable skill, discretion and responsibility for quality, and almost all grinders saw themselves as members of a cooperating team, consisting certainly of grinders, conveyor men and polishing machine operators, and less certainly inspectors and packers. The need to work together, both with other grinders and with the two other occupations, created both satisfactions and frictions, within the team of grinders and between grinders, conveyor men and polishing machine operators. The feeling of interdependence was expressed in many ways typified by some of the comments made about methods of pay.

Almost all grinders were satisfied with the way they themselves were paid, but spontaneously expressed sympathy with and dissatisfaction with the methods of pay of the other two occupations. Quite frequently, spontaneous suggestions for a shop bonus or some group method of payment were made. The bonus system influenced methods of collaboration between grinders. Each day the group set itself a target output which would yield maximum bonus earnings, and each man would agree to produce his quota, which most groups then divided into batches. Because of skill differences and differences in speed of working some men always completed their batch earlier than others, and then waited while the slower workers were catching up. There was a minor amount of helping out between individuals.

One of the topics on which grinders spoke at some length was that of training and again the comments were fairly unanimous: that training at the moment, despite the existence of an official training scheme, was inadequate, resulting in variations in skill and speed of working. This in turn increased tensions within the group, and by encouraging the less skilled men to rush, helped to augment the number of recirculated components.

Supplementing these views was information about the grinders' backgrounds, the most striking feature of which was the complexity of their employment histories. Four-fifths of them were local men with long and complicated histories of coming into and out of the company, and of transfers between different works in the same town. Very few had worked continuously in their present spell for more than two years although many of them had been in and out of the Finishing Shop at various times over the last ten or twenty years. Talk of redundancy (by which was meant not formally recognised redundancy, but rather transfers to other departments on work which the men often felt unacceptable, or voluntary leaving in anticipation of contraction) was a characteristic feature of the shop, and helped to form some intragroup attitudes. There was a need to protect work, and some resentment about a redundancy scheme which meant that older, less flexible or productive colleagues tended to remain in the shop during periods of contraction while the more enterprising men were forced out into other jobs. Whatever the effects, labour instability was seen by most employees as a feature of the department imposed by the firm rather than the employees. This applied to all occupations except the inspectors who tended to have had long and stable periods of employment.

Conveyor Men
The attitudes of conveyor men contrasted greatly with those of the grinders. The majority positively disliked their job and no one expressed satisfaction with it. Most were determined they would shortly either move on to other jobs in the works or leave altogether and most in fact had left within a few weeks of the discussions. The conveyor man's job was perceived as being unskilled and uninteresting, but requiring a great deal of physical energy. These dissatisfactions were reinforced by engineering faults on the conveyor, and by the belief that it was of inadequate capacity. Moreover, tensions between conveyor men and grinders appeared; the grinders were recognised to have free time whereas the conveyor men were 'always sweating to keep up with the grinders' and under pressure from them to keep the conveyor loaded. Recirculation of components (for which the grinders were held responsible) added to pressure of work.

It was difficult to separate dissatisfaction with the job from dissatisfaction with pay, each reinforcing the other. The weekly take-home pay was seen as inadequate in absolute terms, and not only in relation to the high pay of the grinders; but it was made slightly more tolerable because of overtime opportunities in other departments, and because there was some helping out by the grinders as well as expressions of sympathy from them. One comparison which did cause resentment, was between the conveyor men and the packers, whom all the conveyor men saw as having a far easier job with far higher pay. The solution to the pay problem was generally seen as a bonus common to the whole shop. They generally regarded those working in the shop as one cooperating team, despite some differences in interest between conveyor men and grinders and despite the divisions caused by the payment system. Their particular position at the beginning of the process caused difficulties because of the pressures put on them to keep the grinders fully supplied. But potentially the grinders were dependent on them and stood to lose a great deal should the conveyor men refuse to cooperate.

Polishing Machine Operators

The polishing machine operators were not quite as hostile towards their job as the conveyor men, but still saw it as having very little skill or interest, and entailing a great deal of hard physical work and danger, as well as dirty and unpleasant conditions. Again like the conveyor men, dissatisfaction with the job was tied up with dissatisfaction over earnings, which they compared with the grinders' earnings. Polishers' grievances concerned both the level of pay and the fluctuations in it. Again, recirculation of components was one of the factors making for harder work on the part of the polishers, and this was again blamed on lack of attention on the part of the grinders. Closely associated with this were further complaints about poor maintenance, particularly on the polishing machines, and the point was frequently made that despite spare capacity, standby machines were often not set up to cope with the possibility of breakdown.

There seemed to be two potential compensations for polishing machine operators: that the job was a crucial one, on which grinders must rely to get production through the shop, and that therefore the polishing machine played a key role in team work; and that the grinders did in fact cooperate, to the extent that they would occasionally come voluntarily in slack periods and start up a standby machine if one was available, to help clear a backlog.

Inspectors and Packers

Between these three occupations on the one hand and the inspectors and the packers on the other, there appeared to be some social distance. A number of reasons emerged for this. One was the fact that there were two separate authority systems and that the inspectors and packers were not formally responsible to the same supervisors. A second was the difference in conditions of employment and the basis of pay. Thirdly, their work was physically separated from the closely collaborative work round the main conveyor; the intervention of the second conveyor relieved many potential frictions and introduced rather more discretion in the way the inspectors timed their work.

Another reason for the observed distance was the potential role conflict between the grinders and polishers producing the components, and the inspectors on whose judgement both production bonuses and extra work in the form of recirculation depended. This social distance was symbolised during tea and meal breaks by the inspectors and packers remaining for their breaks near their own working positions while the rest of the department invariably went to a local rest room.

The inspectors and packers appeared to have less emotional involvement either positive or negative with their job than the conveyor men, grinders or polishers. The inspectors' job was seen as fairly skilled but lacking in interest, and the packers saw their job as neither skilled nor interesting, but entailing few problems. There were some minor complaints about monotony, and the inefficiency of the automatic washer and dryer, but the comments were by no means as central in the men's minds as for other occupations. There was also considerable division as to whether they were or were not part of a team covering the whole shop. They were less concerned about the pay or the problems of other occupations in the shop, although some muted sympathy was expressed for the polishing machine operator, the occupation to whom the inspectors were closest physically.

The general attitude in the shop to supervisors was very favourable, although the chargehands obviously had no very high status. Men almost invariably spoke highly of the ability of the chargehands, but there was a clear and consistent view as to what their duties were, summed up in the phrase 'jack of all trades'. They were seen as maintaining and keeping the machines working, and as the key element in keeping the whole system operating. The chargehands were seen as structuring their job in such a way as to facilitate the flow of work and allow the grinders to meet their desired performance level. They ensured that the equipment was operational and reallocated men to different jobs, according to the flow of work and to absence. The one disadvantage was seen in the fact that the chargehands were not responsible for the work of the inspectors and packers and therefore they were unable to reallocate jobs over the whole shop.

A SYSTEMS VIEW OF THE ELEMENTS AFFECTING PERFORMANCE IN THE SHOP

One characteristic of perceptions is that they tend to be partial views and to have a particular perspective. Whether as descriptions of the department or as explanatory models, perceptions are incomplete in themselves.

For instance, it is possible by looking at the managers' perceptions of the shop to identify what would be the most important elements in their explanatory model, and also to make some guesses about the lines of causation and interaction which they assumed. The elements included: a

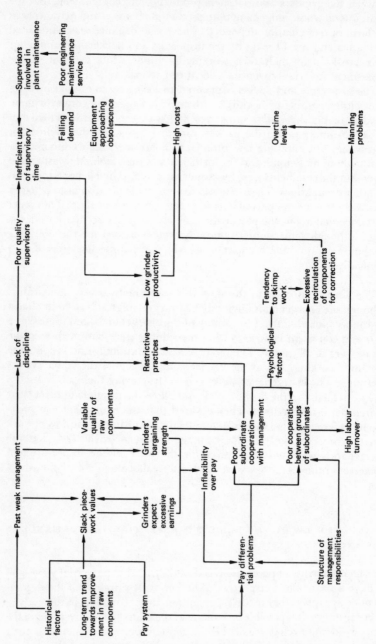

FIGURE 4.2　A management-oriented view of the Finishing Shop

past history of weak management and poor discipline, gradual improvement in raw component quality, grinders' expectations of excessive earnings, excessively low grinder productivity, lack of cooperation by subordinates, both with management and among themselves, excessive recirculation of poorly finished components, poor maintenance standards, inadequate cooperation from the supplying department, poor quality of supervision, work values which were far too slack and a payment system which encouraged high earnings and low productivity. It is not clear whether the managers had worked out explicitly in their own minds the causal relationships between all these variables, but in so far as they had, it would lead to a model of causation which was already fairly complex, though probably inadequate as a basis of explanation of behaviour and performance in the shop. For illustration, one might regard the diagram in figure 4.2 as representing this model pictorially; the arrows in the diagram would indicate the direction of causation or influence between the various elements.

If one turned then to the explanation postulated by the supervisors, one would discover a different model being proposed, in which a central part was played by various elements of the technology, especially the layout of the plant and the balance between different parts of it, the problems imposed by the conveyor system on those operating it, the problem of maintenance and prevention of breakdown. Other important parts would be played by the payment system, the flow of production through the plant and the relationships which existed between various subordinate groups. This is illustrated in figure 4.3. Some elements which played an important part in the managers' model are missing from this one, including the use of bargaining strength, the existence of restrictive practices, deliberate restriction of production, and costs (this last largely because supervisors in this works did not see themselves, and were not seen by management, as responsible for costs).

Likewise, models could be constructed, and illustrative diagrams drawn, of the situation as it affected and was perceived by each of the shopfloor occupations in turn.

The models which are held by different groups within an organisation may contain different elements; and even where the elements are common, the relationships perceived to exist between those elements may be different. Where each participant or group of participants has a different model of the system in his mind, this is bound to affect the relationships between the various participants and react back further on their behaviour. Satisfactions and dissatisfactions, values and conflicts are produced by the technical arrangements, the pay system and other control systems, but in addition to these, the interaction between the varying perceptions held about the system is also crucial in helping to generate patterns of behaviour.

There is a further point: that not only is each partial model inadequate as a total explanation of the situation, but there is no justification for

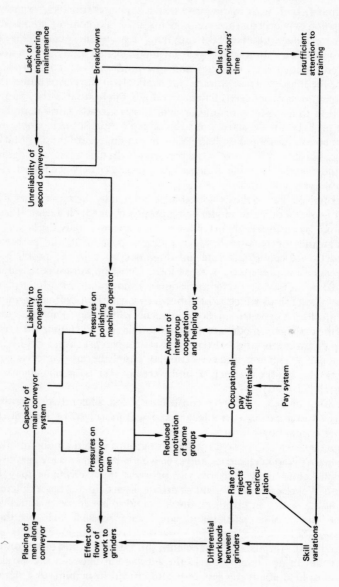

FIGURE 4.3 A supervisory view of the Finishing Shop

assuming that a sum of the perceptions of everyone connected with an organisation would be any more complete. Some elements tend to get left out of all models, and since all of them are likely to contain some elements of misunderstanding, new postulates have to be brought in to reconcile them. It is here that the skills of systems analysis come in.

An explanatory model in systems terms is by definition an interactive model, in which the influences on any particular activity are multiple. This being the case, the particular point at which one begins to construct the model is not important. All the elements we have been describing will interact with a number of other elements, and may well produce a series of nuclear partial explanations of particular features of behaviour, which however will themselves influence and be influenced by other parts of the model. We will begin by examining the effect of certain features of the technology.

The main conveyor is one of the crucial elements, because through it a number of inflexibilities were built into the jobs of conveyor man and polishing machine operator. The former came under pressure from the grinders, especially those at the end furthest away from him, who would be starved of work. The polishing machine operator had to try to discharge the conveyor at the same rate as finished components were being placed on it by grinders. If he did not, the conveyor tended to get congested, and finished components would begin to be piled up around, with risk of damage, and perhaps more important, grinder frustration. The pressures on both conveyor men and polishing machine operators were increased because of the periodic batches of recirculated components, which had officially to be loaded by the conveyor man, and which went through the grinding process more quickly than raw components. They were also increased by breakdowns, and by grinders' conscious variations in their speed of working, in which fear of breakdowns played a part.

Breakdowns had increased over the years because of the age of the plant and inadequate maintenance, but also because the gradual increase in size and weight of components was putting more strain on machinery designed for different conditions. (It is interesting to note here how market trends can have a direct effect on rates of breakdown.) Grinders' perception that breakdowns frequently occurred and put their earnings at risk induced them to put in as much effort as possible at the beginning of each shift, so that in the event of a breakdown, they would still be able to make up their output by the end of the shift or, if the breakdown were prolonged, would qualify for a high 'average' bonus payment on the basis of hours worked. Thus, in the first two or three hours conveyor men and polishers were working very hard (and incidentally the risk of breakdown was being increased by yet further overloading—an interesting interaction between pay system and breakdown rate). The batch system of working already described exacerbated these variations in working speed and meant that the conveyor men and polishing machine operators not only compared their pay unfavourably with the grinders, but saw groups of them standing

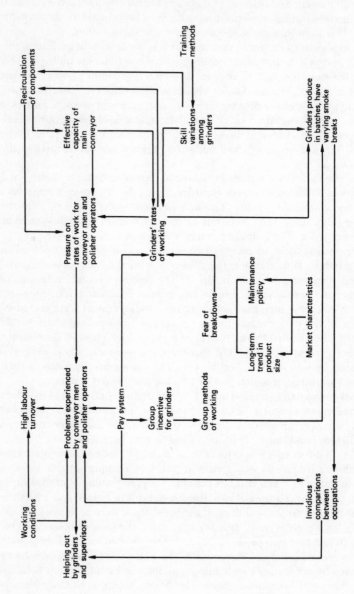

FIGURE 4.4 The sociotechnical system round the main conveyor

around smoking while they themselves were still under pressure from the conveyor.

Already then, in this one small area round the main conveyor, a fairly complex pattern of influence is emerging, and the variables in it may be illustrated (figure 4.4). If the situation had ended there, the system would almost inevitably have broken down. Some mechanisms for resolving the conflicts and tensions must have been established, and in this case the situation was made more tolerable by the grinders and chargehands both modifying their job requirements. While still maintaining considerable pressure on the conveyor men, the grinders nevertheless had unofficially undertaken to reload the conveyor with batches of recirculated components at convenient times, relieving the conveyor men of the frustrating job of, as they saw it, putting the same components on two or three times over. Other grinders would voluntarily start up a standby polishing machine, and work alongside the regular polishing operator for a few minutes to help clear a congested conveyor.

The chargehands were conscious of the tensions around the polishing machines, and therefore of the need to keep them working, to the extent of doing all of the routine maintenance on them, cleaning them out and clearing the blockages which occurred in them, and putting in a hard spell of work during official break periods, in order to clear the washing conveyor and those levels of the main conveyor containing half finished components. Further, the outgoing conveyor men had come to an arrangement to leave the conveyor full of raw components, so that at the beginning of the next shift grinders could come in and start work straightaway, without putting a great deal of pressure on their own conveyor men to fill up an empty conveyor before they could start work.

What appears is that the conflict resolution mechanisms for this part of the system consisted mainly of unofficial 'helping out'. In other circumstances, they might have taken the form of manipulation of the pay system, hours of work, manning arrangements or other controls; or the conflicts might have led to modification of some of the elements of design. Why this had not happened seems mainly to have been a function of management philosophy: some insistence on maintaining discipline and ensuring controls operated as they had been designed. This itself could have been a consequence of the management belief that their shop had in the past had a 'weak' management. Any manipulation of controls like hours, payment rules or manning levels, perceived by management to have a 'disciplinary' connotation, would have been regarded, if openly recognised, as a 'weak' concession to militant bargaining, and if tacit, as a toleration of slackness.

The recirculation of unsatisfactory components affected performance both directly, and indirectly through its effect on attitudes. Another submodel can be constructed round this phenomenon. We have already seen that the grinders' pay system encouraged group methods of working which highlighted the differences in skill and speed between individuals. Skill differences were a result of the non-functioning of the skills-analysis training programme, which was itself partly due to the constraints on chargehands' behaviour and their own perception of what was needed of them. Recirculation, and also reject and wastage rates, were increased by the natural tendency of the poorly skilled men to skimp some of their work in order to keep up with their more highly skilled colleagues. A further factor was the varying quality of incoming components; some were far more difficult to grind than others, and some of the poorer components were likely in any case to be inadequately finished. The influence of quality differences was in turn increased by the working of the conveyor system and the selection of places along the conveyor in such a way that the more highly skilled men had more time to pick and choose which components they would work on, with the natural temptation to leave the worst components to those who had no choice, who were less skilled, and more likely to create rejects or regrinds.

Inspection criteria at the end of the manufacturing process had not been very clearly defined, and there was little understanding by the manufacturing inspectors of the needs of the Finishing Department. Although manufacturing reject rates were fairly high, it was not entirely clear how much relation the criteria for rejection bore to those a skilled grinder would have preferred. At the other end, too, the Finishing Shop inspectors were assessing quality on criteria defined without a great deal of evidence that they fully reflected customers' needs.

Problems however arose in our early attempts to explain patterns of events. The level of recirculation, at approximately 60 per cent of the net output from the shop, was extremely consistent from shift to shift over long periods of time, and seemed to hold irrespective of size, type or quality grading of raw components. A short investigation by the research department into the pattern of recirculation had confirmed this figure of 60 per cent, but there were indications that components were recirculating almost at random, so that any given component passing the inspectors had about a thirty-seven per cent chance of being recirculated no matter how many times it had already gone through the system. These facts had supported managers in their view that recirculation was being 'manufactured' by the inspectors, and that good components were circulating round the system in order to increase the amount of handling for inspectors, packers and polishing machine operators whose bonus depended on quantity handled.

The difficulty with this very plausible explanation was that attitudes towards recirculated components were extremely hostile, and the polishing machine operators expressed perhaps the greatest dislike of all, both of the congestion caused by 'regrinds' and of the extra work. Some of the hostilities expressed towards the inspectors were associated with allegations that they sent too many components back through the system. Almost certainly, social pressures in the shop would have tended effectively to reduce to the minimum the number of components recirculated through the system.

The evidence about recirculated components was thus to some extent contradictory, and for a long period difficult to reconcile. Eventually, other information came to light which it would have been difficult to obtain from those involved: that one should look for a difference between recorded recirculation and actual recirculation. Recording of numbers was wholly in the hands of the inspectors, and it was well known that all inspectors' booking in the factory was very approximate, and was done periodically on the basis of fairly conventional proportions. In this case the conventional proportions overstated the amount of recirculation, and it was suspected (though for obvious reasons this could not be verified) that the inspectors deliberately misbooked in order to raise both their own and the polishers' bonus earnings. Meanwhile, the number of components physically circulating was probably restricted strictly to those which had regrindable faults on them. When a quantified investigation was carried out—a survey regarded by the men as being for control purposes—the number of booked regrinds and of physical regrinds coincided and this was tolerated in the shop during the few hours of the investigation.

Thus by manipulation of the payment system and misbooking of production, some alleviation of the differential between grinders and polishing machine operators was achieved, but the pay of inspectors and packers had been put out of line with the rest.

Another partial model could be constructed around the pay system and direct lines of influence leading to and from it. The pervasiveness of the influence of the pay system is rather striking and that model would be a complex one. Alternatively, a submodel could be constructed around the defined supervisory role and responsibilities on one hand, and the actual behaviour of supervisors on the other.

Rather than look in detail at these particular submodels, however, it may be more beneficial to fit a number of the nuclei together in a general explanatory model in sociotechnical terms of the complex patterns of behaviour in the shop. The kind of causal relationships which would be found are those illustrated in figure 4.6.[2] However, no two-dimensional sketch of this kind can represent completely the complexities of an explanatory model in a situation like this. A diagrammatic representation is necessarily a serious over simplification of the pattern of causation postulated by the model.

We have given a general explanation of behaviour in this shop, within the systems framework outlined in the last section. It would have been possible to have gone into considerably more detail about certain aspects of these relationships. However, sufficient has been expressed to illustrate the kind of explanatory model which can emerge if enough is understood about the interactive nature of the system even in a small department such as this.

The apparent contrast between the new model and the original management perception of the shop in which the important elements were deliberate restriction of output, resistance to bonus proposals, the lack of

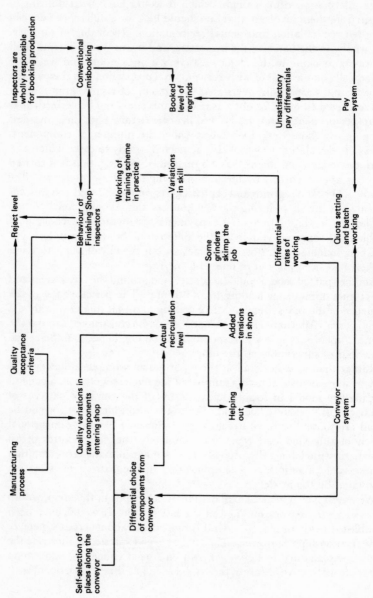

FIGURE 4.5   The recirculation problem

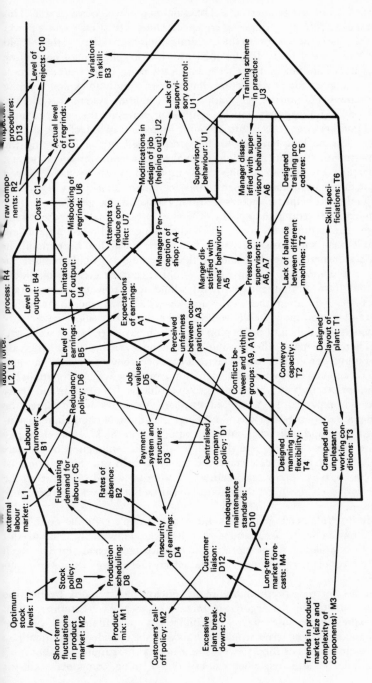

FIGURE 4.6 A sketch of the more important relationships in the socio-technical system of the Finishing Shop

discipline and the grinders' use of bargaining power, is considerable. This is not to say that the grinders were unconscious of their bargaining power or that, had other factors in the Finishing Shop been different, they would not have used it to the full for their own benefit; one cannot say. In the present circumstances, there were manifestly many other reasons to resist any change in the pay structure than a desire simply to exploit a strong bargaining position in negotiation. The conveyer system was already working to full capacity, especially if the pressures on the conveyer men and polishers were taken into account. Moreover, in a declining market there was no long-term or medium-term possibility of increasing the departmental output (although seasonal peaks would continue to occur). Therefore any increase in individual output could only be achieved by a reduction in the number of men employed, and the long history of periodic redundancies helped to increase resistance to such a change. Moreover, the conventional redundancy policy of 'first in last out' meant in the eyes of many that redundancy would affect the younger and more enterprising family men, and particularly would affect those who had been mobile in the past, whereas the older and less flexible employees would remain. To agree to a new pay system which would encourage greater individual output from a smaller department would tend to cause more stress, particularly for the rather slower and less skilled men who, so far as they were older and more stable would remain there, but who were already having some difficulty in keeping up with the average rate of working.

There were many other possible effects. Under existing rules an increase in output per grinder would actually reduce conveyer men's pay and would also make the work studied manning ratios between occupations less appropriate, thus increasing intergroup problems. If a rise in productivity was accompanied by a rise in grinders' pay, this would upset the differentials between grinders' earnings and those of chargehands, conveyer men and polishers, and if in compensation the lower levels of pay were made more adequate this might affect the willingness of grinders (who would in any case have less time) to help out. Since grinders' discretion over speeds and methods of working would be reduced, the effects of breakdowns on their ability to earn a bonus would become more serious.

In general, a change in job values would completely upset established relations between occupations and between individuals, and in this complex situation, where a precarious balance had been attained between all the conflicting elements, the total effects of a change were unpredictable.

Thus there were probably many unexpressed reasons behind the reluctance to consider negotiating on rates of pay and work studied values; unexpressed because they were difficult to articulate, and because discussion in these terms would probably not be considered legitimate by either managers or shop stewards in a normal bargaining situation.

Similarly, although poor quality of incoming components caused genuine difficulties for grinders the frequent complaints and bargaining sesssions about it were probably important mainly in the context of protecting the interests of the less skilled, given the actual training procedures, the conveyor system and the regrind situation.

CONCLUSION

We have in this chapter been concerned with demonstrating a particular method of investigation which was used for the Finishing Shop, and with examining a number of different perceptions about activities in the shop. Further, we have tried to demonstrate how the concepts of open socio-technical systems analysis can be used in conjunction with these perceptions and with other facts, to construct what we would claim to be a more complete explanation of the patterns of behaviour in the department.

If a more satisfactory explanation is obtained by this method, that in itself has considerable practical advantage. Better understanding of the patterns of influence should enable those responsible for operations in the shop to operate with a more realistic model in their minds, be better able to influence the situation and perhaps have more ability to predict the effects of their actions. In this particular case, a more complete understanding might have enabled the managers to operate on some of the other factors under their control like quality, the production schedule, stocking policy, engineering maintenance, technical design and the balance of workflow, and possibly occupational structure, to improve the situation, rather than concentrating their energies on the costs of high wages and wasted man hours.

We shall consider the possibilities for improvement in the Finishing Shop at length in chapter 12, and show there that, complex though it is, the socio-technical systems understanding could help in the formation of a step-by-step strategy for improvement—a proposed movement towards a new situation. In chapter 15 the actual course of events on the change programme is described, and it appears that where the actual implementation of change is concerned, reliance on the socio-technical framework alone as a basis for implementation, as distinct from improving understanding of an existing situation, may be insufficient.

In this part we are mainly concerned with an illustration of the kind of explanation arrived at through open socio-technical systems models and with showing the patterns of causation that tend to appear in a systems study of industrial situations. Other examples appear in the next two chapters, where different patterns emerge.

NOTES TO CHAPTER 4

1. Compare the striking by similar comments on the position of the deputy in Trist and Bamforth (1951) IV, 4 (The Strain of Cycle Control)

2. Readers will note that each of the variables in Figure 4.6 is given a code letter and number. These relate to the classification of socio-technical variables given in the Appendix to Chapter 8. For example, in the terminology of that chapter, the variables lettered A are all attitudinal variables, those lettered D are Designed Mediating Mechanisms, and those lettered T are Designed Technical variables. It is interesting that this diagram (and those derived from investigations in other small systems, such as the Press Room) can be divided off into discrete areas in such a way that almost all the variables in one area are of a particular class. The interactions between classes of variables (e.g. between technical and attitudinal categories) can thus be seen at a glance. The inter-class influences from this diagram may be compared with the more general scheme illustrated in Figure 8.1.

5 The Press Room

This chapter looks at another small production department which, for the purposes of the study, we have called the Press Room.

THE SETTING

Raw materials manufactured elsewhere in the same factory are transformed in the Press Room into a finished product consisting of sections of semicircular profile. The sections pass directly from the Press Room to the warehouse and thence via regional depots to the customer. Customers expect deliveries within a fortnight of placing orders, and production is geared to the present state of the order book with the warehouse providing a temporary buffer between the production department and fluctuations in the product market. There is some seasonal variation in demand and a general trend upward in the size of the market as a whole. Production is by batches, the same basic product being made in a wide range of different sizes. The product and the production methods employed are simple and there has been little technical change or innovation since they were introduced ten or fifteen years before this investigation.

At the time of the study the department had four separate machines, each of which could be used for carrying out the production processes. Production involved a number of distinct steps on the part of small teams of press operators. First, the raw material was collected from adjacent stores, cut to size and 'pleated' on a pleating machine adjacent to the press. Then the pleated material was pressed to shape and cured under the presshead, the length of time required for this curing depending on the size and thickness of the product being made. After pressing, the cured material was sawn and trimmed to give the required final profile. Sections were then stockpiled to await the attention of the quality control inspector, although the operators noticed and discarded most of the faulty items in the course of manufacture.

In all, about thirty men were employed in the shop on each shift and at the time of the study there was continuous seven days a week operation with a 'continental' type four-set, three-shift system. Each set had its own shift foreman, and in addition a senior foreman was on duty on days.

When the Press Room was chosen as an area for investigation, the marketing department had forecast a steady increase in the demand for the items being produced. As demand increased the department was showing increasing difficulty in meeting the calls made upon it. The market was competitive, and if the department was to take advantage of the buoyant market it had to be able to deliver sections of the sizes required, of good quality, at times promised, and at low production cost.

The achievement of these objectives depended in the first instance on having enough sections of the right size in the warehouse at any time. A preliminary study indicated that the technical capacity of the department was, in fact, sufficient to meet the forecast demand provided the presses were fully utilised. Therefore, once a stocking policy appropriate to the demand trend had been chosen, maintenance of the designated stock level at low production cost depended on: the output of a team of men on a given machine in any shift; the incidence of machine downtime and the consistency with which the machines were manned; the amount of materials wastage or rejects of finished products; and the range and proportion of different items produced in any given period of time. Initial talks held with the members of the department also highlighted these same factors and suggested that they were likely to become the key variables in any strategy of change.

EARLY STAGES IN THE INVESTIGATION

The investigating team was to examine the department as a socio-technical system and construct a model of the interactions in that system. We needed, therefore, to try to understand the sequences of events actually occurring in the Press Room and how these events were related to each other and to what was happening outside the works. We would examine the relationships between the technical organisation, resource inputs, nature of the labour market and product market, and variables such as the wage payment scheme and supervisory system, all in relation to their effect on the members of the department and the behaviour which resulted. It was not enough just to look at the relationships between physical features (plant, materials, labour, content of work, etc.) and technical constraints on machine utilisation like cycle times, downtime, expected absence and turnover of labour. It would be important to discover how the whole interacting system in the department generated opportunities, tensions and dilemmas that affected the attitudes of its members, and through these influenced productive behaviour. It might then be possible to trace how change in one aspect of the department—for example supervisory behaviour, the intake of new people, the structure of the pay packet or the layout or capacity of the presses—would influence other aspects of the department and through these interdependences the overall performance of the department. It might also be possible to predict the outcome of any improvement the investigating group might propose, and to formulate a strategy for successful change.

The investigation was undertaken by a team which included the manager and senior foreman from the department concerned, a works study engineer, design engineer, maintenance engineer, the warehouse manager, a marketing department representative, and members of the central change team. An early part of the work included talks with a large number of people—managers, supervisors and operators—about the department in general and their own problems in particular.

From these discussions some early findings emerged. It was generally agreed that working conditions were poor, but that high average earnings could more or less adequately compensate for this. Further (unlike a situation that had existed some two years earlier) there was now a fair degree of satisfaction with employment conditions, reflected in high labour stability, low absence from work and reasonably high individual output and stable earnings. However, it also emerged from the talks that the men on the shop floor and their managers had quite different initial perceptions about the nature of the department as a system. There were divergencies in the way they explained production difficulties. In the management's view the Press Shop was seriously undermanned and efficiency could be raised by improving standards of skill and application of present employees, improving discipline and increasing the actual numbers employed. The men and their supervisors, however, constantly spoke of poor quality raw materials as being a major problem, and the senior foreman in particular insisted that in his experience an increase in numbers employed in the shop in the present circumstances would create many problems without achieving any higher output. In his view an increase in production would require attention to be paid particularly to the quality of raw materials and to engineering maintenance problems, and possibly to increasing the number of machines in the shop.

This divergence in sets of perceptions clearly had important implications in the way the department had functioned in the past. It had precluded active cooperation between management and operators and this lack of cooperation had forced the senior foreman over the previous two years or so to use the discretion available to him so as to act as a buffer between management controls on the one hand and the expectations of the men on the other. It was becoming apparent that his use of discretion was a crucial factor in the way the shop operated.

The discussions also suggested that a number of key interactions dominated events and helped to determine productive behaviour and, indirectly, the level of production in the department. These interactions involved the following variables

(1) the physical conditions in the Press Room;

(2) the structure of the wage packet and level of earnings, including bonus and overtime earnings;

(3) the varying properties of the raw materials;

(4) characteristics of the production schedule (the length of production runs and the range of sizes being produced);

(5) the discretion exercised by operators over methods of work;

(6) downtime for machinery caused by breakdowns and changeovers;

(7) the balance between different parts of the pleating, pressing and trimming operation;

(8) the manning arrangements and size of press teams; and

(9) the total number of men employed in the Press Room, and the proportion of inexperienced new starters among them.

Indeed, it began to appear that the situation was more complicated than had been perceived by any of the parties directly involved in it.

METHOD OF APPROACH

Following the initial discussions it was decided for this particular study to carry out a good deal of statistical work—considerably more than was usual on the programme. There were different interpretations of behaviour, even among the members of the investigating team who knew the department well, and members experienced difficulty in accepting that alternative interpretations were valid. There would thus be problems in confirming the validity of hypotheses, and the investigating team recognised they would need confidence in the model they produced if they were to gain agreement on it among themselves, and to accept some of its behavioural implications. They would also need to be confident about the nature of the system if they were to avoid unanticipated counter-control reactions on the part of subordinate members of the department to any changes that were introduced. To overcome these difficulties it was decided to try to put mathematical dimensions on some of the relationships in the socio-technical model as it was formulated. It was hoped that by using records already existing in the department, measures could be put on some of the more significant relationships, and the relative importance of each of them could then be assessed, so as to increase the plausibility of the final model.

A particular illustration can lead us into our description of the whole socio-technical system. One difference in perception related to the influences affecting the output of a team on a given press in any shift. Statistics of the number of items produced per machine per shift showed that over several months the variance in the number produced on different shifts was very high, and in some products the range had actually exceeded the average number made (table 5.1). Management and shopfloor strongly disagreed about the causes of this variability, and especially the

TABLE 5.1
Number of Sections Produced Per Shift Over a Six-monthly Period
(six major product sizes, two-man press teams)

Product type	Mean output per full shift	Range in output per full shift
2	1502	1109 – 2012
5	1309	759 – 1832
8	1367	597 – 2015
11	1201	626 – 1594
14	1080	620 – 1287
17	959	495 – 1260
21	833	479 – 1067

emphasis that should be given to different contributory factors. In the managers' opinion the variability of output from individual machines running a full eight hours could be attributed largely to the differences in the performance levels of different operatives: that is to say, differences in skill and application. The operatives attributed most of the production problems to fluctuations in the quality of raw materials. The opinion of the senior foreman was that both sets of opinions were, in fact, only partial explanations. He thought the variability in output could be explained to a considerable extent by technical problems induced by the quality of raw materials, although the effect of raw materials was dependent in his opinion on the size of the item being made. The foreman did not wholly disregard the effect of individual operatives' levels of skill on the variability of output, but he saw technical constraints and the consequences of this for their earnings as more important than variability in skill or application.

A series of statistical tests was devised in an attempt to test the plausibility of various opinions about the causes of variations in output between shifts. All the members of the department agreed that some variation in output must be due to differences in skill and effort and, indeed, there were significant differences between the output of different individuals when averaged over a three-monthly period. However, an analysis of variance forced us to reject the hypothesis that most of the variability was caused by characteristics of individual operators, and also that an individual's or a team's output was independent of other circumstances in the department. Certainly, no more than twenty-five per cent of the variability could have been caused by variations between individuals in skill and application.

Further, a series of step-wise regression equations was developed, each attempting to account for the variations in output per team on each shift for a particular size of product. The equations included variables designed to measure or to indicate: the quality of raw materials,[1] the frequency of changing presshead moulds, how accustomed members of the team were working together, the team structure, and the number of new starters in the team.

The results of the equations, in fact, seemed to confirm the foreman's opinion that the quality of material was particularly important in the output of the smallest sizes of product. With the smallest sizes there was a partial correlation coefficient of -0.77 (significant at the 99 per cent level) between the wastage rate and output, suggesting that nearly 60 per cent of past variations in output for those sizes could be explained by variations in certain unidentified properties of the raw material. For the other sizes, however, the correlations were rather smaller, ranging from -0.58 for the next largest to some insignificant coefficients.[2]

Thus, there was some evidence to support the perception that characteristics of the raw material affected rates of production for the smallest items. The smallest sizes, however, accounted for only a small proportion of total production and on the whole the argument that it was the arrival of poor quality material that led to frequent production problems received only limited support.

However, there was a significant correlation between the wastage of raw materials and bonus earnings (table 5.2). The correlation coefficient was -0.72 (significant at the 95 per cent level) for the twelve months preceding the investigations. There thus seemed to be a closer relationship between the quality of raw materials and the amount a man could earn than between quality and output overall. This fact was rather difficult to explain, and it led to a number of possible hypotheses, none of which could be directly confirmed unless we could find some way of getting to understand the whole interacting system in the Press Room in much more detail. This process we will now outline.

TABLE 5.2
Variation in Bonus Earnings
(coefficients from multiple regression equations — data taken monthly over sixteen months)

Variable	Partial correlation coefficient	t – statistic
Percentage of press turns worked with three-men teams	-0.90	6.58
Wastage rate per good item produced	-0.72	3.26
Average number of breakdowns per press turn worked	-0.71	3.19

Degrees of freedom: 10
Multiple regression coefficient for equation: -0.96
Durbin – Watson statistic for equation: 1.43

LATER DEVELOPMENT OF THE SYSTEMS MODEL

Conditions of Work

In the first place, it was clear that the conditions of work on the presses were poor relative to comparable work elsewhere in the company or the district. Working conditions had led to difficulty in recruiting and in deploying labour, and the management had attempted to counter this by paying relatively high wages. Many of the interviewees attributed the labour turnover occurring in the department to what they saw as unnecessarily poor working conditions. The reason they themselves had not left they attributed to the amount of earnings they achieved.

Factors Affecting Earnings

There were, however, constraints on their ability to achieve high and stable earnings or on management's ability to provide them. The company's *pay system*, the broad principles of which were controlled from head office, consisted of fairly low basic wage and time-studied, work content-based, incentive bonuses which had recently comprised anything from twenty per cent to fifty per cent of individuals' weekly gross earnings (see table 5.6). The bonus was a multifactor scheme, and although there was a fairly clear relationship between output level and bonus earnings, there were disadvantages to the system in two directions: that men were unable to predict their earnings in detail or understand in retrospect just how their bonus payments had been calculated; and that the bonus element introduced fluctuations into take-home pay for reasons outside the control of the press teams, and to some extent of the management as well. The men saw their earnings being affected by a number of factors including

(1) the variation in rates of pay (work-study values) for different sizes of product;

(2) the quality of the incoming raw material;

(3) the press on which the man was working: the characteristics of different presses varied, and the rates were not seen to reflect these characteristics accurately;

(4) time lost through machine downtime;

(5) press team size and composition.

To take the first of these factors, the men saw the *work-studied rates* as varying from very tight to slack, depending on the size of the product, and also on whether rates were based on measurement or on synthetic estimates. Values were considered to be tightest at the smaller end of the product range, which at the time of the investigations included the items most in demand in the product market. The perception of values as being slack or tight may show the different perceptions of the operators and the work-study engineers as to the importance of various factors entering into the times, and of various allowances to account for quality variations, mould changes and idle time in the course of the pressing operation.

The view that work-study values were variable between different sizes of product may be given some support by the closer statistical association discovered between bonus earnings and quality of materials than between output and quality (see table 5.2). If, because of tight work-study values, the men found it harder to earn high bonus on the smaller sizes, for which the quality of raw materials was most critical and wastage highest, then there was likely to be a correlation between wastage rates and bonus earnings, and this would not be reflected in output. This is not, of course, conclusive, but other plausible explanations also seem to turn on work-study allowances in relation, for instance, to lengths of production runs.

Whether or not the men's perceptions were justified, it was clear that frustration could be caused when members of a team believed an accumulated high bonus was being undermined by one day's unexpected drop in earnings. A common response in such circumstances seemed to be to refuse to attempt the usual performance level. Output and bonus earnings could thus show marked falls on certain days, and this could go some of the way to explaining variability of output.

On the other hand, when the effort required by the men was favourable in relation to the reward (that is, when high bonus earnings were possible), the bonus scheme appeared to be an effective means of controlling output. The people attracted into the Press Room were prepared to put in considerable effort for high rewards. Some press teams would come in early so that they could use the pleater to stockpile prepared batches for the press before the arrival of the team with whom they had to share a pleater. Other teams worked continuously through their break periods to keep up their performance levels. Each team tended to set its own performance level and there appeared to be few strong pressures on individuals to restrict output. Although some men spoke disparagingly of the high-fliers in the department, there did not appear to by any attempt to restrain the high output of other teams.

Some of the relationships so far emerging are illustrated in figure 5.1. The clear impression coming from the discussions was that high earnings were not by any means always capable of achievement and, as is described later, the senior foreman had instituted a system of discretionary payments to compensate for circumstances preventing men from earning their usual level of bonus.

The *quality of raw materials* appeared to limit the ability of teams to attain their desired performance. In conversation, men tended to attribute most production problems to the quality of incoming raw material, and this question deserved further detailed study. The production processes for the raw material made some variability between batches inevitable. Batches came into the section every few days and were inspected on arrival for physical characteristics. The men argued that the quality was regularly bad—one man claimed that 70 per cent of the material coming into the department was bad—but it appeared that the categorisation of materials as 'bad' covered material with a range of property variations, each of which they claimed affected the speed of either pressing or pleating, or both. Operators and supervisors used fairly uniform definitions as to what comprised good and bad materials, but it was not clear that their definitions corresponded to the criteria used by quality control inspectors.

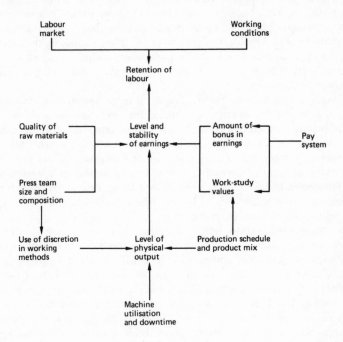

FIGURE 5.1 Relations between the elements of pay, output, earnings and retention of labour

The apparent discrepancy between technically defined raw material characteristics and the perceptions of the men could have had a number of causes. The response of the men to using the material was at least partly determined by the structure and level of the pay packet, and particularly by expectations as to the amount of bonus they could earn with it. The men saw any quality variation that affected output as directly affecting the amount of money they would take home, and what influenced their attitude to the raw material was whether they could satisfy their own expectations as to bonus earnings.

This attitude contrasted with the logic used by the work-study engineers. These latter were quite aware that quality variations produced discrepancies from day to day in the ratio between effort and reward, but they had devised job values on the basis of the *average* quality of the materials and would claim these values were fair overall, taking one batch with another. They would claim that at times the men could make more bonus, in relation to effort, than they should, given the basis of the calculations.

Clearly, however, the operators felt that the variability of the raw material frequently prevented them from making the bonus earnings to which they aspired. There was some evidence from the interviews that the men's earnings expectations were determined by the bonus earnings they could attain, and the effort required to attain them, supposing the material had the optimal characteristics for particular product sizes. This was so even though they were aware that work-study values were based on suboptimal characteristics.

Several points arise from this. Firstly, if these hypotheses are correct, then it was not the average quality of the materials as such, but the variations in it which caused problems for the department. Quite a large step increase in the average quality of raw materials would still have produced the same dissatisfaction so long as some material arrived which was less than optimal. Secondly, one way this dissatisfaction appeared to be reflected in behaviour was in resistance to working overtime during a period where the materials were below optimal standard, and in increasing the willingness to work overtime when they were of better quality. Poor materials also led to restriction of output in the course of a shift. Material which was perceived as bad led many operators not to attempt to make their usual performance and possibly to finish operating the presses early and to wait around idle until the end of the shift. Thirdly, from the viewpoint of systems understanding it was clear that both the operators on the one hand and the managers and work-study engineers on the other were likely to sustain their different expectations and to justify them on grounds that were quite valid, given their own frames of reference. Further, both sides were likely to continue refusing to accept the other point of view as legitimate, though the consequences in behaviour of the opposing frame of reference were recognised and agreed.

There was yet another consequence. Foremen and men believed that variations in raw material quality had different effects according to the size of the product being made. Further, the men said some batches of material were slower and more difficult to pleat; some batches they thought created more waste and a higher proportion of rejects; and both these effects depended upon the size of product. But some batches allowed the operators to fine down the standard curing times under the presshead on some product sizes (the smaller range) only.

So *the balance of effort* between the three main operations on the presses changed with the properties of the incoming raw material and the size of the section being produced. The relation between the time taken for pleating and the time for pressing and curing was changed as a result of the interaction between them. Whereas the technical operating specification made pressing and curing always the longer operation (and thus the critical one for capacity of the plant) a combination of difficult pleating quality of material and shortened curing times meant that in practice the pleating operation could be the longer. With a given product mix, therefore, the varying quality of the raw materials influenced the effective capacity of the equipment in the department via the men's use of unauthorised discretion in working methods.

A relationship also appeared between the quality of raw materials and the operation of the *production schedule*. Detailed production scheduling was in the hands of the senior foreman of the Press Room. Each week the foreman received two sets of figures from the warehouse: the number of products of different sizes needed to fill orders already received, and the numbers needed to achieve the planned stock levels. On the basis of this he worked out a detailed schedule which took into account the availability and anticipated quality of the raw materials, the optimal length of run on each press (which was determined largely by the need to change moulds for cleaning after given periods), the numbers of operators available, both to work the press and for certain subsidiary operations, and finally, the earnings expectations of the operators as he perceived them. As a result, the final schedule was something of a compromise between the requirements of each of these factors, and the Press Room usually supplied the warehouse, partly to order and partly to stock, but not necessarily in the proportions which would best suit the current needs of the warehouse. Further, since neither availability nor quality of the raw material could be accurately forecast, the schedule often needed further modification in the course of the week, either on the arrival of a batch of substandard material, or in response to pressure exerted by the men.

The most important consequence of production scheduling methods was that it became difficult to match the patterns of production to *warehouse requirements*. As a result, it was difficult for the warehouse to meet customers' demand by the promised delivery dates. As demand increased, the shortage of particular products was beginning to delay despatches, both directly because of non-availability and indirectly through the slowing down of the despatch procedure as a whole. Comments made by warehouse packers suggested a number of consequences arising from the shortage of particular products.

Packers were unable to complete orders they had started packing, and thus tended to reduce their own speed of work. At the same time working space was taken up with half-packed orders, leaving the packers inadequate room to work, and reducing efficiency still further. Most complaints in the warehouse were, in fact, about working space. Further, the requirements of the packing job were for a relatively young and active female labour force, but as the job required more initiative than most packing work, the age range tended to be between twenty-five and thirty—an age bracket which produced characteristic attitudes by the packers to their earnings. Given that financial incentives were important, and that earnings depended on the amount of orders they succeeded in packing, anything like shortage of products from the Press Room which affected their earnings was likely to affect the stability of the warehouse labour force.

To the extent that disruption of the despatch procedure could be attributed to events in the Press Room, it was an additional cost which had to be borne by the works. The Marketing Department also feared that delays in despatch might undermine the competitive position of the company.

Thus, there seemed to be a fairly complex relationship between the quality of raw material and the utilisation of equipment which was contingent upon the production schedule and also upon the response of the operatives to that schedule in relation to their expectations about earnings. So the *utilisation of the equipment* which we have already identified as being one of the critical factors in the success of the department, deserved further detailed investigation.

As a consequence of the numerous variables in the design of the production schedule it had become impossible to have optimal batch sizes and optimal production runs. There was, in fact, a wide dispersion in the length of runs for different batches of any one section size (table 5.3). The time lost in changeovers between batches was one factor contributing to the underutilisation of the presses and a source of additional cost.

TABLE 5.3
Range in Length of Run for Seven Important Product
Sizes Over Three months

Product type	Minimum length of run during period	Maximum length of run during period
2	2556	5105
5	3168	4620
8	2427	5625
11	1213	4170
14	400	3622
17	398	4035
21	415	3217
24	390	2585

The men also complained of machine breakdowns, and a partial correlation of -0.71 between reported breakdowns and bonus earnings (significant at the 90 per cent level) seemed to confirm that mechanical faults could have a disruptive effect on earnings (see table 5.2). Although records showed only about one per cent of potential machine hours as being lost through mechanical faults, in fact what were referred to as breakdowns included minor faults such as breakages of saws or misalignment of equipment, requiring the attention of the operators rather than of a maintenance fitter, but still making it difficult to achieve a high level of performance.

The effect on production as such may not have been as clear. Not all the presses were continuously manned and it was possible to reduce the impact of breakdowns by redeploying labour on to unmanned presses. As output in the department rose to meet the expanding market, there would be a decline in excess capacity, and lost press hours were likely to come gradually to represent direct losses in production.

More important than either of these was the relationship between the utilisation of equipment and the *manning level* or team size. The system had been designed to run with a three-man team on each press. One man would be working full-time on the presshead itself, while the other two alternated between the pleating operation (stockpiling pleated material for the presshead) and the trimming operation (running down a stockpile produced by a presshead operator). However, on all but the largest product sizes the capacity of the presshead restricted the amount of work that could be produced by a three-man team, and the two men working on the pleating and trimming operations could not be kept fully employed. Output per man overall was therefore reduced, and this interacted with the payment system to restrict earnings.

Recognising these problems, the senior foreman had, over the course of time, reduced the number of people employed in the department. Fewer men were budgeted for than were required if the machines were to be manned with three-man teams, and many teams had been reduced to two men. With a two-man team, both men were needed periodically for sawing and trimming the sections stockpiled while the presshead was operating. Thus, the presshead had to remain idle during the time taken for trimming—a period which depended on the number of sections produced by each pressing, and the length of time of each pressing cycle. These factors in their turn depended on the size of the sections and the properties of the raw material. Men in two-man teams estimated that the presshead could, in certain conditions, be idle for up to thirty per cent of each shift. However, what did result from this system was high output per man and high earnings; for two-man teams, although leading to more lost machine time, resulted in less 'lost time' for the men, who could thus maximise their own output.

The smaller team size also improved the ability to cope with variations in skill and with individual differences in response to the wage payment system and variations in raw material quality. There tended to be a better match between individuals in two-man teams than when three men were working together. Thus, there need not, in fact, have been a great deal of difference between the output from a press with the reduction in the size of press teams. In fact, with the smaller range of products two-man teams seemed to produce regularly about 80 per cent of the output of three-man teams.

The men were convinced that the present deployment of labour in the department had favourably affected their effort–reward bargain, and these claims were confirmed by a negative partial correlation of -0.90 (significant at the 99 per cent level) between bonus earnings and team size (see table 5.2). There was some evidence from work-study values to support a view which was expressed, that men working in a two-man team could make a '120' performance with the same effort as was required to make only a '90' performance with three men. This was partly because of the difference in work-study values for the two team sizes and partly because three men were less able to maximise individual output.

Figure 5.2 illustrates some of the relationships just discussed. Obviously there is already evidence of considerable rather subtle manipulation of the formally designed system, resulting in increased individual satisfaction and increasing stability of earnings. At the same time the level of output and pattern of production had been affected via production scheduling techniques and the intensity of machine utilisation.

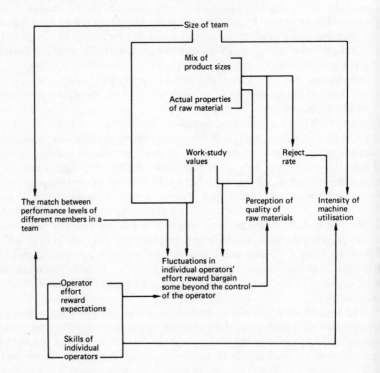

FIGURE 5.2   Relations between deployment, raw material quality, machine utilisation and effort – reward bargain

The utilisation of equipment was also affected by the *total numbers of people employed* in the department. Firstly, it was not possible to keep all the presses running, even when they were all mechanically sound (table 5.4). This was partly planned by the senior foreman so that if a breakdown occurred teams could be quickly redeployed to a spare machine, without great loss of earnings potential. It was partly an indirect result of the use of two-man teams, since if one man was absent without cover it was almost impossible to keep that press running and his partner would have to be redeployed elsewhere, either to make up a three-man team, or to effect a temporary arrangement of five men working on two presses.

TABLE 5.4
Running Time and Press Time Lost for Various Causes over Three Months

| | Hours | | | | |
| | Press running time | | Press time lost | | |
	manned by scheduled press team	manned in course of shift by redeployed labour	on shifts where scheduled press team is available	on shifts to where no scheduled press team is available	Total
Press I	1664	22	120	370	2176
II	1660	30	112	192	1994
III	1084	46	141	908	2179
IV	1544	63	71	?[a]	—

[a] approximately 500 hours

The flexibility the various methods of redeployment had introduced into the organisation of labour kept production at a fairly high level, despite the reduction in the numbers employed. In cases of absence the foreman was occasionally able to redeploy a man from one of the subsidiary activities to keep the presses running, and with certain products a group of five men could be used to man two presses in order to increase the output from each. However, the most important way of compensating for loss of urgent production through absence or undermanning of presses was to bring people in on overtime (table 5.5).

Overtime as a means of balancing production with the needs of the warehouse produced a number of problems. In the first place, nearly a third of the absences occurring in the department were unexpected. This made it difficult to enforce the shift changeover scheme when the oncoming shift contained no reserve of labour; it hindered the effective deployment of men on to press teams; and it prevented the foreman giving adequate notice to those required to work overtime. Secondly, there were difficulties in persuading press men to work more overtime than they were

TABLE 5.5
Manning of Presses over Previous Calendar Year

Month	Total hours worked	Percentage of press hours worked		
		with less than two men per press	*by men redeployed from other jobs*	*through overtime*
January	5667	–	–	3·8
February	4639	0·9	2·4	7·1
March	4566	0·3	2·2	11·5
April		data not available		
May		data not available		
June	4636	0·5	–	5·5
July	4224	–	–	7·0
August	3818	2·7	0·9	6·7
September	2903	3·3	–	12·5
October	5584	5·2	–	7·6
November	4741	6·1	–	6·9
December	4684	3·9	–	7·7

inclined to want, particularly on the Monday to Friday shift turns when rates of overtime pay were lower. Given the level of earnings within the normal shift cycle, combined with the difficult working conditions, most men said they would welcome only limited overtime, and some commented during the interviews that already they were working more than they wished, in order to help out with production difficulties. Again, as one man implied, to work overtime could have a detrimental effect on one's performance during the shift. Overtime work on the part of some individuals may cause deteriorating performance, reduce the bonus earnings of their team, and lead to conflict and subsequent absenteeism. Further, when production difficulties occurred through raw material problems there was a tendency both to restrict output in the course of a regular shift and to decline overtime. This could lead to wide fluctuations in the output of the shop. In any of these circumstances, and given his objective to maintain high morale in the Press Room, the foreman was probably inhibited from pressing his subordinates too hard to work extra overtime.

There were several possible ways in which men could make use of overtime opportunities to increase their own satisfaction: to supplement incomes so as to generate higher average earnings; to stabilise earnings as bonus fluctuated in the course of the regular cycle; and to redistribute their effort between regular hours and overtime hours, so that they were able to put in less effort during the regular shift and make up their earnings during overtime. Different men would use different criteria, and the same men might well operate different criteria at different periods.

For all these reasons, dependence on overtime for maximising output and optimising plant utilisation was not likely to achieve the best results. It was therefore important for the investigators to understand the place of overtime in the performance of the Press Room. To this end a breakdown was made of the weekly earnings of a sample of operators over a period of twelve weeks (table 5.6). Most overtime was worked as complete extra shifts, but there were remarkable differences between the amount of

TABLE 5.6

Overtime Hours Worked by Individual Press Operators, Related to Total Earnings and Bonus Earnings

Overtime hours			
Ranking of operator	Hours worked	Rank position of operator's total earnings	Bonus earnings as per cent of total earnings
1	175·5	1	41
2	168	3	26
3	131·75	16	21
4	129·25	2	40
5	120	6	33
6	112	4	43
7	90·5	20	24
8	71·25	13	38
9	63·5	9	41
10	56	7	43
10	56	17	39
12	40	11	—
12	48	22	36
14	40	19	42
14	40	20	35
16	32	23	28
19	24	8	42
19	24	12	40
19	24	16	—
19	24	25	27
19	24	26	43
19	24	27	42
23	23·5	14	36
23	23·5	27	26
25	20	5	35
27	16	10	42
27	16	15	49
27	16	24	32

overtime different men had worked in the period. Six had worked for more than 100 overtime hours, and five of these were among the six highest earners in the whole department. It may be concluded that these five men (about one-sixth of the sample) were using overtime as a means of generating high earnings. Two of them had worked an average of at least two extra shifts every week.

There was evidence to suggest that a few men may have been redistributing their effort and working fairly long overtime hours to compensate for low levels of effort during the shift, but the majority were obviously putting in overtime as required by the department, rather than to satisfy earnings needs. There was no indication that more overtime was worked following a week of low bonus or low total earnings.

TABLE 5.7
Variation in Overtime Worked

Variable	Partial correlation Coefficient	t-statistic
Average number of breakdowns per press turn	0·35	2·07
Ratio of new starters to experienced employees	0·47	2·93
Percentage of labour Force under forty years old	−0·36	2·09

Degrees of freedom = 30
Multiple regression Coefficient = 0·728
Durbin – Watson statistic = 2·3194

A regression analysis of factors influencing overtime appeared to confirm that overtime hours were more closely associated with departmental requirements than with earnings expectations (table 5.7). High partial correlation coefficients were found with the number of inexperienced new starters in the department and the incidence of breakdowns. There was no significant correlation between bonus earnings and level of overtime. This seemed to confirm that it was departmental requirements rather than individual satisfactions which were most significant in the amount of overtime worked.

Thus, the foreman's ability to use overtime to compensate for underproduction during shift hours was dependent on the willingness of his subordinates to cooperate with him in the system he was managing. Indeed, it appeared that the number of press teams volunteering for overtime in advance was regularly below the number required if production was to be maintained (table 5.8). This was especially so on press turns from Monday to Friday. The fact that men were not prepared to work as much overtime as was available, together with the use of two-man teams during shift hours, meant that a rise in labour turnover or absence could cause an immediate and direct effect on output. The balance in the department was therefore very critical.

TABLE 5.8
Overtime Runs Available and Worked in Previous Year

Month	Monday to Friday		Saturday and Sunday	
	Press teams known to be required for overtime runs in advance	Press teams volunteering for overtime in advance	Press teams known to be required for overtime in advance	Press teams volunteering for overtime in advance
January	$23\frac{1}{2}$	19	$15\frac{1}{2}$	9
February	$33\frac{1}{2}$	22	$10\frac{1}{2}$	12
March	$39\frac{1}{2}$	23	15	13
June	$11\frac{1}{2}$	10	$5\frac{1}{2}$	6
July	$17\frac{1}{2}$	19	$5\frac{1}{2}$	7
August	17	10	7	14
September	59	25	$16\frac{1}{2}$	13
October	71	23	$22\frac{1}{2}$	15
November	33	14	13	13
December	29	35	$10\frac{1}{2}$	9

Data for April and May not available

The fact that machinery was underutilised suggested that increases in the *number of men employed* could improve the low production figures. This, however, was strongly contested by the senior foreman, who maintained that an increase in the number of men would, in fact, reduce efficiency in the department. Although he agreed that small numbers employed reduced utilisation of equipment below its potential, the fact was that past attempts to increase numbers had led to considerable disruption. For the period in which recruitment was taking place, there was a rapid rise in *labour turnover* in the department, particularly of new starters remaining in the Press Room for a week or less. Labour turnover then remained high, and stability was regained only as numbers began to decline again. While much of the turnover could be explained by difficulties in recruiting—the induction crisis for newly engaged men—difficulties in retaining established labour were also increased owing to changes in the pay packet associated with larger numbers and with the influx of inexperienced new starters. The effect of inexperienced newcomers on the bonus earnings of established operators was considerable. Newcomers joining a three-man team would, over the period of some months, tend to hold back the earning capacity of the team to which they were attached. If, at the same time, a two-man team was increased to a three-man team, then the inherent loss of earnings would reinforce this problem. Some men objected to three-man teams regardless of whether bonus earnings were protected, simply because of the bottlenecks that occurred, resulting in idle-time for the press men, and also because of the difficulty of getting three men to work together. With three-man teams, labour turnover was always higher and the problem of new starters, therefore, always had to be dealt with and always tended to aggravate it.

The causes and the effects of labour turnover constituted one of the most difficult issues facing the investigating team, and a considerable amount of statistical analysis was done to test the hypotheses just stated. The fact that two separate processes underlay labour turnover, one related to recruitment and one to retention, was confirmed to some extent by the data available about those leaving the department in the previous two years (table 5.9). About a third of those leaving had done so before completing the five-week training period. This could be regarded as the measure of the difficulty in recruiting new labour, and it might be supposed that recruitment difficulties could be explained in terms of working conditions

TABLE 5.9
Number Leaving by Length of Service over Previous Two Years

Length of service	Percent of total leaving
Less than one week	7·0
One week and less than one month	25·6
One month and less than three months	30·2
Three months and less than six months	19·8
Six months and less than twelve months	12·8
Twelve months and more	4·6
Total	100·0

for those unaccustomed to the department. The difficulties in retaining established labour were more likely to be related to changes in the pay packet, and this was confirmed to some extent by a correlation of 0·6 (significant at the 90 per cent level) between average earnings in the department each month and labour turnover in that month.

Another significant negative correlation was discovered between labour turnover and the percentage of people who had been recruited from the immediate neighbourhood of the factory. Given the tightening labour market, an attempt to increase the numbers employed would encourage recruitment from some distance. If labour turnover regularly increased as the numbers of employees from outside the immediate locality increased, then larger numbers employed would inevitably raise labour turnover (table 5.10).

TABLE 5.10
Variation in Labour Turnover

Variable	Partial correlation coefficient	t-statistic
Average earnings divided by retail price index	−0·37	2·00
Percentage of employees starting that month	−0·13	0·64
Percentage of press turns worked by three men teams	−0·25	1·32
Percentage of workforce recruited from local district	−0·49	2·77
Number of unemployed in district	−0·16	0·79

Degrees of freedom: 25
Multiple regression coefficient for equation: 0·76
Durbin−Watson statistic: 1·9382

It was interesting that a regression analysis run in parallel on the causes of *absence* from the department (table 5.11) also showed significant associations with the number of new starters in the department, and the percentage of people recruited from outside the district. There appeared to be no correlation between bonus earnings and absenteeism, and this lack of association had been predicted by the foreman who felt that the factors

TABLE 5.11

Variations in Percentage of Scheduled Hours Lost through Absence, Leave or Sickness

Variable	Partial correlation coefficient	t-statistic
Average number of different sizes produced per press turn	−0·25	1·37
Number of new starters	0·34	1·94
Total number employed	0·26	1·47
Percentage of workforce recruited from local district	−0·37	2·12

Degrees of freedom: 29
Multiple regression coefficient for equation: 0·80
Durbin–Watson statistic for equation: 1·8267

likely to influence bonus earnings on any shift were not likely to be known in advance by the men, who would, therefore, have no opportunity of making an informed decision whether or not to stay away from work.

Thus, although the low numbers employed in the Press Room could restrict utilisation of the equipment, the solution was not straightforward. The supply of labour to the Press Shop was a finally balanced system, very sensitive to the composition of the workforce, as well as to fluctuations in total earnings and the structure of the pay packet. Past attempts to increase numbers had worked in conjunction with the reward system to upset this balance. The reward system was an indirect cause of underutilisation of equipment, regardless of which of the various alternative manning levels and deployment policies had been introduced into the department.

Some of these relationships are illustrated in figure 5.3

Other important factors in the efficiency of the Press Room were the *wastage rate* of raw materials and the *reject rate* of sections partly or fully processed. Raw material represented over 60 per cent of the production costs, and since low costs were needed for the satisfaction of the market, performance could be influenced significantly by the rate of wastage. Further, since the rate of rejects helps to determine the effective capacity of the department, to minimise the rate of rejects would considerably increase its ability to satisfy the needs of the warehouse and product market. The current reject rate appeared to be partly a consequence of raw material characteristics. Clearly, however, raw material quality affected rejects differently for different sizes of product, and the overall consequences of

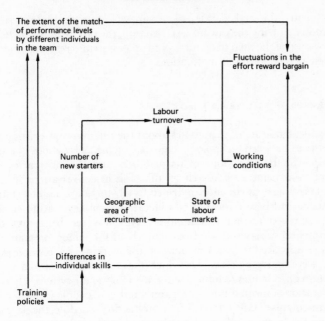

FIGURE 5.3 Interrelationships between fluctuations in earnings, working conditions and retention of skilled labour

raw material properties depended on the production schedule. The senior foreman's modification of the production schedule in accordance with properties of incoming raw materials may have helped to reduce the rejects, but the current degree of flexibility in the production schedule was only possible because the warehouse was short of almost every type that could be produced. If the stock position were improved, then greater constraints might well be put on production scheduling, and rejects might increase as a consequence.

The reject rate was also influenced by the incentive bonus scheme. The fact that some operators were induced to maintain their earnings by fining down curing times could have meant that they were risking incurring a high reject rate and thus causing higher costs in wastage of materials and products, as a result of attempting to work faster than either the design specification or the quality of the materials would permit. The men may have been encouraged in this practice by the fact that a variable percentage allowance was given for rejects which had been caused by process and material faults beyond the control of the operators. Since most rejects were discarded by the men before the inspection process took place, the exact nature of the fault would only be known to the operators themselves.

Once again, therefore, a significant factor in the success of the department—the reject rate—was subject to a multiple system of causation involving the raw material quality, the production schedule and the response of the men to features of the pay system—responses mediated by their perceptions and motivations.

THE ROLE OF THE SENIOR FOREMAN

A complicated series of hypotheses about the relationships existing in the department between technology, control systems, perceptions of different participants, the behaviour of its members and the efficiencies which resulted, was being constructed on the basis of conversations held with members of the department, confirmed by existing data, and by statistical tests based on these data. On consideration, one key feature stood out which deserved further examination. This was the behaviour of the departmental supervisors, and particularly of the senior foreman, whose decisions appeared to be a key factor in the working of the whole system. There were four major ways in which the senior foreman had used the discretion open to him to influence the workings of the system. These were his alteration of the manning levels and number of people employed in the department, his detailed design of the production schedule, the payment of average bonus to members of production teams under certain circumstances, and his allocation of overtime.

By reducing the numbers employed and modifying the manning level for the presses, the senior foreman had obviously reduced the potential output of the department well below the designed or theoretical optimum. In doing so he had, however, increased the satisfaction of subordinate members of the department, and ensured that his working force was a stable and highly productive one. In his own terms he had transformed a department that some years earlier had had a chronically high level of labour turnover and considerable discontent about earnings, and in which grievances were common, into one requiring little attention from higher management and, in fact, still probably producing as much as previously in quantitative terms. Among adverse effects of his actions, however, were the increasing failure of the department to satisfy the needs of the warehouse and product market, both overall and from the point of view of product mix. His behaviour had also helped to raise the expectations of the men as to effort and reward in the department, and this created some later difficulties for the foreman himself.

The senior foreman had formal responsibility for production scheduling. However, the weight he gave to factors other than the current requirements of the warehouse and optimum batch size for the presses was not formally expected. In particular, he would not normally have been expected to pay a great deal of attention to raw material quality and its effects on reject rates and the earnings potential of the operators of particular presses. The way the production schedule was designed had some adverse effects, since it helped to distort the output of the Press Room, and the priorities of the warehouse for particular types of section were not wholly met. Further, like the alterations in team size, it helped to raise the current expectations of the men about their effort–reward bargain, and if these expectations were not met, problems occurred within the department. On the other hand, so far as the modifications did effectively reduce reject rates, the cost, morale and output of the department were improved.

TABLE 5.12
Hours Worked by Method of Payment over Nine Weeks

	Actual hours worked		
Week no.	*hours worked for which bonus paid on work-study values*	*hours worked for which an average bonus paid*	*per cent of hours worked for which average bonus paid*
1	891·25	107·75	10·7
2	1007·25	69·25	6·4
3	984·00	70·75	6·7
4	966·75	111·25	10·3
5	940·75	100·00	9·6
6	922·09	110·50	10·7
7	924·50	72·00	7·2
8	529·00	392·00	42·6
9	634·00	394·00	38·3

The third kind of action by the senior foreman was to extend a discretion which was formally his, to give 'policy payments' to operators when through no fault of their own they were unable to achieve a reasonable output. In fact, he commonly paid teams of operators on an average of their current bonus earnings when there was evidence that they could not achieve their usual performance, either because of raw material properties or because of redeployment of individuals from two-man to three-man teams (table 5.12). Policy payments to operators in emergencies seem to have no adverse consequences, at least for the utilisation of equipment. Indeed, in some ways they are beneficial. The foreman was able to make a fine distinction between the skills of different operators, and there was no evidence that the men received such payments unless they had made the appropriate effort. Thus the supervisor, who had an intimate knowledge of operators' normal level of earnings, retained some sanctions and did not have to exert continuous direct control over operators while on average bonus. Indeed, the men expressed considerable approval for the way in which the supervisor 'left them to get on with the job' and several of them

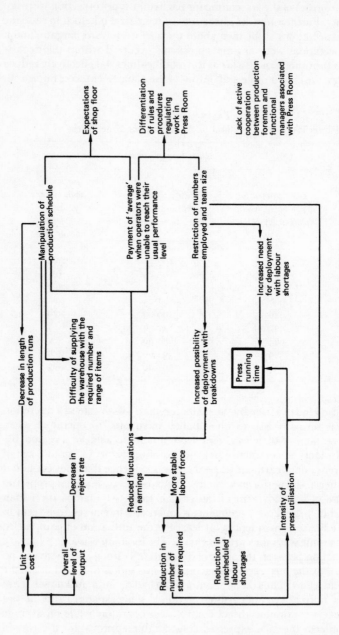

FIGURE 5.4 Consequences of foreman's use of discretion for the production process

commented that bonus payments were much fairer now as a result of these actions. One further result was that operators were prepared to respond by cooperating with additional effort in the event of extra pressure on demand. The main factor which may have argued against this sytem was the high cost (including the administrative costs) of operating the pay scheme in this way and it was certainly frowned upon by the industrial engineers. Further, it again acted to raise men's expectations as to the appropriate relationships between effort and reward and the stability of that relationship.

The classic method of exercising foreman discretion in production departments is by the manipulation of overtime hours. In the Press Room, the foreman had used his discretion on overtime in conjunction with his other manipulations to maintain a certain balance in the system. In this, as we have said, he was not wholly successful. Whereas in the classic case, overtime manipulation is carried out as a means of satisfying employee earnings needs, in this case the earnings needs of the majority had already been dealt with fairly satisfactorily through the other discretionary actions of the senior foreman, and overtime for him was an attempt to make up the production requirements of the department. For this he had to rely on the goodwill of his subordinates, and although this was evident the extent to which he could call on it as an inducement to work overtime was limited.

The use by the senior foreman of these various areas of discretion is illustrated in figure 5.4. It deserves a much fuller treatment than we can give it here. The foreman had taken over the department some years earlier at a time when it still had excess machine capacity in relation to market demand. As demand slowly increased (at a time when the local labour market was becoming tighter) the attempts to increase production by increasing manning levels had led to the kind of disruption already described. Some years before the investigation the department appears to have been in the early stages of a regressive spiral[3] and, given its patterns of output, it was likely to have become increasingly difficult to meet orders. Recurrent crises in production would thus have been likely to occur, necessitating shorter runs and increasing inflexibility in production scheduling. To extract the department from this spiralling situation, the senior foreman had seen the creation of a stable labour force as an overriding necessity, and he believed that this could be achieved only by maintaining a relatively high and stable level of earnings. Consequently, he had first persuaded management of the need to change from five-day shift working to seven-day continuous working, and this had enabled him to reduce the manning on each shift and also to raise the average level of earnings through increased shift differentials. However, he still perceived a need to reduce some of the unpredictable fluctuations in the effort–reward bargain, and to make the relationship between earnings and effort consistent with the men's expectations. This he had done by exercising his discretion in the four ways described, and providing the section with a

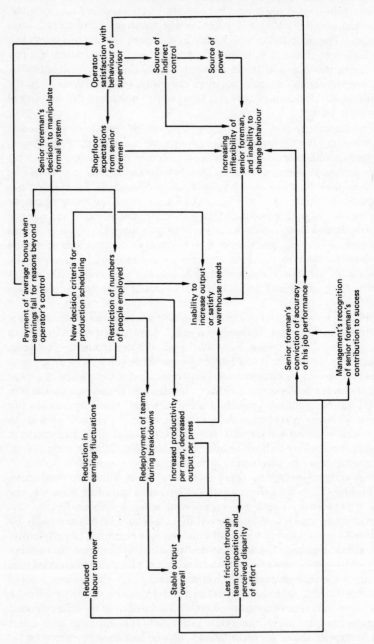

FIGURE 5.5   Sources of inflexibility in senior foreman's control of Press Room

consistent supply of experienced skilled labour and considerable flexibility in the use of resources.

What, however, the foreman's model did not take into account was that a sudden rapid increase in demand should occur, part of which was the result of a new company sales and marketing policy introduced some months before this investigation. Indeed, the success with which he had solved the production problems of the department may have been a factor in preventing him from dealing adequately with the current situation. The foreman had become convinced that the way in which he performed his job was the most appropriate way of keeping the department running effectively. He had a very good understanding of the department and the likely consequences of any changes that might be forced on it which ignored the problems he had earlier been faced with. However, simply because of the past success of his methods, his own expectations may have become inflexible.

Further, the senior foreman's intimate understanding of the department and knowledge of the skills and expectations of each of the operatives (which was required in order to make a success of the discretionary payments system) made his presence indispensable to the day-to-day running of the department. More personal power had become attached to his job than had been formally designed into it, or than it had originally had. At the same time, the general satisfaction within the Press Room about the way the department was run had given him considerable prestige. Not only was the senior foreman's job performance influencing his expectations as to the way his job should be performed, but was also leading to new rewards for him which had not been previously attached to the job.

The expectations on the part of the senior foreman were matched by shopfloor expectations: that once a system of production scheduling modifications and payment of average bonus had been established, it would always continue, in order to maintain operators' perception of a fair effort–reward bargain, and to minimise fluctuations in this bargain. The situation that had developed is illustrated in figure 5.5.

The senior foreman was, of course, not wholly independent in the way he managed the shop. He was formally responsible to a departmental manager, and other departments like Industrial Engineering and Work Study were responsible for designing and advising on the control systems. The senior foreman had achieved this degree of discretion for reasons which were partly historical. A new manager had taken over the department at the time when labour disruption had been considerable, and he had necessarily relied on the advice of the senior foreman, and recognised the success with which he coped with the problem. The fact that the foreman was performing his job effectively, and that he was becoming indispensable, led the departmental manager finally to leave most decisions to him. Similarly, the Industrial Engineering department, though aware that the rules and procedures were not being implemented in accordance with company policy, was also fully aware of the disruptive effect on the department of trying to change the foreman's behaviour. Consequently, little attempt was made to influence him and, in effect, the formal requirements of his job were changing to match his own behaviour. His initial use of discretion had become an integral part of the way in which he performed his job, and many of the discretionary decisions in his role had become non-discretionary components.[4]

If these hypotheses were correct, they would have to be taken into consideration in any strategy the investigating group wished to impose. The future position and policies of the senior foreman were factors which must be dealt with satisfactorily if a change strategy was to be successful.

CONCLUSION

What appeared in practical terms to be a small and simple production department that was experiencing some unidentified difficulties in reaching the output demanded by an expanding market, has been shown on investigation to have many complex and rather fascinating patterns of interaction.[5] Some of these interactions were noted at the beginning of this chapter: those between physical working conditions, the wage system, variability in raw material quality, plant layout, manning arrangements and the varying perceptions of operators, supervisors and managers about these matters.

It is particularly interesting to note the part played in the generation of attitudes and relationships by the different perceptual models held by different parties in this case. For example, the senior foreman's model, in which his ability to satisfy the needs of press teams played a major part, conflicted with that of the warehouse manager, for whom the Press Room was relevant mainly for its ability or inability to satisfy warehouse requirements. Attitudes were generated by this, which further influenced behaviour in the department.

As another example, the perceptions of operators about the effect of the pay system, raw material quality and the production schedule on their effort–reward bargain contrasted with the perceptions of work-study engineers and the departmental manager about the function of rewards and of controls. The conflicting perceptions again helped to generate attitudes on the part of both groups, towards the system of controls and towards each other's behaviour, and these, in turn, influenced behaviour in the Press Room.

An interesting point arises from this last example. The approach, and the framework of analysis used in this chapter, avoid making judgements about whether particular responses or particular patterns of behaviour are right or wrong, legitimate or not. However, among the people in the system—managers, work-study people, operators and others—there were quite clear views about the legitimacy or otherwise of others' responses.

The perceptual models on which these groups were operating included concepts of legitimacy that were often in conflict with each other. One of the reasons why managers and men found mutual communication or cooperation in making improvements difficult was this conflict in their ideas about legitimacy—a conflict that was considerably greater than any disagreement about causes or consequences of behaviour. So we have to take account of the perceptions about legitimacy held by actors in the system, while avoiding imputing legitimacy ourselves into the model.

So far, then, we have used our analytical framework to bring us to some fairly clear understanding of events in the Press Room. In chapter 13 we show how we believe the understanding could be used to help formulate a strategy which would allow the department to cope better with its market needs. The actual events in the department did not, in fact, follow this pattern, and we shall summarise in chapter 15 what actually occurred. The points we have just made are very relevant to this contrast between a strategy arising out of the systems model and the actual course of events. As we suggested earlier, conflicting perceptual models were held from the beginning by members of the investigating team (who included members of the department), and although the work of the team and the moves made to verify the model quantitatively resulted in a considerable measure of agreement between team members on assessment of consequences, the team never resolved differences among its members about the perceived legitimacy of different forms of behaviour or responses to that behaviour. These retained ideas helped to influence the decisions eventually made as to what should happen in the Press Room. Of course, this fact in itself has lessons for the structure and strategy of an organisational change programme, and we shall have to look further into this difficulty.

NOTES TO CHAPTER 5

1. It was impossible to find a precise indicator of the different properties of incoming raw materials. However, variability in wastage of raw material per similar-sized item was chosen as being a reasonable indicator of whether the incoming materials were likely to be the cause of other difficulties, including the rate of rejects at the production stage.
2. However, tests for autocorrelation in the residuals suggested that a significant variable was missing from the equations for the middle range of sizes. Listing the residuals of the equations with low Durbin–Watson statistics as a time series showed that over time the high positive and the high negative residuals did tend to occur in clusters that were independent of the machine being worked or of the operatives working it. This was consistent with the missing variable having something to do with the properties of the raw material. Significantly, in the light of the men's comments, the residuals were about equally negative and positive, suggesting tentatively that the missing variable was not the frequent arrival of bad materials but the arrival of materials with properties that varied consistently. However, the inclusion of

this variable could not have accounted for much more than an additional ten per cent of the variation.

3. For elaboration of the concept of a regressive spiral see Legge (1970), and Gowler and Legge (1973).

4. A general model in terms of which the senior foreman's position can be analysed is proposed by Gowler and Legge (1972). In terms of this model, once the senior foreman had used the discretionary components of his occupational role in such a way that his department was running more successfully, a number of influences had come to bear (from the workings of the modified socio-technical system, the expectations of others in the system, and his own perception of his appropriate role) to ensure that the various components of his occupational role had become integrated, and no longer discretionary. A subsequent change in the environment providing a new set of job requirements for him led him to revert to ritualistic repetition of manipulations that could no longer meet the situation.

5. Roy (1953, 1955) also points out 'The discovery of complexity where simple lines of relationships had generally been assumed to exist' and 'complication in a picture that has come to be accepted as simple in design'. This complexity seems to be as common as its understanding is rare.

5 The Lower Foundry

The third study concerns a very different system—the Lower Foundry—which employed comparable numbers of people (varying between 100 and 180) to the Finishing Shop, but had a fairly heavy technology based on melting and casting of alloy. The working conditions were naturally characterised by heat, dirt and oil, but a considerable amount of highly mechanised equipment was employed and the disposition and activity patterns of employees in one-half of the foundry at least were quite closely constrained by the nature of the process and the plant.

The Lower Foundry was part of a larger factory which incorporated another, rather more advanced foundry working in parallel with it, and also a number of assembly departments preparing the various products for the market. Responsibility for operations up to and including the melting process was in the hands of a factory-wide melting department. The system we define as the Lower Foundry comprises the processes from the control of molten metal in the 'forehearths' of the furnace through to the testing and inspection of the products at the end of the line, before they were transferred to intermediate storage areas.

THE PRODUCT RANGE

The factory as a whole had long specialised in highly technical products made to rather difficult specifications and requiring considerable expertise in design and in control of dimensional and other physical characteristics. This was true of two of the three main product lines of the Lower Foundry which we shall call cups and grilles. There was a third main product line, boxes, which technically were not very sophisticated in that rather greater manufacturing tolerances were permitted, but in the production of which this factory had almost a world-wide monopoly. In addition, some miscellaneous products were produced from time to time in relatively small quantities for specialist clients. In terms of the weight of alloy used (and individual items were of fairly comparable size between the three main lines) cups currently comprised about half the total output, boxes something over a quarter and grilles just over a fifth. Other products formed about two-and-a-half per cent of the total.

Cups had been produced in the Lower Foundry for about twenty-five years. After many years the domestic market had recently rapidly declined

with a change in technical requirements and attempts had been made b
the divisional sales department to enter certain foreign markets on a larg
scale. Export markets now took up eighty per cent of output.

Two problems had been created by this diversion overseas
Specifications in each overseas country were different, both in dimensiona
characteristics and in the technical requirements laid down by nationa
standards. As a result, a great deal of experimental and design work had t
be carried out before the technical requirements of each new area and eacl
new usage could be met. In fact, a range of about twenty basic type
varying in weight between 1 kg (2lb) and 10 kg (22lb) were produced
but with a large and growing variety of design modifications to mee
specified technical properties. The second problem was that there wa
much more competition internationally. The company was, in effec
competing in most markets against similar products made by foundries i
the United States, Western Europe and Japan.

Grilles were a product line that had evolved from some traditional good
produced since prewar years, mainly for the building industry. Produc
developments on the continent had transformed what had originally bee
a purely functional component into an aesthetic feature, and thes
developments had been accepted by the architectural profession i
Western Europe and the United States. The success of Europea
producers had encouraged management to believe that a potential marke
existed in the UK and that if the purely engineering image of the origina
product could be forgotten, the architectural profession might take up th
new generation of grilles and feature them on a fairly large scal
Manufacture of the new generation had thus been started under licenc
and considerable design development followed. The main manufacturin
problems were in dimensional tolerances and in ensuring an acceptabl
high quality and durable appearance. Since grilles had developed int
virtually a new building product, the main marketing problem was 1
obtain wide acceptance for it from architects and building clients, i
competition with other building components.

Boxes were made in a range of sizes weighing between 0.6kg (1½lb) an
5 kg (11lb). They had thirty or forty years earlier been the principa
outlet of the Lower Foundry. The original high demand for boxes ha
suffered from rapid technical development in the user industries combine
with changes in materials, and the output had fallen drastically over th
years. Although the market was now relatively static, boxes were seen b
the factory management as a useful 'loader' and contributor to revenue, 1
be retained for the next few years but probably to be sacrificed if th
expected profitable expansion in grilles took place. If manufacture was 1
continue in the longer term then it was felt considerable price increas
would be demanded from the principal remaining customer to compensa
for the greater opportunity cost their manufacture would then entail. N
attempts to expand sales or to find alternative markets were to t
contemplated. Nevertheless, the factory had a long-term relationship wit

his particular customer, and the company was a little reluctant to bandon the relationship entirely.

Other *miscellaneous products* were of much the same technical complexity s grilles and boxes, and were produced occasionally in small batches as obbing items in response to particular orders.

HE TECHNOLOGY

The piece of plant that dominated the Lower Foundry was the furnace, a arge continuously fed oil-fired plant, incorporating complicated temperaure and air-flow control mechanisms. There were technical as well as conomic reasons why the actual throughput of the furnace should not vary too greatly from the designed capacity, and the size and cost of the urnace may have been one of the principal present-day constraints on patterns of productive activity. Because of its obvious importance, the management of the factory and the division tended to act on the assumption that the needs of melting technology must determine production patterns.

The basic casting process for all products was similar, and consisted of pouring measured amounts of molten metal into a mould and pressing hem into shape by downward pressure from a top plunger. However, here were two quite different technologies, with different degrees of mechanisation and capitalisation. In effect, the furnace had four different outlets, all of which could in theory (within the constraint on maximum hroughput) have been in use at one time. Three of the four outlets were automatic feeders from temperature-controlled forehearths which gave directly into automatic casting and pressing equipment, and each of these hree was associated closely with one product line: no. 1 for cups, no. 2 for grilles, and no. 3 for the miscellaneous small-batch products. In fact, the second and third outlets tended to use the same personnel and parts of the same production line and were scarcely ever in operation at the same time.

These three lines were fairly highly mechanised production lines based on automatic multiple-head hydraulic presses. Although the 'autos' were over twenty years old, they were complex and adaptable machines capable when fitted with suitable moulds of pressing almost all sizes and shapes of product, so long as these were produced in any quantity. Following the casting and pressing process on the two main lines, products were conveyed to other mechanised processes. Cups were tempered and cooled before nspection and shock testing. Grilles went through a 'sealing' process and were then annealed before inspection.

The fourth outlet from the furnace was quite different. Molten metal was ladled by hand out of access points in the side of the furnace and cast in a number of hand and power-assisted presses. All boxes were produced on these hand and power presses, as were many short-run and development-type cups and grilles, and a small number of miscellaneous products. Boxes and most miscellaneous products were put directly into the annealing process after the pressing had been effected, but short runs of cups and grilles and some of the miscellaneous goods had to be tempered or sealed using the facilities of the main product lines.

As with any similar large furnace it was necessary to keep the melt going for fairly long periods, twenty-four hours a day and seven days a week, and to achieve a fairly steady throughput. It was technically feasible (though for the sake of economic usage of equipment and metal quality not desirable) to close down the actual casting and manufacture of product during the weekend. In fact the lines tended to operate continuously and some production was taking place from the furnace at some time during the whole duration of one 'campaign' during which the furnace was operative.

Over the previous twelve months, during which the furnace had been continuously in operation, the two main auto lines had worked on average for about 65 per cent of their potential working hours, the power-assisted presses for about 60 per cent on average, but the small hand presses for only fifteen per cent and the third auto line for only three per cent of potential. For twenty-two weeks of the year (in three separate spells) one or other of the main auto lines had been closed down altogether. If productive efficiencies had been higher when plant was actually running (in other words, less waste produced) then the current market demand would have been met with shorter working hours still.

As a result of the variations in workload there had been considerable variations in the number of people required, to the extent that can be judged from table 6.1.

These variations necessarily created a problem of labour redeployment which was a marked feature of the Lower Foundry, and indeed of many areas in the factory. Almost everyone who had worked there for any length of time had experienced either redundancy or redeployment to another department. The reasons included the history of surplus capacity, and underutilisation of the manufacturing facilities, and also the periodic shutdown both of this furnace and of the parallel furnace in the other half of the factory. Sometimes during these shutdown periods men the company wished to retain would be redeployed to work in the Upper Foundry or in another factory in the same town, or given standby maintenance work. Sometimes during a shutdown in the Upper Foundry workers from there would be drafted across to supplement the Lower Foundry working force. Problems to do with labour deployment for these or other reasons kept cropping up during this inquiry.

All the products of the Lower Foundry used the same basic alloy type but each product line had its own physical characteristics, which were best met by its own detailed alloy specification. All were being produced simultaneously from the same melt, and the alloy used had therefore to be one that would meet the requirements of all the products. Technically, this caused few very serious problems, but it had economic consequences. For

TABLE 6.1

Labour Requirements in the Lower Foundry in Different Production Situations
(including inspection and testing personnel)

	Numbers required assuming four-set working and		
	Full operation of two lines and side presses	*No. 1 line and side presses only operating*	*No. 2 or no. 3 line and side presses only operating*
No. 1 auto (operators, quenchers, inspectors, machine hands, etc.)	66	66	—
No. 2 or no. 3 auto (operators, machine hands, inspectors, etc.)	40	—	40
Side press men (cutters, ladlers, takers-in etc.)	40–55	40–55	40–55
Constant requirements (cleaners, recovery men, etc.)	24	24	24
	170–185	130–145	104–119

example, because of the need for a durable high-quality appearance in exposed situations, it was essential that grilles were cast in an alloy containing an expensive ingredient that was quite unnecessary to the technical requirements of any of the other products. This added perhaps £30000 a year to costs, over half of which was borne by cups and over a quarter by boxes, while the grilles for which it was needed used only about a fifth of the metal.

Possible solutions to this problem all created technical difficulties or high costs. Given different marketing decisions it might have been possible to arrive at a product mix whose alloy requirements were more compatible; or given present production patterns it might have been possible to produce sequentially and manufacture the whole output of grilles in three or four months of the year, reserving the more expensive alloy for this period. This, however, would have created inflexibilities and additional storage costs, and if the grilles market expanded greatly the solution would no longer be open.

A more radical alternative would have been to replace the furnace by a number of smaller and more flexible ones, each able to specialise on one product line. Although technically feasible, this would have been quite alien to those accustomed to one dominant furnace, and unless carried ou when furnace rebuilding was inevitable after the normal life of the existing furnace, it would have entailed very high capital expenditure. The step had not hitherto been contemplated by the local management, which did not see it as a possibility open to them. It was assumed that fundamenta redesign would be ruled out by the parent company in a factory which wa not seen as very profitable, and in the conditions of uncertainty facing all the major products of the Lower Foundry.

The only other major input which need concern us in this study were the tools (mould parts) used for casting and pressing, for which the usual source of supply was a tool-room/machine-shop run as part of the factory engineering department. Tools provision is another recurring theme of the study.

THE COMPANY AND THE FACTORY ENVIRONMENT

The Lower Foundry was part of a larger factory, and the factory was par of a division of a much larger company. Activities in the foundry were constrained by policies laid down elsewhere in the factory, the division and at company centre, and decisions had to fit in with some conception of overall company, divisional and factory needs.

Policies of the company centre affected the Lower Foundry in two ways Firstly the company, whose activities were fairly highly concentrated in one locality, retained considerable control at the centre over such things a capital expenditure, the patterns of activity and the markets served accounting procedures and controls (including overhead allocations, the charging out of central service functions, budgets and budgetary control and expected contributions to profits of particular activities). Pay rate were centrally negotiated and salary scales centrally decided, and the wage payment system was a company-wide scheme whose operation was monitored closely by central personnel and work-study departments.

Secondly, there was a perception at the centre that the factory was problem area. The division was a relatively small one, and neither it technology nor its rather diverse markets fitted very well with other company activities. For a long period the factory had not, in the Board view, made an adequate contribution to profits. The Board's concern with its contribution and the desire to see costs reduced were communicated clearly and often to the division and equally clearly by the Divisional Management Board to the factory manager. The effect of this on the divisional and works managements was mainly to make both act in such way that the company centre would have no cause for outright condem nation. Although the senior managers of the works and the division recognised that they were given considerable freedom by head office to make decisions affecting the efficiency of the factory, they in fact were discouraged from being venturesome, and tended to assess any proposal in the light of the attendant risks. More than in some other divisions, there was an emphasis on enforcing central work-study manning and payment systems rules, central recruitment and grading policies, and standard budgetary and costing procedures; and there was perhaps exaggerated compliance with Board requests for cost reduction or demanning or prohibitions on relatively small items of capital expenditure. Certainly no overt arguments took place with the Board on the reasonableness of central policies towards the Division or alternatives to them. We may mention three particular consequences that affected operations in the Lower Foundry

(1) One effect of the pressures on senior management in the works was that those managers imposed fairly tight controls and a rather inflexible monitoring procedure on the activities of middle managers.[1] Departmental performance was controlled strictly on the basis of manning levels, machine utilisation, reject rates and overall production, against budget targets, and managers were called to account for short-term deviances from target. As a result, the energies of departmental managers were concentrated on attaining these short-term targets, to the exclusion of longer-term development. Longer-term thinking was further discouraged by the knowledge that permission for capital expenditure for schemes initiated by departments was almost impossible to obtain. As will be seen in a later section, the tight controls created problems for the manager of the Lower Foundry and also produced some conflicts between him and one of the departments he was supplying.

(2) The Lower Foundry, as we have suggested, was the less glamorous of the two foundries in the factory. Consequently, cost saving tended to have a differential impact, and its efficiency had been affected in a number of ways. Its technology was older; many of the side presses were forty or fifty years old, and the multihead autos were of a type made obsolete in the Upper Foundry some ten years earlier. Working conditions were poor and facilities like restrooms and showers inadequate. Marketing effort had been reduced, the foundry staff felt themselves to be treated as rather second rate, and when recruitment problems arose the Upper Foundry's labour requirements were given precedence over the Lower Foundry.

(3) The factory engineering department was particularly affected by cost reduction. It was recognised by senior management that engineering had indirect effects on production efficiency, but these effects were not immediately apparent. When it was impossible to respond to central pressure by reducing manning or other costs in production areas, therefore, there was a tendency to reduce engineering staff for the time being on both the works maintenance side and the provision of tools for casting and pressing operations, and again the Lower Foundry was given lower priority than other areas in the competition for scarce engineering

resources. Both maintenance problems and inadequate provision of too[ ]
affected work at shopfloor level, and caused frustrations.[2]

Thus, there were contrasts in perspective between the Board's view o[ ]
what the company needed from the factory and the Division, the foundr[ ]
manager's view of the needs of his department, the assembly plan[ ]
managers' views of their requirements from the foundry and, in betwee[ ]
them all, the perspectives of the senior management of the works and th[ ]
Division about what was needed for their own survival and the survival o[ ]
the factory in this situation. Some effects of these contrasts in perspectiv[ ]
are implicit in the remainder of this chapter.

THE EMPLOYEES AND THE LABOUR MARKET

The traditional way local men were recruited was by word of mouth o[ ]
recommendation of employees already working there. There was thus [ ]
fairly long tradition of family employment in the factory. However, ove[ ]
the last three or four years there had been increasing difficulty i[ ]
recruiting. The senior management supposed that men with the kind o[ ]
outlook they wanted were no longer available because of changing socia[ ]
and educational standards. Some criticism of the personnel departmen[ ]
and its recruiting methods and pay rates was voiced but the managemen[ ]
was unwilling to institute a serious recruitment campaign. Partly, it woul[ ]
have been a break in tradition for the company. Partly, other compan[ ]
works in the same town had periodic labour surpluses, and company hea[ ]
office expected to be consulted when recruitment was taking place, or wa[ ]
contemplated, lest one factory should be recruiting when another factor[ ]
was seeking to redeploy or make redundant some established workers[ ]
Partly, there was a suspicion that the kind of employee who might b[ ]
attracted by advertisement would not 'fit in'.

In fact, a number of new light industries had recently arrived in th[ ]
locality and the local rate of unemployment had for some years been low[ ]
Further, over the last decade, the demand for labour in the factory ha[ ]
shown extreme fluctuations, rising no more than five years earlier to a pea[ ]
of 1700 men, and falling over the following two years to no more than 750[ ]
It was now about 1200. The deliberate drastic reduction in number[ ]
employed, together with unpleasant conditions and an impression of lov[ ]
basic rates and widely fluctuating total earnings, had created a ba[ ]
reputation for the works locally, and this was likely to stay with it for som[ ]
time.

Since demand over the last year or so had been increasing, the works ha[ ]
been forced to recruit through the Department of Employment and ha[ ]
had an influx of men from outside the immediate neighbourhood, some o[ ]
them immigrants from Ireland or the tropical Commonwealth. These me[ ]
came to the works in search of high earnings, and were attracted ther[ ]

because for the time being, owing to the shortage of labour, there were opportunities for working long hours of overtime. However, the influx of strangers, who were seen by local men not to fit easily into the traditions of the industry, had induced some of the more stable local workers to leave, which increased the shortage. Older workers also left to avoid strong pressures to work overtime, and the opportunities for overtime encouraged differential recruitment of men willing to work long hours for high earnings. Thus, at the time of the investigation, about thirty-five per cent of the men in the Lower Foundry were from outside the district, and this proportion was increasing fairly rapidly.

Rates of labour turnover in the department were on the whole very high, and this was particularly so for low-status occupations, for two of which the rates over the previous twelve months had been well over 200 per cent. Labour stability was correspondingly low; 57 per cent of foundry employees had had less than one year's service and almost 70 per cent had been there less than two years. Because of the retrenchment a few years earlier, no one at all had worked in the foundry between three and five years, and only just over a quarter had worked more than five years. All those with over five years' service were from the immediate locality. Almost all the outsiders had low-status jobs.

Outsiders were usually in their thirties and early forties. Many of them travelled to this works because as unskilled men with large families or other commitments, they needed fairly high earnings. So long as high bonus earnings and high rates of overtime were available they would remain, but when the demand slackened or redeployment to a lower paid job threatened, they left for highly paid work elsewhere. Therefore, the initial shortage of labour which had produced a high demand for overtime had enabled the department to recruit from a new source. This had, in turn, forced the department into a situation of constant high rates of overtime in order to retain the new sources of labour. Indeed, the overtime level was self-regulating. If the level of overtime dropped, men would leave the factory and the rate would be forced up again. The advantage of a highly mobile labour force was that so long as demand for labour fluctuated widely it was possible to run down the numbers employed rapidly simply by reducing the amount of overtime demanded. The problems of redeployment when either the furnace or one of the auto lines was closed for a few weeks were less serious than they might have been. On the other hand, problems of induction and training were greatly increased by instability.

As would be expected on a four-shift system with high rates of overtime, voluntary absence was high in the two lowest-paid, low-status jobs, where overall absence rates were eighteen per cent. Absence was usually taken without notice, and problems were caused for foremen attempting to allocate men to jobs on shift. They frequently had to plead with men just going off shift to stay and work either for the whole of the next shift, or for a few hours until replacements could be found. Alternatively, some foremen tried to estimate likely rates of absence, and brought men in from other shifts on overtime in anticipation of needs—a practice that was not popular with regular men on that shift if these highly paid overtime men then spent their time sleeping or sweeping up.

Differential rates of absence ensured that the foremen's problems were worst on the unpopular and less well-paid Monday to Friday day shifts. All shift foremen saw manning and deployment of men to positions on the line as their most troublesome problems.

Data on the distribution of overtime earnings help to confirm the role of overtime. Fewer than a third of the foundry workers took two hours a week or less overtime, and most of these in conversation said that they tried to avoid overtime, because of health or domestic circumstances, or because as single men or married men without dependents the earnings net of tax were not worthwhile to them. Over half the men had worked on average between five and fifteen hours a week, earning something between one-eighth and one-third of their earnings as overtime; and most of them tried to work a regular one or two shifts of overtime every week, sometimes on their days off, and sometimes by working double shifts of sixteen hours. Some of them complained of insufficient overtime opportunities. Finally between ten and fifteen per cent of the men regularly took home over a third of their pay as overtime earnings, and these men made it clear that if high opportunities for overtime were not there, they would not stay in the foundry. This group of men were seen by the majority as unfairly favoured by the foremen, and there was a lot of talk about the behaviour of the foremen and their methods of overtime allocation. From the foremen's point of view men who would work overtime on unpopular shifts were in a fairly strong bargaining position when it came to allocation at other times. Those who asked to work overtime on the more popular weekend shifts often found their requests refused in favour of men who had already worked on a day or afternoon shift during the week.

The whole recruitment and employment situation was an obvious one that would interest the investigating team if they were to devise a strategy for change.

PRODUCT MARKETS AND MARKETING ARRANGEMENTS

The immediate market for cups was another part of the factory where cups were incorporated into what we shall call a 'cup assembly' in a technically difficult and quite closely specified assembly process. The management and staff of the assembly plant had a quite different set of orientations from the Lower Foundry and saw themselves as a small business to which the Lower Foundry was a supplier. As well as the normal production and warehousing sections the assembly plant had a highly qualified technical design and testing department and associated laboratories.

The manager and his technical staff were in fairly close touch with customers and gave considerable thought to both new product development and technical development of existing products. They had close liaison with the R & D (Research and Development) function of the parent company, and had access to one small press in the Lower Foundry that was kept available for development work on the prototypes for new designs. For formal sales and marketing activities, however, they relied on a divisional sales department whose representatives were not regarded by the plant management as having adequate technical expertise, either to satisfy all the needs of the final customers or to recognise opportunities for new developments in the market.

In the final marketing of cup assemblies technical knowledge was more important than selling skills, and (whether for home or overseas customers) it entailed close technical collaboration with user industries and often with technical standards institutions of the countries concerned. Both the technical staff of the assembly plant and people from central R & D therefore got involved in marketing, and the former necessarily had to have some knowledge of the production problems and techniques of the Lower Foundry (as well as of the problems and techniques of their other suppliers).

The assembly department's ability to act as a small business (producing and marketing highly technical products of which cups were only one component) was constrained by the fact that the assembly plant manager was responsible directly to the factory manager and through him to the divisional managing director, whose orientations were towards foundry technology and for whom the efficiency of production in the foundries was of more interest than the economics or the technical problems of assembly and marketing. The differences in orientation between staff of the assembly plant and the senior factory management created problems, in that the former were highly committed to the success and the development of cup assembly as a business, whereas the latter were concerned that foreign markets were unfamiliar to them and seen by them to have considerably higher risks than they were used to. They saw the markets for cup assemblies mainly as an outlet for the production facilities of the Lower Foundry; and since they perceived the needs of survival in a competitive market in terms of costs and prices rather than collaboration in terms of technical properties and technical services, there was a concentration on reducing costs so as to allow the foundry, and the assembly plant, to contribute to their share of revenues.

The factory management had, on the other hand, put considerable thought and enthusiasm into developing and marketing the new generation of grilles. They were, however, being marketed to an industry (and a profession) of which the factory had had little previous experience. Eventually, by agreement with company head office, responsibility for launching and marketing the new product had been put in the hands of another division's marketing department, which decided to market it through wholesale channels it already used. This decision was unpopular in the factory, as it was suspected that low priority was given to the promotion of grilles by a division which stood to gain little from any success they achieved.

As has been suggested, little other marketing effort was made for Lower Foundry products. The managers of the foundry and the warehouse concerned were in fairly close contact with the customers for boxes and for the miscellaneous lines. They knew the technical and market requirements of these customers well. However, apart from the fairly recent developments in grilles and some unofficial market research by the highly committed design team for cup assemblies, little had been done by the factory or the Division to develop new markets or new products to increase the loading for the Lower Foundry.

One of the points to be considered by the investigating team would therefore be whether the existing product range was appropriate at this time, and what changes, if any, it would be rational to bring in. Should the management of the foundry aim to expand markets for existing products? Should it develop quite new products for new or related markets which were still suitable to the existing production facilities and expertise in the foundry? Or, if the technical and marketing expertise built up for the requirements of a specialist market were a valuable and scarce resource, should this specialist expertise dictate the production patterns for the future, even at the cost of a change in the dominant production technology?[3]

In fact, the dominance of melting technology and the expertise which went with it, had so influenced management attitudes that the answers to these questions might be less open than the team might have wished.

MANAGEMENT AND SUPERVISORY STRUCTURE

The Lower Foundry was under the control of a foundry manager. He had responsible to him a senior foreman, two day foremen who had certain responsibilities over the side presses and the auto-lines respectively, and a foreman on each shift. The responsibilities of the senior foreman and of the day foremen were largely technical and concerned with pressure, temperature and dimensional settings for the multihead presses, for tools and mould parts and for advice on obtaining the required rates of output and minimising rejects and wastage. Much of their effort was concerned with experimental work when new designs were being developed. The shift foremen, on the other hand, had responsibility for routine production and for allocation of men working on the autos and side presses to meet production plans laid down for them by a production planning department. Also, on each shift was a chargehand auto operator. A chargehand temperer worked on days and had much the same responsibilities for the tempering machine as the day foremen had for the autos and presses.

One striking fact about the supervisors was that almost all were within a

ew years of retiring age. During the retrenchment a few years earlier many
of the less senior foremen had been made redundant. At the time of the
subsequent re-expansion the Upper Foundry was given the advantage of
newly promoted younger and supposedly more flexible foremen to tackle
problems which were seen to be more difficult and more important, and
the Lower Foundry took over the more senior men.

The Foundry Manager was supported by the usual service functions,
and could call for assistance from the technical department of the factory,
and from the company's R & D function. A production planning
department translated the needs of the market, or of the cup assembly
plant, into production plans suitable for the needs of manufacturing. For
any new types or designs, however, lead times were long and the
production plan relied on the production and verification of new press tools
to fit in with manufacturing dates.

The engineering department provided important services both in
maintenance of equipment and by providing the tools for casting
and pressing. In both respects the Lower Foundry management saw itself
as being in competition with the rest of the factory for scarce engineering
resources.

Recruitment was in the hands of the factory personnel department
which also laid down the conditions of employment. Both personnel and
work-study departments were involved in designing the details of the wage
payment system and monitoring its operation.

There was also a fairly new quality control department, whose main
contribution at present was sample inspection of hot castings immediately
off the presses. Inspection of cups at the end of the process was done by
employees of the cup assembly plant, responsible to one of its technical
managers. Other products were inspected by employees of the main
warehouse. Final inspection was done as much for monitoring of efficiency
and bonus control for foundry workers, as for compliance with customer
requirements.

THE SOCIO-TECHNICAL SYSTEMS

The description so far has been management-orientated, and has outlined
some perceived problems about economic and technical efficiency. A
complete (or, we believe, a really useful) understanding of the foundry
requires some knowledge of the system as perceived by those involved for
the time being with operations on the plant.

The technologies in the Lower Foundry created an interesting situation.
Several quite different sociotechnical systems existed side by side but were
related to each other through the use of common technical facilities and the
occasional redeployment of labour from one to the other. We describe
these systems in considerable detail because they show again that, at
whatever level the analysis is made, there are complex patterns of

relationships, perceptions and influences, and that the different systems
and different levels of analysis are relevant for each other.

We will begin with an outline of the socio-technical system around the
hand and power presses, and later see how this compares with and, to some
extent, interacts with the 'auto' systems.

THE SOCIO-TECHNICAL SYSTEM ON THE SIDE PRESSES

The teams on most presses were of three men, known respectively as cutter,
ladler, and taker-in. Typically, in a three-man team the sequence of
operations was for the ladler to ladle molten metal from the access point for
that press, carry it to the press and pour it into the mould. The cutter, who
was recognised to have the most skill and responsibility of the three,
watched the pour and when he judged the right quantity of metal to have
been poured he tapped the ladle as a signal and 'cut' the stream of molten
alloy. He then operated the press to form the article being cast, and after
the requisite period lifted the plunger and indicated to the taker-in that he
should carefully remove the article from the press (usually by collapsing
the mould sides) and transfer it to the annealing process. The cutter then
reassembled the mould, cleaned it and oiled it for the next pour.

On all the presses the task was a highly cooperative one and because of
the danger and unpleasantness of dealing with molten alloy the team had
to work closely and harmoniously together and have considerable
confidence in each other. They invariably took their tea and meal breaks
together at convenient times, brewing up near the presses and starting
work again immediately the meal was over. Some teams arranged to take
their holidays at the same time, to avoid the team being split up.

Almost all the side press men were local men. Many, particularly among
the takers-in and ladlers, were keen young men in their early twenties. The
more senior cutters tended to be in their forties and to have been in the
foundry some years. The job, like most in the foundry, was thought to be
too heavy and unpleasant to remain in much after fifty years old. Normally
a man started on the side presses as a taker-in and this job was usually
obtained by a machine hand from one of the automatic lines who had
made himself known to a cutter or one of the foremen, shown at interest in
the presses and perhaps come over fairly regularly to lend a hand during
the frequent rest periods.

The younger takers-in would usually be looking for an opening as
ladlers, and the usual progression was from ladler to cutter, though by no
means all ladlers would be seen as capable of taking on the responsibility of
cutters, nor would some of them have wanted to. Training was almost
entirely on-the-job and consisted of working alongside the more experienced members of the team, gradually picking up the techniques of other
members. There was no obvious feeling that this was wrong, but men did

complain about the effect on their earnings when an inexperienced new man joined a team for a spell.

The wage payment system was an important element in the attitudes of press teams. It consisted of a fairly low basic wage (which varied somewhat from press to press), together with a shift supplement where appropriate and differential payments for night work and weekend work, such that the supplement for men working a four-set system raised their basic rate by forty-five to fifty per cent. In addition to the basic rate and shift supplement there were fairly high rates of work-studied incentive bonus, which were related directly to the number of good articles produced during the shift, but subject to a cash maximum. The rate varied according to the type of article being made and the press on which it was being made, each press having different characteristics from the others. Standard allowances were incorporated to compensate for such things as teething troubles at the start of production on a new type. The bonus was calculated on the work done by the cutter, and his teammates received varying proportions of the same bonus. Typically, the ladler received 75 per cent of the cutter's bonus and the taker-in 66 per cent. These rates, of course, magnified the basic differentials between the three occupations. Whereas the basic rate, including shift supplement, differed by only about £2 per week between cutter and ladler, and by a little over £3 between the cutter and taker-in, the maximum earnings of a cutter within the shift cycle might be £3·50 per week more than his ladler, and as much as £7 per week more than his taker-in. Although bonuses varied considerably, it was quite common for them to approach the maximum, which meant that thirty per cent of the wage packet of a cutter might consist of bonus, compared with about twenty-two per cent for a ladler and eighteen per cent for a taker-in. Much of the culture surrounding the side presses was influenced by these facts. The men believed that their earnings could be considerably higher than on the autos, and that they were largely within the control of members of the team.

The payment system introduced some tensions into team work. Takers-in and ladlers, although on the whole favourably disposed towards the system of pay, had some complaints about their earnings potential as compared with their teammates. They felt the team to be 'in control of the bonus because you are in control of your production', but the tensions arose from this same fact: 'The cutter has to be interested in the job. If he couldn't care less, then he ruins his money and he ruins your money, and then you couldn't care'. Not only the cutter, but any member of the team could spoil an item through carelessness, and it was important for there to be a good match between the effort – reward bargain desired by each member of the team.

A second form of tension was between teams working on the same shift, but on different presses. There was a feeling that work was harder on some presses than others, and that some presses were treated more favourably than others by both job-evaluated basic rates and work-study values.

There was considerable debate about the relative difficulty of the jobs on different presses.

Nevertheless, the majority of men working on the presses appreciated and were reasonably satisfied with the general system of pay. There were four aspects of the job on which some dissatisfaction was expressed all of which, in fact, tended to lead to fluctuations in earnings outside the team's control. These were the work-study values for different products and different presses, the standards of inspection at the end of the line, the state of the tools, and frequent redeployment.

Since the payment system was for the pressmen a real incentive to production, there was widespread interest in and knowledge of the exact details of it. Cutters in particular generally knew the rates for every product produced on their own presses, and many had compiled tables giving at least the numbers of good products they had to make for particular shift bonuses. There was considerable emphasis in conversation on the perceived differences in rate for different products, and a few anecdotes were told about the progress of particular grievances over rates that were seen to be far too tight. In some cases teams had worked for months at much reduced effort and low earnings in attempts to get rates changed.

Given acceptable rates, press teams generally worked for a target output of good articles on each turn, and the tempo of work thus imposed on them was known universally as 'working for their number'. On presses which worked continuously on four shifts this target output, which was nicely judged to take account of a gearing in bonus rates, was tacitly agreed between shifts, so that each worked for the same target. This had considerable importance in bargaining with the work-study department and hints were frequently dropped about friction between shifts when targets were not kept to. Reprisals like deliberate cooling down of tools, or dirty moulds could ensue when one shift suspected that its predecessor had produced significantly more than it need have done to attain its target output. It was explained that if a target was exceeded, then management and the 'time-study people' as they were still known, would put pressure on a succeeding shift to increase its output to a comparable level and in the end work-study values, both for that product and generally, might be tightened. There was considerable hostility towards time study, the inequities of which were felt to have created a number of tensions in the department. It was difficult to discover whether the battle with time study was not ruefully enjoyed, but in any case it was universally indulged in.

The keen interest of press teams in their own production figures created some further problems. The bonus was calculated on the number of good articles passed at the end of the line. Although the press teams themselves rejected and threw away to scrap boxes which were obviously faulty at the time of casting, there was a natural tendency to send borderline cases through the annealing process in the hope that the inspectors might pass them. However faults undetectable at the time of casting were believed to develop during annealing, and the annealing process was so lengthy that feedback from the inspectors was not available until about two hours after the item had been cast.

So, given that reject rates were high, production was a bit of a lottery and although on a familiar press and producing a familiar article the rate of rejects could within broad limits be predicted, in unfamiliar production conditions the teams were never sure what the inspectors were likely to pass. Further, because of the slowness of feedback, the teams, particular at the beginning of a new run, were always anxious lest after two hours or so of production they should discover the inspectors rejecting the whole of their output. If a constant fault was discovered by the inspectors at this stage, it would be impossible to make any worthwhile bonus during the whole of that shift and the tendency was then to stop trying.

The conflict between press teams and inspectors was influenced by three facts: that press teams were of longer service and higher status than inspectors and as they saw it of much higher skill; that inspection had been instituted in this form (and was treated by management) as much for bonus control as for market-orientated quality control; and that the inspectors' shift system was quite different from that of the foundry workers, so that a team did not work regularly with one group of inspectors. There was a suspicion that quality standards varied from one inspection shift to another, and that they could be lowered during periods when a product was in heavy demand and raised when it was being produced for stock.

The comments made by press teams about tools and about the maintenance of presses, were also coloured by the effect on bonus earnings. It was felt that the poor engineering service received by the presses was an indication of the low status of the presses compared with the Lower Foundry autos; compounding the impression constantly given that the Lower Foundry itself had low priority relative to the Upper Foundry. Poor tools and the difficulty of persuading foremen to replace faulty tools, were thought by press men to put quality out of their control and therefore to produce high and unpredictable rates of rejects.

Unofficially, many press teams did a considerable amount of maintenance work on their presses. However, management opposed this practice for fear that reprisals from engineering craftsmen would affect standards of engineering maintenance both here and in the rest of the factory. There were therefore delays, particularly when breakdowns occurred on day shift as it was more difficult then to get away with unofficial practices. Further, men felt that press design modifications that could have been made during closedown periods would have helped solve the demarcation problem. They wondered why management could never be persuaded to undertake these. As downtime was paid at either basic rate or a nominal rate of bonus, idle time meant teams were not only losing bonus but also bringing down their 'average' which had significance for other reasons.

The most serious cause of grievance amongst press teams was frequent redeployment. Redeployment took a number of different forms, each with its own effects on the earning capacity and satisfaction of those concerned. The main occasions for redeployment were:

(1) long-term redeployment when the furnace was closed down altogether for a period;

(2) redeployment on to another press because of urgent orders or for production scheduling reasons;

(3) redeployment on to the auto when there was no work available for the press (shortage of orders or lack of tools);

(4) redeployment on to the auto at times when the latter was undermanned due to absence or sudden loss of personnel;

(5) sickness, absence or unplanned leave of a member of the press team.

Relatively mild complaints were made about shutdown of the furnace. Despite considerable loss of earnings, this appeared to be accepted as technically necessary. Warning was usually given, and some men actually left the factory in anticipation of such redeployment, with the intention of returning on restart.

Production scheduling complications, or urgent orders, or possibly faulty tools on the team's regular press, sometimes caused the whole team to be transferred onto an unfamiliar press. In this case the team was guaranteed a bonus at the notional 80 units an hour of the time-study scheme, with the opportunity of earning more than this should their output exceed the notional figure. However, teams transferred to another press were unlikely to make their normal bonus and this, combined with unfamiliarity of work on the new press, caused complaints. Some teams claimed that their presses were more subject to this kind of redeployment than others, and therefore they suffered more than other teams; other men believed that the reason they were called on frequently was because of their greater skill and flexibility, for which they received no recognition, but rather lost earnings. Some of the tension between different presses was caused by the feeling that some presses and some teams were penalised more than others by this system.

Usually, when a press was closed down because of shortage of work on that range of products, some notice was given to the press team concerned and they were then transferred over onto the auto line to work as machine hands or spare operators. In these circumstances the men would be paid as though they were regular auto workers, and the moves were unpopular, because of breakup of the team and dislike of the machine-controlled conditions on the autos. Earnings potential on the autos was also believed to be less than on the presses.

Even more unpopular (though of increasing frequency) was redeployment at short notice from one of the presses over onto one of the auto lines to make up for unexpected undermanning on those lines. It was customary that men transferred for these reasons should be paid their 'average' bonus for the month. However, redeployment was still unpopular because the group had been broken up, the work was disliked and the regular men on the auto line were thought to resent the high wages the pressmen were still earning.

Equally important, redeployment on to the auto line gave the press men a clear indication that the autos had operational priority over the presses. If the autos were undermanned the press groups were broken up to keep the auto manned. On the other hand, if through absence a press was undermanned it was extremely rare for a man to be redeployed from the auto to a press team. If the cutter or ladler was absent from a team, the press team was normally inoperative and those present were either given their basic wage to do odd jobs as 'spare men' or were redeployed onto the auto line on auto rates. If it was the taken-in who was absent, then on occasion the team would be made up with a spare man from another press, or a man on overtime, though they would still suffer monetarily from working with an unfamiliar teammate.

To sum up this system, work on the presses was a cooperative activity between members of small teams. Satisfaction was created by this, and by the fact that the incentives in the pay scheme gave men the feeling that earnings were within their own control. The circumstances detracting from satisfaction were technical problems connected with poor engineering service, defective moulds or presses (which left men out of control of their production) varying inspection standards and especially redeployment. All of these went to destroy the feeling of being a team in control of the effort–reward bargain. The complicated rules made to cover redeployment were symbolic of the perceived complexities in the situation and the care needed to keep it in balance.

THE SOCIO-TECHNICAL SYSTEM ON THE AUTO LINES

The men working on each auto line formed a cooperating group whose work and whose earnings were determined by the operation of the line as a whole. Efficiency required the whole group to work in time with the auto presses and maintain a rather delicate balance between different parts of the line. Interdependence created common orientations for the whole auto group, but within the wider system were some closer-knit nuclei, to some extent overlapping and sometimes in conflict, of which the two most pronounced were around the autos and around the tempering process.

Each of the two principal automatic multihead presses was manned by a semiskilled operator who was the key man on the line. A chargehand operator was usually present and his job was to oversee both autos when both were working. Generally the chargehand worked alongside the operators, making some of the adjustments to the press to meet varying conditions, or to correct quality faults in the castings. Between them the chargehand and the operators controlled the casting and pressing process and their object was to obtain as high a yield as possible of acceptable products.

The jobs of the operator and chargehand operator were recognised to be complex and responsible ones giving them high status. They tended to be either fairly long-service men in their late thirties or early forties, or newly trained operators in their early twenties who as machine hands had shown initiative and mechanical aptitude and interest in the casting process. Usually promotion had been from machine hand via a spell as 'spare' operator.

There were frequent 'rough turns' on the autos when almost the whole time was taken up with operating problems. Casting is still an art, and it was generally recognised that an operator must work for at least two years before being able to get the feel of the job. The challenge, and perceived responsibility for the output of the line, was a source of satisfaction for the operators and their most common complaints were about the restrictions placed on their control over the job, partly by the activities of the chargehand and foremen, who tended to make adjustments or correct faults on the machine without reference to the operator; and partly by the maintenance fitters who set up the machine at the start of a new run. Operators respected the superior knowledge of the chargehands but would have preferred them to have had a training role. Attitudes to the day foremen and technicians were more hostile.

Also involved on each line near the autos was the quality control inspector, inspecting a sample of the hot castings particularly for dimensional characteristics. The work of this man, who was generally known as the 'hot sorter', was designed partly (for newly introduced products) to relate the characteristics of the hot castings to final inspection criteria, and partly to give rapid feedback of adverse trends to the operator. This feedback was recognised by the operators to be essential to their own job.

The nuclear group around the auto included the hot sorter, and on no. 1 line a machinehand transferring cups from the auto to the bottom of an inclined conveyor, using a handling device and asbestos gloves. The role of each member of this group was recognised to be indispensable, the chargehand for his superior skill, the operator for his responsibility for production over the whole course of the shift, the machinehand, not only for his part in unloading the multihead press, but (if he was experienced) for his ability to recognise a number of the faults as they came off the machine and to give immediate feedback to the operator. The hot sorter was, of course, relied upon for the main feedback on trends, particularly on dimensional and other characteristics not immediately visible. The closer the hot sorter worked to the machine, the more useful a member of the team he was seen to be.

Close integration between these four was emphasised because 'It would come out in earnings if we didn't work together'. The payment system consisted of a low basic rate, shift allowance and multifactor incentive bonus that was subject to a cash maximum. The scheme attempted to reflect the contribution of the men to the output of the line, but because of the many factors other than individual effort which could affect the output of good quality products, numerous allowances were made for length of run, type of product and differential rates of reject. The men believed that the scheme in effect gave a higher bonus the greater the number of good quality articles produced and the lower the rate of rejects, and they aimed to produce as many good articles as possible in the course of the shift.

The main problem was that hardly anyone understood how the bonus was calculated and it was never possible to estimate what bonus earnings would be for a particular week. Operators spoke of the paradox that the 'rough turns', when work rates were extremely high, usually resulted in low yields and therefore low bonus earnings; whereas during the quiet times they could be standing back and doing very little, knowing that high bonuses were resulting. Fluctuations in bonus earnings had little to do with fluctuations in individual effort or even skill, but were caused rather by uncontrolled quirks of the technology, by occasional faulty tools and by the activities of foremen and technicians whose interference with settings, often for experimental reasons, could, it was believed, cause many hours of difficulty for the operators.

Another clearly identifiable subgroup on the autos was the tempering team on no. 1 line. From the top of the conveyor on this line cups were transferred by a machinehand into a temperature equalisation kiln prior to passing through a quenching process in a tempering machine. The team consisted of a skilled temperer (responsible for controlling the speed and temperature of both equalisation kiln and tempering machine and for conditions in them), an assistant temperer (who had some knowledge of the temperer's job and was able to control the machine in the temperer's absence) and an unskilled machinehand. Temperers were much involved in their job, which they saw as highly skilled and responsible. They talked a great deal about timing, temperature setting and handling and seemed to put a great deal of thought into suggestions for improved methods. Timing was important, for if the kiln or the tempering machine got out of balance or any of the heads on them were defective for a period, there would be product losses. The three men on the tempering machine, even more than those around the auto, worked together closely as a team. Experience, and the ability to work together and to discuss methods of operation were all seen as important. Resentment was expressed when a new machinehand was allocated to the team without being given full briefing. Other members of the team had then to watch him continually, demonstrate faults to him and gradually integrate him into the work.

Complaints about poor maintenance, poor conditions of work and lack of protective clothing were many, and there seemed to be sources of conflict between the temperers on different shifts, largely revolving around the unofficial modifications each made to the job. Settings were never correct on taking over a new shift and it took some time before the process settled down to the liking of the new team. Supervisors who tampered with the settings were also a focus of resentment.

On no. 2 line the operation of the sealing machine was performed by teams of machinehands who worked in spells of forty minutes in every hour, because of the generally very hot conditions. Normally four machinehands (with two others resting) were engaged on a completely unskilled set of operations, consisting principally of carrying hot castings from one position to another. It was characterised by a high level of physical energy in hot and unpleasant conditions, and requiring a certain amount of care (for reasons both of safety and quality assurance).

Machinehands knew little about the basis of their bonus and often expressed the feeling that 'you can't weigh your money up'. They had little influence over the quantity or the quality of products made or the amount of work they had to do. When after a heavy spell of work they saw a high rate of rejects, frustration about loss of earnings was evident. It was this group of machinehands, many of whom travelled in from another town, who tended to stay least long in the factory, because of lack of interest in the work, feeling of being frequently moved from place to place, the fluctuations in earnings and fluctuating opportunities for overtime.

Redeployment was a characteristic of the auto lines. When no. 1 line was closed, the operator was made a machinehand or spare operator on no. 2 line, and for a few months lost his operator's basic wage as well as the corresponding bonus; the tempering team was broken up and the senior temperer was made a machinehand on no. 2. Thus there was a loss of status and self-esteem for operators and temperers and a considerable loss of earnings opportunities for everyone on the line. Machinehands from no. 2 line were commonly redeployed as cleaners or sent to other poorly paid jobs and they eventually left. When a furnace shutdown took place, then all the employees in the Lower Foundry were either transferred to other work or dismissed. Many left the foundry voluntarily at least for the few months of the shutdown. Cooperating teams were thus broken up almost in the same way as on the side presses.

To sum up these few pages, work on the auto lines was a cooperative undertaking, relying on groups of people working together and coordinating their efforts to produce high yields. Despite its deficiencies, the effect of the pay system was to reinforce this cooperative effort. What detracted from it was nothing in the design or the motivation of the men, but the unpredictable technical faults (some of which were due to faulty tools, poor maintenance and delays in getting repairs done), the inexperienced newcomers and the demotivating effects of redeployment, exacerbated as they were by the way pay rules were enforced. Although the atmosphere on the auto lines was quite different from that on the side presses, the features creating dissatisfaction were much the same.

THE INSPECTION PROCESS

All process workers had suspicions about inspection criteria. High rates of reject by the inspectors directly affected the bonus earnings of everyone on the lines and side presses and any evidence of variation in inspection standards aroused strong feelings. For a number of reasons, including physical separation and a different shift system, the inspection and testing teams formed a quite separate social group from the auto and side press workers. We examine here only the interface between inspection and production.

Basic pay rates for inspectors were low and bonus rates (based on the number of items handled) did not allow high earnings. Those doing the inspection were short-service men of equivalent status to machinehands, recruited directly to do the job after a short spell of training. Little respect for them was expressed by operators or press teams, and problems were caused for their employing departments because of the high rates of turnover among them and difficulties in recruitment, which again resulted in high overtime. At one time during the enquiry inspectors were working regularly on a twelve-hour shift system.

The fact that the inspectors were not known personally to the men on the autos and presses made it more difficult to exert pressure on the inspectors to pass doubtful production. Pressure however there was, and for this reason a number of more senior checkers were employed to do a sample check of the inspectors' work. If unacceptable items were found by the checkers, the inspector concerned would be officially reprimanded and his bonus could be forfeit. Rejected items were not checked, but inspectors were discouraged from throwing good items away to the reject area by a differential in the bonus, which gave them more for items they passed than for items rejected.

One feature of the inspection process was its subjective nature. For cups and grilles there were two final inspection processes: a dimensional check and a visual inspection. The former caused few problems. Items that fell outside the specified tolerances were rejected. The visual inspection was for both technical and aesthetic defects, and again the technical defects were clearly specified and their presence led to rejection without great dispute. The most common faults however came under the heading of aesthetic faults, and though inspectors had fairly clear criteria for rejection there were always grounds for dispute whether particular items could, in the ruling circumstances, pass or not—disputes in which the managers concerned could become involved.

Another source of interaction between inspectors and process men was the fact that some visually identified defects (technical and aesthetic) were caused by faults in the alloy and others by casting or handling failures. Since process workers could not be blamed for metal faults, they naturally tried to put pressure on the inspectors to safeguard bonuses by overbooking metal faults among the rejects and this was yielded to, to the extent that the melting department at one stage came under misinformed pressure from senior management to improve the quality of alloy it was providing.[4]

The fact that inspection had the dual purpose of quality assurance and bonus control, meant that inspectors were under conflicting pressures. There were parallel sources of conflict between the foundry manager and managers of the departments he was supplying, and these we must examine.

ROLE DIFFICULTIES OF THE FOUNDRY MANAGER

The foundry manager was a knowledgeable and experienced man who had in the past worked both as an operator and a cutter, and had at one stage been a foreman in the Lower Foundry. He had been appointed to the post only a few months earlier, apparently to help improve efficiencies in the department, and was in the process of restructuring the supervisory and technical organisation.

Because of his background the differences in perception between managers and shopfloor evident in the other cases were absent in the Lower Foundry. They were however replaced by wide differences between the perspectives of the foundry manager and the senior management in the works. These can perhaps best be illustrated by analysing some sources of role conflict between the foundry manager and two of his colleagues: the assembly plant manager responsible for the quality of cups, and the production planner.

The assembly plant manager saw quality control as a battle, partly because of the low skill and efficiency of the men he was forced to employ as inspectors, but also because of the problems he had with the foundry. At the start of a run the assembly plant had to insist on getting the best possible standards, and it tried to delay full production until these were attained. The production people were anxious for a long run, resisted the delays and often seemed reluctant to make corrections requested by the assembly plant until threatened with 100 per cent rejection. Should a fault develop in the course of a run, say because of a dirty mould on one head of the auto, the foundry manager would be reluctant to change because 'it would lose us an hour's production'. Inspection standards were thus a field for perpetual battle between the production manager, who continually felt good production was being rejected, and the assembly plant manager continually pressing him to get standards up to specification.[5]

The management of the assembly plant would have preferred that the foundry produced to set standards laid down by an independent quality control department, that the foundry manager and his staff were fully cognisant of the technical requirements for cups and that they should take responsibility for the quality of their own production, with advice from a quality assurance service. This, however, was contrary to the policy of senior management and would not have fitted the control system generally used in the factory.

Each of the managers appreciated and sympathised with the problems of the other. However, the foundry manager was forced by circumstances to act as he did. Factory controls on the Lower Foundry meant that he was judged on criteria such as the quantity of production, the ratio of rejects to total output, machine utilisation and final output per man employed, all of which were reduced to the extent that he succumbed to pressures from the assembly managers (or the warehouse manager where grilles and boxes were concerned). Moreover, given the recruitment and retention problems for men on both sides of the production process, it was necessary to maintain the level of bonus earnings as far as possible.

One way of satisfying earnings needs would have been by 'policy payments' when through no fault of their own the men were not producing good products. These the foundry manager made exceptionally, especially for side press teams, but the practice roused the extreme hostility of the personnel and work-study departments, and the conflicts had been taken in some cases to works manager level, where, because of the situation reported earlier *vis-à-vis* division and head office, the foundry manager's actions were not usually supported. There was thus much pressure on the foundry manager to try to keep production going as long as possible, for the sake of satisfying both factory control systems and the earnings needs of his subordinates, and retaining the latter in the foundry.

Reasons for high reject rates included the poor maintenance standards, the inadequacy of some of the plant, and faulty mould parts. The reluctance of foremen and managers in the foundry to change faulty moulds was due to the pressure to reduce engineering costs, and the knowledge borne of long experience that new tools were not forthcoming in response to orders. The foundry therefore carefully conserved stocks of deteriorating tools, despite pressures both from user departments and from operators and press teams to change faulty tools more frequently. What did happen was that the foundry concentrated on ensuring documentary evidence was available that new tools or tool repairs had been ordered on time or maintenance work requisitioned, or capital expenditure requested. If then the cup assembly plant, for instance, answered criticisms of unmet deliveries by demonstrating that the foundry had produced oversize and unacceptable cups to meet the order, the foundry could demonstrate in its turn that this was due to worn-out moulds, and that new ones ordered perhaps months earlier had not been produced by the engineers, who could in turn point to their inadequate staff and usually show that senior management had directed them to give specific priority to other work.

No one cared for this situation, but it helped develop certain skills, perhaps at the expense of departmental performance. It is not clear whether the real costs to the organisation of inadequate tool provision outweighed the savings made by the staff reductions in engineering.

The role conflicts between the foundry manager and the production planning manager were less serious and less evident, though again they had consequences for efficiency. Because of the surplus capacity in the foundry, the production planners had been given the task of planning so as to maximise output per man employed. The aim of the plan was generally to achieve long runs, within the constraints imposed by market and stocking policies. However, the efficiency of the planning process could be upset by non-availability of suitable tools for the runs proposed, or by lack of replacement tools should a fault occur. These were among the factors that caused the frequent short-term redeployment of men from one press to another, from the presses on to the auto lines, or from one auto line to another. The foundry manager recognised the problems frequent re-deployment caused and tried to mitigate some of the effects, though the constraints of maximum stock levels, unexpected market variations, and, it was said, occasional intervention by senior management into the plan with instructions to carry out certain work at once, made this smoothing process difficult. The foundry manager's concern about redeployment was of course partly due to the reactions on him of men whose pay had been adversely affected.

CONCLUSION

In the Finishing Shop and the Press Room the interactions between different perceptions of the situation were important in generating some of the processes we discovered there. Conflicting perceptions helped to influence the relationships between people, and these in turn influenced behaviour. In the Lower Foundry some quite complex processes were generated by the interactions between technology, production patterns, pay systems, engineering services, manning arrangements and other aspects of the situation, and perceptual differences between members of the department were less pronounced, though they did exist, as for example between side press men and auto men, between local employees and newcomers, and between some foremen and shopfloor workers.

However, in this case various levels of management are shown to have held very different perceptual models of the factory, and of the Lower Foundry in particular, and the processes generated by these differences were at least as important in the whole pattern of performance of the foundry as were the interactions within the foundry system. Company centre, divisional management, works manager, assembly plant managers engineering department managers and the foundry manager himself, each appear to have operated with different models of the situation as it affected the foundry, and the effect of those different models was to place constraints on the behaviour of those concerned, to the extent that is evident in the role difficulties found by the foundry manager, some of which have been outlined.

The foundry manager's position was an interesting one. His aim was to run his department efficiently and to increase its performance over time, and he recognised the need to improve the efficiency of equipment, to improve maintenance standards, and to build up the skills of his foremen and subordinates. However, he was under continual pressure to reduce costs, and was forced to economise on maintenance and tools, and on minor supplies. Although he had been given freedom to reorganise the department and to make procedural experiments, approval had to be obtained for extremely small amounts of capital expenditure, and this approval was often not forthcoming. He believed his ability to make any fundamental improvements in the department was therefore severely limited. Other managers in the same factory recognised that they were so constrained and had decided to accept the situation and work to the rules provided for them. Much of the behaviour of the foundry manager, recently appointed as he was, was due to his continuing enthusiasm for the potential he believed the foundry capable of; and his attempts to work within the constraints imposed on him towards this end.

Whether the manager would ever achieve a more efficient department was open to question. Much of his current energy was taken up with short-term battles and he required both greater stability and considerable expenditure to achieve his goals. The foundry, and possibly the factory as a whole, was in the grip of a regressive spiral that affected many dimensions of performance: market satisfaction, technical efficiency, the employment of labour, and so on. One task of the investigating team would be to try to uncover some means for the foundry to emerge from this spiral and begin on a path of improvement, if that were possible within the necessary constraints. Some of the thinking of the team about how these improvements could be started is given in chapter 14, where it will be shown that there were many constraints on its ability to begin any implementation of these changes.

NOTES TO CHAPTER 6

1. R. H. Guest (1962) chapters 2 and 6, has described a somewhat similar situation.
2. Legge (1970), and Gowler and Legge (1973) have examined the idea that a regressive spiral can quite frequently be identified in the internal labour market of firms which have experienced an unfamiliar product market change to which they have made inappropriate adjustments. We suggest that the Lower Foundry was also in a regressive spiral, but one that operated through the technology as well as the labour market: perceived lack of profitability had led to tightening of cost controls, reduction in engineering services, greater inability to produce efficiently and hence even lower ability to meet market requirements.
3. The fact that these questions were felt to be of importance to the work of the team is of course consistent with the approach we have used. It does however

    illustrate one of the main differences between this programme and what is generally entailed in a programme of planned organisational change or development.

4. Summaries of a number of similar counter-control measures in engineering factories are given in Roy (1955), Lupton (1963), and Jones (1969).

5. Pugh (1966) describes other examples of role conflict between production and inspection departments.

7 The Three Cases Compared

We have now reported on three quite different cases studies. The studies differ in at least three ways: (a) the approach and method of investigation has differed between the three; (b) the departments studied, their problems and the patterns of behaviour in each were very different from each other; (c) and the way in which the cases have been reported differs. As we have suggested in chapter 3, methods of investigation will vary with the different circumstances of the system being investigated, for the open socio-technical systems approach allows those doing the investigation considerable discretion to suit their detailed methods to the nature of the organisation. There is a second reason why investigation methods may be different: the structure of skills and the relationship between members of the investigating team, and the circumstances in which that team finds itself during the investigation. Methods of analysis have differed between these cases for both these reasons.

In the Finishing Shop study the collection of data, whether from departmental records or through interviews, almost wholly preceded any attempt at the formulation of explanatory hypotheses about causation. Data were collected and summarised, views listened to and behaviour observed before any conscious attempt was made to relate all these sources of information together or to make tentative explanations about causation or to try and fit together the different perceptions. The Press Room enquiry was done by a project team set up with specific terms of reference, namely to find means of rapidly increasing output. The project team included members who knew a good deal already about the characteristics of the shop, and it also included members of the central change team. Because of the specific task given to the team and the dynamics of team structure, the process of hypothesis formulation began much earlier in the investigation and some hypothetical models of behaviour were being discussed soon after the preliminary overview of the department had been made. Many of the decisions about the facts to be collected resulted from the need to obtain information with which to back up or to falsify alternative explanations. There was less need in this study to undertake lengthy exploratory enquiries into the nature of the socio-technical system, since much of the system was already known to experienced members of the project team.

The third case, the Lower Foundry, lies somewhere between the two. The circumstances of the team were similar to those of the Finishing Shop team, in that no specific terms of reference were given to it other than to formulate a method of analysis which could eventually lead to improvement in the foundry. However, as the team began work in the foundry, the complex nature of the relationships between technology, resource markets, product markets and company policies became evident and the investigation lasted considerably longer than the Finishing Shop enquiry. Moreover, changes occurred in the investigating team over the course of the project, and the final outcome integrated the findings of a number of separate strands.

The methods used in the Finishing Shop and in the Press Room are in a sense at two extremes: one in which the socio-technical framework was used to build up a detailed picture of relationships and attitudes in the department, from which an explanation of behaviour was eventually derived and confirmed, mainly by discussing the explanations arrived at with existing members of the department and obtaining their agreement or disagreement to them; and the other where the understanding was obtained through a classic method of hypotheses formulation and testing. Most investigations on the programme in fact, fell between these two extremes, and the Lower Foundry is possibly an example of a more common approach, where some of the relationships became manifest from the earliest stages of the enquiry, and tentative partial models were built while data collection was still proceeding, some of which data might yield further insight into the same problems.

One legitimate reason for differences of approach between one departmental investigation and another is that industrial situations differ so greatly from each other. In the three cases we are considering these differences are manifest. The Finishing Shop was a system no one was satisfied with. It was now a declining department, and for long had been seen by everyone to have problems (though as we have shown there were many different perceptions as to what the problems were). Whatever the Press Room's problems were, they were different from those of the Finishing Shop, and its members expressed far more satisfaction with it as a system. If it had not been for its inability to meet a rapidly expanding market, neither management nor shopfloor men might have wanted radical changes made. In many ways, these were two quite comparable small production departments with simple technologies which had been in effect managed in almost diametrically opposed ways. Not only were the states of efficiency and product market satisfaction different, but the manifestation of problems was very different in each.

By comparison, the Lower Foundry was a rather complex system with a dominant and difficult technology, also working in difficult market situations, and in which it was difficult to achieve a good fit between technological requirements, market requirements, social requirements, and the control systems within which men had to work. Emphasis had to be given to influences from outside the department. Although analysis of the detailed socio-technical systems as they affected members of press teams and auto lines was essential for a full understanding of behaviour, a description of the shopfloor socio-technical systems alone would be insufficient to explain adequately many of the events in the Lower Foundry, and would certainly be an unsatisfactory basis, taken by itself, on which to formulate a strategy for improvement.

Given the differences, in the circumstances of each investigating team, in the nature of the departments as systems, and in the way in which each has been reported, nevertheless the general framework of the open socio-technical systems approach is evident in each of the studies. The framework would almost certainly require some consideration of the inputs into the organisation, the outputs going to a product market of some kind, and the interplay between such internal elements as the technology, control systems and social structure. The relevance of these elements, and particularly of the relationships between them, is evident in all three studies.

For example *the material inputs* into each system have relevance in each case, but they have had a very different impact on behaviour in the Press Room study compared with the Lower Foundry study. In all three studies the principal materials entering the system came from another department of the same works and characteristics of the manufacturing process were relevant in explaining the patterns of events. Quality also affected departmental behaviour. In the case of the Lower Foundry, quality variations were important mainly for the effect on inspection – production relations; but for technical reasons the melt was more costly than was needed for 80 per cent of the output of the foundry. In the other studies quality variations reduced the ability of members of the department to produce efficiently and affected the rewards they received for given inputs of effort. In the Finishing Shop the technically imposed need for large warehouse stocks could have been beneficial and permitted much more flexibility to be introduced to the finishing process than was in fact taken advantage of.

Similarly *the inputs of skills and energies* from the labour market are an important theme in each study. Each department used unskilled or semi-skilled men drawn from a local labour market still regarded by the employers as fairly benign, with little alternative employment and an expectation among local people that the conditions of employment offered, including shift work, were normal. In each case, this situation was changing and each department was experiencing some difficulty in consequence. Conditions of employment offered were different in each department, and they had attracted men with rather different character-istics. In the Lower Foundry in particular there seemed to be two different groups: local men who had chosen the more highly skilled and rewarding jobs, and men from another town whose main motivation was the high earnings available from long hours of work. In all three studies it was clear that self-selection of employees had resulted in membership of the department by men with fairly clear characteristics and with backgrounds and patterns of motivation that it was possible to match fairly clearly to the employment conditions offered by the departments in which they were working.

Since all three studies took place in the same company (although not the same factory) the effect of *central company policies* is evident. The company imposed fairly tight controls over divisional performance and had fairly strict definitions of what was expected in terms of management responsibilities and style. Company policy defined the type of pay system in operation in all three areas and the characteristics of this pay system were among the most important influences on productive behaviour.

Central controls encouraged line managers to yield fairly influential roles to, for instance, work-study engineers. Where this happened the system of controls had created conflicts for those working in the system, and notably for the supervisors who had in one way or another managed to resolve the conflicts through *manipulation of the system*. The consequences of this manipulation were evident in each case, but they were most profound for the Press Room foreman, since the course he chose not only constrained the behaviour open to him in the future but also affected behaviour at the interface between the Press Room and the warehouse, and between the company and its market. In the Lower Foundry, the recently appointed foundry manager had begun to take on a few of the balancing activities that the Press Room senior foreman had undertaken, though apparently under greater constraints from the controls imposed by his supervisors.

Contrasts in perception of the situation between shopfloor and management were very evident in the Finishing Shop and to a somewhat smaller extent in the Press Room and these perceptual differences interacted with other features of the socio-technical system to generate attitudes and conflicts that influenced behavioural patterns. In the Lower Foundry it was rather the various levels of higher management and functional management who held conflicting perceptual models of the foundry as a system and who consequently placed a number of conflicting constraints on the operation of the system and on the behaviour of those within it.

No industrial study can ignore *the technical arrangements* of the department being studied, and these naturally form a central part of each of the three studies. In each case the effect of the technology on the characteristics of the socio-technical system is clear, and the way the values and relationships it created reacted back on technical efficiency is evident, particularly in the Press Room and Finishing Shop studies. In the Lower Foundry the operation of the auto lines was for technical reasons less open to modification than in the other cases, and for all its deficiencies, the fit with the reward system was better. As with the layout of equipment, so the influence of other technical features such as maintenance and training policies have to be given due weight, and in all three studies these influences forced themselves on the attention of the investigators.

A central theme of any socio-technical study is of course *the way the technology and formal procedures have affected the social system*, the reactions of people in that system to the formal arrangements under which they are constrained to work and the effect those reactions have on the operation of the formal procedures. The three studies show the distinctive ways in which the technical systems described have generated conflicts, values, attitudes and relationships among people, and how those have characteristically affected behaviour, including the willingness of some members to remain in the department at all. The Finishing Shop is a case of a rational design by management and the industrial engineers of technical and procedural arrangements which management were determined to work as they had been designed. These arrangements had created serious areas of conflict and difficulty for those attempting to work them, resulting in continual conflict with the technical constraints, with other members and with management, as well as some unofficial practices on the part of both shopfloor workers and chargehands. The Press Room was almost at the opposite end of this continuum. The supervisor had been tacitly allowed to initiate many modifications to the formal system of procedures, controls and rewards which had increased the satisfactions of those involved, but had, as we have stated, led to tight constraints on his ability to change, and consequently some inability of the department to improve performance. On the side presses in the Lower Foundry, by contrast, the nature of the work as formally designed, and the designed payment system, together created considerable satisfactions for those involved—satisfactions which were frustrated by undesigned features like poor tools and necessary redeployment of men for technical, market and administrative reasons.

Finally, it was impossible in any of the cases to neglect the influence of the *product market*. Problems in the Press Room were largely due to the inability of that department to satisfy the market, while in the Lower Foundry the markets then being supplied were insufficient for the capacity of the department, and in the Finishing Shop changes in the product mix demanded by the market had made the conveyor system inadequate, while the large market fluctuations imposed on a gradually declining demand, had in the past caused cyclical redundancies, which also helped form some of the attitudes typical of the department. The interface between each department and its market via the inspection process and warehouse policies also influenced patterns of activity, and in two of them the relation between market size and productive capacity had led to engineering standards being affected adversely.

One point raised by the different approaches is the question of *verification* of the relationships discovered in the model being studied. If the model of the production situation is to be used as a guide to making changes, and if those changes are not to have serious and unexpected adverse consequences, then it must be possible to place some confidence in the details of the model. Straightforward collection of the kind of data required in a socio-technical systems model relies a great deal on the skill and objectivity of the investigator. Much of the information is necessarily gathered in the course of interview, and even the most experienced interviewer cannot avoid the danger of bias, either in the answers he obtains to interview questions, or the way he selects from and reports on the information he has obtained. In the case of documentary and statistical evidence, the question of selection is still not entirely absent.

There seem to be three ways in which this problem can be resolved. We suggest in chapter 11 that if a step-by-step strategy for improvement can be agreed on and implemented, then the most effective confirmation of the socio-technical model can take place through continuous monitoring of the effects of the strategy against predictions derived from the model. This requires some confidence in the processes of implementation, and it is important that the initial steps in strategy should be chosen so that the consequences are fairly confidently predictable in terms of the model. A second way in which verification can be arrived at, used for example in the programme in verification of the Finishing Shop model, is by feeding back to those involved in the department the model which had been derived from their comments, and inviting departmental members to criticise the model and express agreement or disagreement with it. If, starting from a situation of contrasting perceptions about the department, the relationships in the final model appear reasonable to all those involved with the department, this in itself can give the investigators some confidence in their findings. Moreover, the feedback process itself can act as a preliminary step in the change process, already changing perceptions of members of the department, and enabling them all to work with greater understanding of the total situation.

A third way of attempting to verify the socio-technical model is the one used in the Press Room study, namely through the use of statistical and other tests of as many as possible of the hypotheses included in the model. Since the socio-technical model deals largely with relationships between variables, verification of this kind will be largely confined to the discovery of correlations and patterns of association between variables which can be used to falsify or to add to the plausibility of the hypotheses suggested. In fact, in the Press Room project many more such ventures into statistical testing took place than have been reported in the study, and this, as has been made clear in chapter 5, was due to the existence on the team, as well as among local managers, of different perceptual models and different ideas of what kind of subordinate behaviour could be recognised and given some measure of legitimacy. These differences discouraged one group from accepting that another group was giving the right importance to some of the relationships. Unless some quantifiable evidence could be produced some groups would continue to reject the model, and the other two means of validation would necessarily be ruled out.

Which of these three methods of verification is used will therefore depend on the circumstances in which the investigating team finds itself both in its own internal structure and relationships, and in relation to the ways it perceives itself to be constrained in putting any proposals for change into effect. In the case of the Press Room, for example, the experience of members of the project team, together with their interpretation of what kind of behaviour was acceptable, and their perception of the risks inherent in implementation, to some extent decided the means used for model verification. Each form of verification has its own place and its own consequences, and none can be said to be superior to any other.

Throughout this part of the book we have been concerned with means of gaining greater understanding of the intricate patterns of events taking place in organisations. We have demonstrated how the use of the open socio-technical models can produce plausible explanations of events, activities and patterns of behaviour in organisations, and we have argued that if a better appreciation of the interactive nature of organisational life can be obtained in this way, then those involved in decision-making in industrial situations may be helped to change their perspectives and perhaps begin to act on the basis of more complete analysis of situations.

This kind of study does not necessarily bring in any new variables of which managers, supervisors, shopfloor workers and others are not already aware. It does bring some factors like attitudes, values and interpersonal relations more to the fore than happens in more orthodox studies and enables these to be considered legitimately. Most of the factors we have dealt with are, however, well documented in management literature on business administration, management decision and control techniques, corporate planning, industrial engineering and so on. However, we suggest that what our approach uniquely provides is a framework that enables all the relevant variables to be incorporated into a dynamic explanation of interacting events, and eventually of performance. To this we attach considerable importance. Industrial managers, accustomed to working in departments like those we have reported on (which on the face of it are quite small and simple production systems) tend always to seek, and are encouraged by some of the authorities to seek, check lists of procedures, decision trees, problem-solving techniques and other ways of tackling one problem at a time. One possible lesson from these three case studies is that simple models of causation, leading to simple techniques of control can be among the important causes of conflict and inefficiency in industrial situations, and can exacerbate the problems inherent in managing an industrial system.

That is one advantage of the more detailed understanding arrived at through the open socio-technical systems approach. There were two further specific uses we had in mind in advocating the use of open socio-technical systems models of the departments under consideration. One was to see if it were possible to say anything new about the state of departmental performance in systems terms. The other was to see if systems understanding could be used in the development of more certain and more satisfactory forms of strategy for organisational improvement than is possible through the orthodox techniques usually available to management. In part III of this book we discuss these developments, first in general, rather theoretical, terms, and then in terms of practical ways o measuring performance, devising strategies for improvement and monitor ing their implementation. We then discuss in part IV the application o these ideas to the three case studies.

A General Framework for Analysis

8 A Generalised Model of the Open Socio-technical System

We have suggested in part II that open socio-technical systems analysis of particular production systems can provide an understanding of the patterns of behaviour in the system and of the causes of that behaviour. We have also implied that this understanding could provide a basis for a programme of departmental improvement. A socio-technical model of a department would suggest some of the consequences likely to arise as a result of change, whether that change is planned or is imposed by changes in product or resource markets, or characteristics of people or control systems. However the patterns of causation in many apparently small and simple production departments are much more complex than is frequently asserted, and considerable skill and expenditure of time and effort is needed to make a satisfactory prognosis in socio-technical terms.

Two features of sociotechnical models are worth pointing out. Firstly they are particular to particular situations and although behind the model are general assumptions as to what is or is not likely to be important in influencing behaviour, nevertheless each system is looked at as being unique, and there is no assumption that the relationships between variables in the model of one system correspond to those of any other system. The second feature is that the use we have made of the model is expository, answering questions about the reasons why certain events occur, and (less explicitly) predicting what might occur if certain things happened. We have so far not said anything as a consequence of using this analytical framework, about performance or effectiveness.

We are concerned in this chapter to construct a generalised framework of analysis for examining production systems in socio-technical terms. We do this partly as a basis from which to develop a definition of organisational performance, but we also want to derive some general principles about formulating a strategy for improvement and devising a pathway from an existing situation to one where performance is known to be better.

Perhaps the two ideas of a contingency approach to organisation theory and a generalised socio-technical model seem contradictory. However, when a number of models of production situations have been constructed it becomes clear that certain kinds of variable enter into most models, and that some kinds of interaction are common. Moreover, some of these variables seem to perform the same kind of function in a number of different situations and the way parts of the system are related together can begin to be predicted. All we mean by generalisation, then, is an attempt to extract and group these common elements and to suggest ways in which they tend to be related in most situations.

A socio-technical model of a particular situation usually deals with a large number of specific variables (manning levels, rates of absence, working conditions, plant layout, levels of stocks, length of production runs, output per man, reject rates, market trends and very many others) and describes the relationships which exist in that specific situation between these variables. For the more general model we move away from specific variables and particularly from specific relationships between variables, into relationships between categories of variable. Starting from our general understanding of the working of systems, we have grouped the many variables into a number of categories, the definition of these being chosen carefully according to systems concepts and with certain clear purposes we have in mind. The interclass relationships which then occur have a rather different significance from intervariable relationships.

CLASSIFICATION OF SOCIO-TECHNICAL SYSTEMS VARIABLES

There are many ways in which elements of a socio-technical system may be categorised, and each of these may be appropriate to a different analytic purpose. For our purpose, a nine-fold classification has appeared to be the most appropriate.[1] The nine groups which we identify are

(1) Product market variables
(2) Resource market variables
(3) Labour market variables
(4) Designed technical variables
(5) Designed mediating mechanisms
(6) Attitudinal variables
(7) Unofficial manipulatory devices
(8) Behavioural variables directly influencing performance
(9) Dependent cost and technical performance variables

What particular variables enter into each of these groups will depend on the system being examined, and they will vary according to the technology being used, the product market and labour market situation, and so on. The appendix to this chapter, see p. 167, shows some of the specific variables which entered into each of these groups in the cases described in part II. Given a much extended list of situations from different environments, this list would obviously expand to include many more variables, but we do not believe that even many more cases would alter significantly the lines of interaction between these categories. In the next few paragraphs, we hope o show that each group has a more or less crucial role to play in the operation of the socio-technical system, and yet that the characteristic functions of each group are rather different from those of any other group.

Let us look at the first three groups of variables: those related respectively to *product markets, resource input markets* and the *labour market*. To a large extent, the features of these are determined outside the organisation, and, decision-makers within the organisation will be unable directly to influence them fundamentally. They have 'low manipulability' in one meaning of the term as defined in chapter 10. But it is possible to underestimate the extent to which members of the organisation can influence them. New markets can be sought and entered, and the features of an existing product market can often be modified through marketing policy or pricing policy or through technical collaboration with customers, and discussion of mutual needs. Relationships with the labour market can be affected by changes made to reward systems, training, conditions of work, shift requirements, the specification of the skills or backgrounds required, or in the last resort by geographical relocation. Generally, however, product market, labour market and resource market variables have to be influenced indirectly, through some mediating device such as marketing policy, purchasing policy or personnel policy.

The fourth and fifth groups—the *designed technical variables* and *designed mediating mechanisms* are features designed into the system overtly by decisions of its management. Technical design involves the translation of production requirements dictated by product policy into plant, processes and equipment. It includes the design of the machinery through which the product is processed, engineering solutions to the physical, chemical, mechanical or other problems which have to be overcome; the way the product will flow through the plant; the flexibility of the equipment, its capacities and the balance which exists between one part of the equipment and another; and eventually the whole layout of equipment and working positions and to some extent the conditions in which people will work. Technical design is also concerned with things like the designed procedures for allocating work between parts of the plant or between groups of people; with designed manning levels, skill specifications and so on; and with a range of similar engineering or quasi-engineering problems.

In most large organisations a great deal of attention will have been paid to the design of a whole range of variables of this kind. There is a natural tendency for specialists to look for optimal solutions to each technical problem separately, and this tendency to overspecialisation and sub-optimisation is sometimes overcome by long discussions in technical working parties to determine how all the aspects of technical design can be integrated together to form an optimal system of process, workflow and procedure.

The mediating mechanisms are also designed from within the organisation and their function is mainly to allow the technical design to become operational. They include such things as a personnel policy, marketing policy, purchasing policy and warehousing and stocking policy, which mediate between the system and various aspects of its environment or other subsystems in the same organisation. They include things like the definition of supervisory and management structures and the job definitions of supervisors and managers; like quality control and budgetary control procedures; payment systems; and possibly a set of job values associated with a payment by results system. These, together with things like engineering maintenance policy, training policy, and principles of production scheduling, mediate between different aspects of the technical design, and define how these various aspects will operate together. The larger the firm, and the more skilled its management, the more attention is likely to be paid to possible incompatibilities between various aspects of technical design, and between technical design and these various mediating mechanisms.[2]

The sixth group, of *attitudinal variables*, consists of the attitudes, expectations and perceptions of people in the organisation, and the values and relationships which have been created among the people employed there. Expectations may be about the working of the system or of particular elements in it, or about the behaviour of other people and other groups. They will include the expectations people have about the effort–reward bargain, their attitudes towards hours of work and overtime, their perceptions about their own roles and opportunities and the constraints on their behaviour, and about the roles and the proper behaviour of other groups in the system. They will include the relationships (of cooperation or of conflict) that exist both within groups and between groups, and the values and dissatisfactions people find in the performance of the tasks they are set. They will include subjective perceptions about raw materials, components and products and about the nature of the organisation and the state of motivation within it.

It does not seem too difficult to identify and describe these attitudinal variables. They do, however, cause a number of practical difficulties. Firstly, they are less open to direct observation and measurement than other features of an organisation: to get access to them, they must be inferred from observed behaviour, or from the responses made by people during informal talks or formal interviews. Secondly, open recognition of their existence and importance, and objective discussion of their effects is unusual in industrial situations, and rather unconventional for people who normally work there. Thirdly, variables in this group cannot be 'designed' or directly created as a result of managers' conscious decisions, but they are the result of other influences which come both from within the system—things like the technical design, the pay structure, and managerial behaviour—or from without. Influences from outside the system include such factors as age and family background, educational experience and past work experience. Finally, the analysis of these attitudinal variables is a complex process, and requires considerable skill and expenditure of resources.

The group of attitudinal variables is among the most important in creating patterns of behaviour in the workplace. The seventh group—the *unofficial manipulatory* devices—is, however, among the most important in providing understanding of the workings of the whole system. These devices include particular examples of supervisory behaviour, tacit creation of overtime opportunities, the actual methods of work allocation as opposed to designed procedures, the actual methods of calculating pay for a job, tacitly agreed misbooking of production and so on. Manipulatory devices of some kind exist in virtually every production situation. Their importance is quite evident in the three cases in part II, and their purposes are generally to supplement the designed mediating variables, help satisfy the expectations of people working in the system, and resolve and manage conflict. They are very similar to the types of behaviour which Dubin (1958), chapter 4, has called non-formal and technological behaviour, and the whole system of manipulatory devices helps to maximise the material, social and psychological satisfactions of the people within the system (or some of them), and to reduce areas of internal conflict in the system (perhaps by transferring it elsewhere). In some cases it renders the situation tolerable for those working in the system and allows the organisation to function without destroying its social fabric.

In contrast to the technical design and the designed mediating mechanisms, these manipulatory devices are by definition unintended from the point of view of higher levels of management, and are outside their direct control. But they are under the control of people within the organisation—shopfloor employees, supervisors, departmental managers and others who cooperate in, or turn a blind eye to, their operation. Those who cooperate in their operation may be doing so unconsciously, or at least without any recognition from others; or the manipulations may be consciously introduced by a group of subordinates, or by an individual manager or supervisor to resolve a difficult situation or increase the amount of 'fairness' in the situation.

The eighth and ninth groups of variables are somewhat similar to each other, and the line between them is drawn somewhat arbitrarily. Further, the names we have given them, and the place we have given them in the nine-fold classification are also rather arbitrary at this stage, since we have not yet considered the meaning of the word 'performance'. Within these two groups some of the orthodox measures of organisational performance are to be found. The *behavioural performance variables* result directly from the behaviour of individuals and groups of people within the system. They include things like rates of absence and labour turnover, the level and variability of output so far as this is determined by individuals or groups, the level of earnings, the variations in skill and effort exhibited by people and the number of disputes of various kinds which occur. The *cost and technical performance variables* tend to be of a different nature, and include such measures of performance as unit cost, the rate of mechanical breakdown, losses of materials, components or products consequent on features of the technology. The main reason for separating these last two groups is that the lines of influence tend to be less complex with the second than with the first, although of course each of these two classes tends to influence the other considerably.

Neither of these last two groups of variables can be changed directly by senior management decisions, and if it is true that a lot of valid measures of organisational performance can be found in these two groups, then to improve performance they have to be influenced indirectly, and the lines of causation must be understood reasonably well by those for whom improved performance is important. Indeed the need for indirect intervention, and the implications this involves, are among the main reasons for this essay in generalisation.

RELATIONSHIPS AND INTERACTIONS BETWEEN CLASSES

We have now described the classes of variables and some of the characteristics of each class. However, what is most interesting and important is the series of relationships and interactions which are found to exist between the various classes. We have said already that there is some consistency in the patterns of relationships. If we analyse a number of empirical situations, classify their variables in this way, note down the causal relationships and then examine the interactions between variables of one class and variables of other classes, we find fairly consistent patterns of influence emerging.

Figure 8.1 has been constructed in this way. It has been devised to represent the interactions found in a number of production departments, including the cases examined in part II. It shows the direction of and the importance of the influences between classes as distinct from the interactions between variables within each class.

For instance, the main external influences on the initial technical design are usually the characteristics of the product market: product policy is usually the main determinant of technical production arrangements (though, as in the case of the Lower Foundry the direction of influence can be the other way). Technical design in its turn helps to decide the mediating variables, and the variables in both these boxes, together with factors brought in from the labour market, help determine the attitudes and expectations which exist in the system. As the direction of influence is traced through the model from the product market towards the criteria of performance, so the lines of influence become more complex and more interactive.

Some of them are in fact very complex. The ways in which the mediating mechanisms affect attitudes, and the interactions between mediating mechanisms and the manipulatory devices are especially important. There is also a complex series of relationships in both directions between attitudinal variables and the manipulatory devices: the way in which

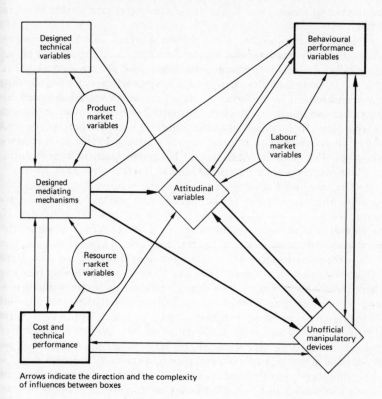

Arrows indicate the direction and the complexity
of influences between boxes

FIGURE 8.1 Interactions between classes in socio-technical systems.

people perceive the situation and the conflicts which they experience will help to determine what they do to modify the system to compensate for the problems it has created for them; while the existence of manipulation and its success or lack of success in reducing tensions, increasing satisfaction and eliminating problems, will affect the perceptions and expectations which then exist among the groups affected by the manipulation; and these in turn will lead to yet further attempts at compensation, and so on. Moreover, how effective the manipulations which exist in the system are in resolving conflict or in allowing expectations about effort and reward to be satisfied will determine the state of some behavioural performance variables, including levels of absence, labour turnover and output. Obviously, the richness and variety of these influences cannot be illustrated in a two-dimensional black-and-white diagram. As we suggested in chapter 2, the whole pattern of behaviour in organisations is very complex. There is, moreover, an important time dimension in the formation of attitudes and values, and in the establishment of interactions between them.

It is fundamental to the socio-technical approach that there are many interacting influences on behaviour at the workplace. The purpose of this more general model is to formalise the influences. We are proposing that behaviour, including those aspects of behaviour which enter directly into the measurement of performance, is especially strongly influenced by unofficial manipulatory devices, attitudinal variables and mediating mechanisms. In its turn, behaviour interacts with the perceptions and expectations which exist, and also helps to shape some of the manipulatory variables. The cases described in part II showed many of these features, and illustrate how these categories tend to interact with each other.

Let us now look a little more closely at the manipulatory devices and examine their significance to the management of a production department. These devices play a large part in sustaining the balance of relationships in the socio-technical system. Theoretically, it is within the prerogative of management to tighten up on discipline or to stamp out many of the practices they know to be operating. However, once they have become established, there is so close and complex a relationship between them and the social system, the values found there by people working in it and the performance level of the organisation, that the constraints on changing any of them are extremely tight. An attempt to tighten up on discipline in a situation of well-established practices and patterns of behaviour will influence some of the most important values and relationships in the organisation, and may upset the way in which many of the conflicts are perceived and resolved.[3] To change patterns of behaviour in one direction is likely to affect behavioural patterns in many distant apparently unrelated parts of the system. Changes imposed on any of these manipulatory devices through actions by higher management are likely to create ripples throughout the socio-technical system, the extent of which it might be impossible to forecast.

CONCLUSIONS

In the light of these ideas it may be valuable to set out some conclusions about the nature of sociotechnical systems which we can use in the next two chapters as a basis on which to begin to think about the definition of performance and the means of improving it.

(1) Let us first look at the two groups of variables whose design is in the hands of organisational decision-makers—the designed technical variables and the mediating mechanisms. These are the only two groups whose parameters are decided on overtly by management. Now, although there may be real constraints on some aspects of design imposed by product market and resource market characteristics or by what is technically necessary in

order to produce a given end product, none of these constraints is usually very tight. The management, at least before capital has actually been sunk into the technology, has much more real choice about technical design than it has about most other things in the organisation. Almost invariably there are a number of technical alternatives to any production or design problem, each alternative giving a different breakdown of costs or a different pattern of compromise over technical efficiencies. There is for instance a wide area within which the solution to the problem of plant layout or capacity, or even technically specified levels of acceptance and rejection, can be set. The final technical solution is inevitably a matter of judgement. The point where a solution is fixed is likely to determine the characteristics of a set of social and psychological perceptions, of values and satisfactions, of relationships and eventually of typical patterns of behaviour. If it can be accepted that it is the perceptions, attitudes and relationships between people that are most crucial in the determination of standards of performance, then it must be seen as unfortunate that the effect of technical design on these social and psychological variables is so rarely taken into account.

In much the same way, management decisions about the mediating mechanisms are relatively free of constraint in the initial stages of design, before attitudes and expectations have developed and before a social system has become well established in the organisation. However, once these are established, mediating mechanisms play an important part in creating and helping to sustain all the complex patterns of values and relationships. Constraints on changing any of an established set of mechanisms are considerable. It may be possible to change an existing payment system, but to do so affects levels of earnings and the ability of organisational members to control or influence the effort–reward relationship and it may affect individual and group output, social structure, absence from work, labour turnover, the occurrence of disputes, and in some circumstances factors like the reject rate, the rate of mechanical breakdown, and so on.

Thus there are relatively few initial constraints on either technical design or design of mediating variables—far fewer than is generally assumed at the design stage. However, there may be considerable difficulties in changing an established system once it is established and operating.

(2) It is clear that we are looking at the organisation from a quite different standpoint from that of a design engineer or an industrial engineer, or most other specialists concerned with systems design. What we have called technical design and mediating mechanisms may well be seen by designers, work-study engineers, personnel managers and others as problems for which there is one optimal technical solution, and to negotiate or otherwise to arrive at a compromise solution different from the conventional optimum may be regarded as an inefficient concession to the human element in the organisation. We would maintain that both the

technical design and the mediating mechanisms should have as a prime target to arrive at that solution which would best serve the performance needs of the whole organisation. They should not merely satisfy some partial techno-economic criteria or some textbook solution. There is no straightforward direct link between a technically optimal design and organisational performance. The real objective of the designer should be defined in terms of overall organisational performance, and because every organisation has a unique set of relationships and interactions, the 'optimum' must always be defined in relation to the needs of that particular organisation.

(3) Since all organisations are in some sense unique, analysis of any given situation will bring out many features and interactions special to that one organisation, and there is no inevitability about the box in which to place any particular variable in this general model. There is a good deal of blurring at the edges of many of the categories. Even the distinction between variables in the technical design category and those which we have called mediating mechanisms is somewhat arbitrary. Perhaps the best way of distinguishing between them is the fact that mediating mechanisms tend to have more complex and more interesting effects on the rest of the system than do the technical design variables.

As an example, we have suggested that maintenance policy, warehousing policy and the production schedule are mediating variables. Industrial engineers would usually claim that they were essentially technical problems with an optimal technical solution. Which group they are classified under will depend partly on how their importance and their influence on the socio-technical system are perceived, and partly on the motives which have determined the designers to arrive at one solution rather than another. If the designers have tried to find the best technical solution, then they might be treated by the investigator as technical variables, whereas a clear recognition by the designers that the 'optimal' solution will create conflicts which ought to be allowed for might lead him to place them firmly among the mediating mechanisms.

Similarly, the line between behavioural performance variables and technical performance variables is not clearly drawn, nor is that between behavioural performance and some of the unofficial manipulatory devices. For instance, if individuals in controlling their own output and thus their own level of earnings, have in mind their own effort–reward bargain, the investigator would probably classify 'output per man' as a dependent element of behaviour which directly influenced organisational performance. If on the other hand group processes had helped to influence the level of output perhaps as a means of integrating members into a group, or resolving some area of conflict, then it might well be treated as a conflict-resolving manipulatory device.

(4) One feature of this approach is the absence of any moral implications about behaviour or its effect on performance. The model helps us to understand the way the system operates, and to analyse the

processes leading from initial design to eventual performance. The approach shows it is invalid to evaluate performance in terms of how closely behaviour approximates to the designer's initial intentions and assumptions, or to criticise management efficiency just because effective manipulation exists. We conclude that those interested in assessment should look at the adequacy of overall performance, and given the state of performance treat as somewhat irrelevant to the assessment the fact that rules and procedures are or are not being manipulated or that controls have or have not been eroded. We should analyse the situation in terms such as this

> the technical decisions and other policy decisions made by management, together with certain attitudes and expectations brought into the system by people working there, have helped to determine what behaviour actually takes place in the organisation and thus have eventually helped determine performance levels.

Rather than judging the behaviour as being right or wrong, we then look at the state of all the variables in the organisation, and the relationships between them and we treat these as being interesting and probably inevitable features of organisational behaviour which follow from the initial design. If performance is to be changed in a given direction, then all these influences must be taken into account in devising a new design.

(5) As a consequence of our analysis of organisational design we conclude that in practice the effective design of an organisation is always a joint effort between managers (who have constructed a number of formal elements of design) and their subordinates (who have tacitly modified and added to these elements with a number of perhaps subconscious motives in view). Thus we necessarily disagree with the writers on organisational control who assume that efficiency is improved to the extent that the organisational controls have the requisite degree of sophistication and are internally consistent.[4] Unless the workings of the socio-technical system are understood by the initial designers (and writers on organisational planning and control rarely allow for this), then for every element of design created by management that is dysfunctional to the workings of the socio-technical system, there will be a corresponding counter-design by the lower levels of the organisation, and the counter-controls may be in conflict with the requirements of formally designed organisation. To discuss this further would bring in arguments about the place of involvement and participation in organisational design, which are not a central concern of this book.[5]

SUMMARY

In this chapter we have grouped the many variables which commonly occur in socio-technical systems into a number of categories, and we have described the relationships which tend generally to occur between these categories. The model thus outlined helps in our understanding of the workings of socio-technical systems in general, and it can guide the investigator through the likely patterns of influence in the sociotechnical system. We also believe that understanding of the general nature of socio-technical systems can give guidelines on where to look for both the starting point and the end point in a strategy for improvement. If we assume for the moment that the end point will often be found through some change in either behavioural performance or technical performance variables, and if it is agreed that those responsible for managing the system cannot operate directly on either of these two groups, then it can be seen that the end position can only be reached by making changes in those variables it is within management's power to manipulate. The principles of how this might be done comprise the subject of strategy formulation which we discuss in chapter 10. First, however, we must look further into the meaning of organisational performance.

NOTES TO CHAPTER 8

1. The model resulting from this grouping was inspired by models of the labour market and reward problems facing an organisation, first proposed by Gowler (1969), and by Lupton (1969). An independent development of this original model to much the same effect as here is in Gowler and Legge (1970).

2. The crucial influence on performance of the processes of design of the technical variables and mediating mechanisms in production situations repeatedly came to the fore in the course of this research. There is a lack of social research into the actual processes of technical design, or design of operating systems (as distinct from advice to designers, or standard procedures for design) and little is known even within industry about the decision processes and how they are taken. Little can be done to change the behaviour of design teams until more is understood about the actual modes of decision making and the constraints on them.

3. A familiar example of this is in Gouldner (1954). Gouldner's main concern was to explore the implications of a rather different framework of analysis, but, as has been shown in other studies, the case he describes can be adapted to a number of different analytical models.

4. See, for example, Arrow (1964), Anthony (1965), Beer (1972). An exception to the general tenor of these texts is the excellent work by Mills (1967). Further, Charnes and Stedry (1966) make an ingenious adaptation of the formal 'command and control' model to meet this kind of point.

5. The implications of this argument for work participation in decision making are taken a little further in Warmington (1974).

APPENDIX TO CHAPTER 8

Classification of Some Typical Variables in Sociotechnical Systems

Market demand variables
1   Product mix
2   Short-term fluctuations in order pattern
3   Trends in product design and specification
4   Long-term trends in forecast demand
5   Competitive nature of product market

Resource market variables
1   Fluctuations in materials market
2   Quality variations in materials
3   Alternative sources in resource market

Labour market variables
1   Labour availability (state of labour market)
2   Family and social backgrounds
3   Age structure of workforce
4   Skills typically available in area
5   Earnings levels elsewhere in locality

Attitudinal variables
1   Expectations of effort and reward
2   Attitudes to overtime
3   Worker's evaluation of fairness of rules and controls
4   Manager's perception of his role
5   Manager's perceptions and expectations of shopfloor behaviour
6   Manager's expectation of supervisor behaviour
7   Shopfloor expectations of supervisor behaviour
8   Supervisor's perception of his own role
9   Intragroup relationships of cooperation and conflict
10 Intergroup relationships
11 Perceptions about raw materials and components
12 Values and dissatisfactions found in job itself

Unofficial manipulatory devices for avoiding or reducing conflict
1   Supervisory role behaviour
2   Operator and supervisor work allocation devices
3   Training system in practice
4   Limitation in and variation in individual or group output
5   Overtime level in practice
6   Misbooking of production, rejects, work content etc.
7   Working of conflict resolution mechanisms in practice

8 Manipulation of designed production schedule and product mix
9 Manipulation of job values or of designed payment procedures

Designed technical variables
1 Design and layout of plant
2 Flexibility of equipment and process, capacities and extent of balance in throughput
3 Working conditions
4 Designed work allocation procedures
5 Designed training procedures
6 Specification of skills required
7 Optimal stock levels

Designed mediating mechanisms
1 Formal control procedures
2 Supervisory structures and supervisory job definition
3 Payment systems
4 Bonus fluctuations built in the pay system
5 Job values
6 Redundancy policies
7 Selection procedures
8 Production scheduling
9 Stock policy
10 Maintenance policy
11 Purchasing policies
12 Marketing policies

Behavioural performance variables
1 Labour turnover stability
2 Rates of absence, sickness etc.
3 Skill variations (as far as significant for operation of process)
4 Output per shift
5 Level of earnings
6 Actual manning levels

Dependent cost and technical performance variables
1 Unit cost
2 Rate of mechanical breakdown
3 Level of rejects
4 Level of recirculation, runs etc.
5 Demand for labour inputs
6 Percentage of trainees in workforce
7 Actual stock levels
8 Plant utilisation level
9 Manpower utilisation level

9 The Criteria of Organisational Performance

If one looks through the literature on planned organisational change, one finds surprisingly little attention being paid to a precise definition of the aims of a change programme. Most writers seem to assume that there is a specific objective which the client organisation wishes to attain—frequently the smooth introduction of some technical or structural innovation—and that the function of the behavioural scientist–consultant is to enable that particular objective to be achieved with the fewest possible adverse complications.[1] Or it is assumed that change is inevitable in present-day society and the function of the consultant is to help the organisation to become more responsive to economic, technical and social changes which it is inevitably meeting.[2]

'Behavioural science' writers are usually also rather reticent about the nature of the improvement coming from new relationships, changed styles of management, or new forms of organisation. Rensis Likert is perhaps the most explicit and gives the most careful treatment. Much of his writing concerns high-producing groups and high-producing managers, and in several passages he writes of an efficient organisation as one with high productivity, low costs and low turnover and absence of labour, together with high motivation and satisfaction among members of the organisation.[3] He does not go very far in analysing the relationships existing between these dimensions, nor, despite his discussion of intervening variables, does he explain how precisely they are affected by such things as management style or methods of decision-making or control.

Argyris also states fairly clearly his conception of an improved organisation. What he appears to be seeking is a creative, innovative organisation in which healthy individuals can gain high motivation and self-actualisation by working in line with the objectives of the organisation. For this, changes are needed both in individuals (especially in increasing interpersonal skills) and in the organisation (in terms of authority and methods of control).[4] Although Argyris seems to dislike rational organisations in the sense of organisations which control and constrain individuals' behaviour in line with detailed goals, he does not greatly criticise the objectives set for the organisation by its management. The objectives are apparently the usual ones of high technical efficiency, productivity and profitability, but the means of attaining these must be such as to satisfy human and social needs.

This view would probably have been shared by McGregor[5] and certainly by Herzberg,[6] who writes at some length about mental health. Our difficulty about these views, as about those of Likert is two-fold. In the first place, we see problems with the internal logic of their models. One might share their apparent desire for industry to pay greater attention to human and social values, to the dignity and fulfilment of people in industry; one can see the advantages of high motivation and psychological satisfaction; but it is difficult to find in behavioural science texts a reasoned argument demonstrating how this is related to implicit measures of performance in specific, defined, technical and market settings. How, for instance, can the directors of a steel mill, a heavy engineering works or a textile firm set about the detailed process of creating conditions to increase social and individual satisfaction while managing to live with the technological and environmental constraints which determine technical efficiency and market satisfaction? A leap is made over the whole vexed question of how to measure overall organisational performance. It cannot be assumed that so long as attitudes are more favourable, job satisfaction increased, rates of absence and separation improved, then the organisation is necessarily performing better. Specific, unidimensional improvements in, say, increased social or psychological satisfaction, tend to ignore the complex, interactive nature of the whole organisation. We still need to search for a satisfactory definition of performance.

That is the first part of our difficulty. The second relates to the wider philosophical and theoretical problems we have discussed in chapter 2. In particular, we are concerned about *who* defines the conditions of work, who defines what is meant by satisfaction and motivation and what are the underlying unspoken assumptions. Whose motivation are we to be concerned with, and why? What, for instance, is the evidence that the human and social values propounded by academic scholars or by middle-class industrial consultants are necessarily those that would be held by the people most directly concerned?

To turn from psychologically oriented theories to sociological studies gives little more immediate assistance. In fact, sociologists tend on the whole to concentrate on explanation and to be less interested in criteria of performance or in the nature of improvement. Among those who do by implication state some criteria, there are Trist and the other Tavistock researchers who originally formulated the concept of the socio-technical system. They use the concept of the primary task to identify what the organisation is there to do. For example, Emery and Trist (1960) say that 'the primary task in managing the enterprise as a whole is to relate the total system to its environment . . .' and for Rice (1963) chapter 23, 'the leader of any enterprise has to manage the relations of the enterprise and its environment in such a way that the primary task of the enterprise can be performed efficiently'. To perform the primary task there has to be some fit between the demands made by the organisation and its technology and the requirements for a satisfactory social organisation of work. In their earlier papers these writers seem to have compared situations largely on the basis of rates of absence, labour turnover and labour productivity, lack of aggression and the 'quality' of the social organisation, including the amount of cooperation between groups.[7]

Other attempts have been made to adapt systems ideas to the definition of organisational effectiveness. Georgopoulos and Tannenbaum (1957) suggested that effectiveness be measured as 'the extent to which an organisation, as a social system given certain resources and means, fulfils its objectives without incapacitating its means and resources and without placing undue strain on its members'. Etzioni (1960), developing these ideas, suggests that organisational effectiveness has frequently been assessed in relation to achievement (or, rather, non-achievement) of the goals set for the organisation.[8] He advocates instead employing a multifunctional systems model, through which effectiveness is assessed via the organisation's ability to use its resources optimally in relation to a defined function. Both of these can be seen as closed systems ideas.

Further advances towards an open systems definition were made by Katz and Kahn (1966).[9] They divided efficiency (the ratio of energic outputs to inputs) off from other aspects of effectiveness, notably the organisation's transactions with its environment, and they suggested that both aspects were necessary components of overall effectiveness, which they measured in terms of the maximisation of total returns of all kinds. They also distinguished between short-term and long-term effectiveness. However, having thus defined effectiveness in systems terms, Katz and Kahn discuss at length the types of human behaviour needed within the organisation to produce high effectiveness: 'People must join and remain in the organisation; they must perform dependably the roles assigned to them; and they must engage in occasional innovative and cooperative behaviour beyond the requirements of role, but in the service of organisational objects'.[10] The way this is expressed is significant. There is a tendency for the organisation and its system objectives to have taken over and have become the masters of its participants. There is a dilemma in attempting to measure performance in these terms, and we shall return to it.

Yuchtman and Seashore (1967) take the concept of effectiveness a good deal further by suggesting that the best measure of effectiveness would be the ability of the organisation to exploit the environment in the acquisition of scarce and valued (that is, relevant) resources (including among the resources the energies of its members); and its optimum procurement of these resources, where optimum is defined in relation to its long-run ability to survive. Finally, Lawrence and Lorsch (1969) provide a somewhat similar, though less detailed and sophisticated, measure. They suggest[11] that development of the organisation can only take place if there is a good fit between the organisation and the demands of its environment or a good fit between the organisation and the needs of individual contributors to it, or both. So if the organisation is making more efficient transactions with its environment and if at the same time people within the organisation are better satisfied and better able to contribute to its efficiency, then, these writers suggest, the organisation is performing more effectively.

A measure of the efficiency of an organisation's transactions with its environment matches well with open systems concepts, but it is based on a 'rational' view of the organisation. There is dilemma which Lawrence and Lorsch do not discuss: how to balance any conflict there may be between environmental fit and the organisation's ability to satisfy the various needs of individuals and groups within it. It is by no means certain that individual satisfaction and a high degree of fit with the environment are positively correlated in given real-world situations and there is little discussion in the literature about how satisfaction of the needs of one group affects the satisfaction of other groups. This brings us back to the dilemmas we discussed in chapter 2, following on our acceptance that there was a plurality of values and objectives in any social system. Burns (1966) maintains that the rationality model of an organisation defines the objectives which are held by those who direct the organisation with rational assumptions in mind, but that it takes no account of the fact that there are many other players in the organisation (individuals and groups) who do not share these objectives and who behave accordingly. Burns, however, while stating the problem, does not resolve it. Indeed, he may have intended to imply that the multiplicity of objectives in an organisation is so important a phenomenon that no social scientist without taking a particular standpoint can define one situation as being an improvement on another. This is certainly the position we have been forced to adopt in chapter 2. We have to have a standpoint and it is preferable that this be made explicit.

We have in fact chosen to use a measure of performance approximating to the first criterion which Lawrence and Lorsch suggest, namely the fit between the system and its environment, or the success of the system in satisfying its environment. We shall examine this definition in more detail a little later. In deciding on this measure of performance we were, of course, influenced by the open systems model and the view of the organisation that gives us. We were probably also influenced by the need to satisfy expectations among our managerial colleagues to have some apparently objective, quantifiable, measure of organisational improvement. As we have suggested in chapter 2 the question of criteria for performance was a cause of a dilemma. But the fact that the decision had to be made also provided a challenge.

A set of evaluation criteria based on systems ideas appears to be more satisfactory than the rather crude and simple criteria which accountants, industrial engineers, operations research people and perhaps corporate strategists sometimes appear to use, but it in no way relieves us of the need to recognise its partiality. It is true that the organisation's ability to satisfy environmental needs is important: if environmental fit is not good enough, the organisation is in danger of ceasing to exist, and thereby ceasing to satisfy any of the needs of its members. It is also true that socio-technical analysis forces us to consider the values held by the individuals and groups comprising the organisation, the relationships existing between them and the satisfactions and dissatisfactions which exist; and although we do not consider these values as ends in themselves, there is some likelihood that measures of improvement instituted as a result of systems analysis will not grossly interfere with the existing interests of members of the organisation, or the values which they now find in the system. To make too many disturbances to existing value systems could well result in adverse reactions and prevent performance (in rational terms) being optimised.

In effect, by deciding on a rational definition of performance we have abstracted from many of the important aspects of organisational success (notably the needs of individuals and groups) and concentrated on one important, but easily defined, aspect of it. We must in this case always bear in mind that these other aspects exist. We are in fact unconvinced that the dilemma of choice between the plural goals of an organisation is ever amenable to resolution except in the crude sense of resolution by use of the power that comes from control over important resources. It may be that the systems approach cannot ever lead us directly to the choice of one 'right' criterion of organisational performance.

THE CRITERIA FOR SUCCESS

We have suggested that socio-technical systems analysis in itself says nothing about performance. It is concerned mainly to describe and explain what is happening in the system. There are no criteria of better or worse implicit in the analysis. However, it is possible to establish some 'rational' criteria for success by the introduction of a few other fairly simple concepts. The first of these is the identification of what Rice and others[12] have called the primary tasks and what we prefer to call the focal activities of the system: what essentially has to be carried on if the interaction of the organisation with its environment is to continue to be effective enough for the organisation to survive and develop. The focal activities of the system have to be properly defined in relation to the needs it is serving (it being recognised that these needs are subject to change over time) and then the criteria of environmental satisfaction can be chosen with some confidence. The focal activities arise from the current requirements of the market and the other parts of the environment on the system and there are certain conditions which permit it to pursue these activities most effectively over the long term. These conditions will include the performance of certain support tasks: that is, tasks and activities whose function is to permit the focal activities to be pursued effectively and to be sustained and developed over time. The importance of proper identification of focal tasks was clear in the Press Room study of chapter 5. The behaviour of the senior foreman there was very effective in satisfying the needs of one aspect of the environment—the internal labour market—but his concentration on this desideratum shows either that he had not clearly defined the focal activities the shop needed to pursue efficiently or that he found these task requirements irrelevant to his own needs, or the way he was assessed, or that because of constraints on his role behaviour imposed by the expectations of subordinates he found them impossible to achieve in present circumstances.

The second concept is that of cost, in the economist's sense of the most efficient combination of resources to produce a given physical output, or perhaps better, the most efficient combination of resources which will allow the essential activities to be undertaken and production to be assured over the long term.[13] In systems terms we are defining here the efficiency of the transformation process within the system boundary and the Finishing Shop was a system where fairly clearly this internal cost efficiency was low. Efficiency in the transformation process involves not only minimum costs, in the sense of the smallest ratio of resources to product, but also the right balance between resources devoted to focal activities and those to support activities: these must be combined so that the interests of each are subjected to the sustained satisfaction of environmental needs. The balance between resources devoted to engineering support tasks and those devoted to focal activities may have been wrong in the Lower Foundry, for example. The resources devoted there to engineering services may have been insufficient to allow it to sustain its major focal activities.

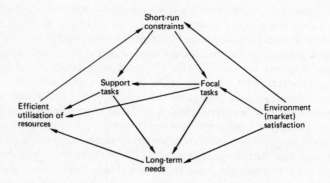

FIGURE 9.1   The dimensions of organisational performance

This scheme is illustrated in figure 9.1. Within it there lie the roots of three different oppositions or polarisations, all of which have to be recognised and satisfactorily dealt with in any assessment of performance.

firstly, there is an opposition between cost criteria and satisfaction of environmental needs. High performance involves maximum efficiency in the use of resources, only to the extent that this is compatible with the main objective, which is to obtain and sustain over time the best fit between the organisation and the relevant parts of its environment. As most managers are very well aware, and as we suggest was the case in the Lower Foundry, these two may well be in apparent conflict. Pressure for immediate cost reduction can lead to a reduction in the system's ability to satisfy the market, and to develop satisfactorily in future. Conversely, better market satisfaction and consequent growth and development of the organisation is likely to entail rather higher immediate costs, and thus apparently to be opposed to the efficiency criterion. A judgement may have to be made between them, and the force of each will have to be recognised in the context of that system at that time. The extent to which costs must act as a constraint on rapid development and progress should be apparent from a study of the system in its environment.

The second opposition is that between the resources which can be devoted to the focal activities and those needed by support activities. The focal activities are those on which the efficiency of the organisation depends, and we seek to maximise the efficiency of the support activities only in so far as this does not impede the effectiveness of the focal activities, and therefore of the organisation as a whole. One of the most commonly experienced phenomena in organisations is the self-centred pursuit of departmental objectives, in which each function or department is pursuing its own efficiency, sometimes at the expense of overall organisation efficiency.[14] The advantage of the focal/support dichotomy, though it is not always as clearcut as we have just implied, is that it gives us the ability to identify those activities which are directed immediately to environmental satisfaction, whose efficiency directly influences the organisation's success, and those other activities (commonly maintenance engineering, quality control, workstudy, general administration) whose main function is to satisfy and support the focal tasks and whose performance can best be judged in relation to their satisfaction.

There is a third potential source of conflict: that there are both short-term and long-term desiderata, and although most of the emphasis must be on the satisfaction of long-term needs, short-term needs act as constraints on the long-term solution. Presumably the long-term development of the organisation is usually being sought, but short-term needs will have to be satisfied, and the problem is how best to create conditions in the short run which permit the organisation's immediate survival, but which do not impose any great threat to the development of the system over the longer period. The short term should act only as a constraint, and its needs must not dominate one's whole view of organisational performance.

To recapitulate, what we have been discussing is some means of identifying the nature of organisational performance. We have suggested that to get any idea of what constitutes improvement in a particular situation, one must use a contingency approach. This entails a clear systems understanding of the way the system works at the moment and what are the constraints on it; and some criteria for assessing performance in that particular situation.

These criteria, with the need to balance a number of opposing measures of performance, could probably be developed theoretically into a fairly elegant and sophisticated performance measurement. However, in the great majority of field studies there is no need to elaborate the concepts much more than we have done already. Usually, an examination of the working of a system reveals fairly clearly what are the environmental, the technical, structural and behavioural constraints on its operation, and where detailed information is available about the makeup of costs of the various activities in the system, the implications for economic efficiency can be discovered. Thus, by examining in turn cost efficiency and the fit with the environment, the relation between focal and support activities and between short-term constraints and long-term needs, a number of broad alternatives to the present state of the organisation can usually be defined, all of which would, taking into account the necessary constraints on the organisation, constitute areas of better overall performance than the present. In chapters 12 to 14 we show briefly how these considerations apply to our three case studies.

The problem of planned change is then to devise a strategy which would move the organisation progressively towards one of these areas, while producing the fewest possible adverse or unforeseen complications. Using the contingency approach, and the techniques of open sociotechnical systems analysis, a management team should be able, with the involvement of people from within the system, to devise and implement a strategy which will move it towards a defined area of improvement in progressive steps over a considerable period of time. By monitoring events and opening the strategy to continuous modification as more is learned about reactions of the system to particular changes, the success of such a strategy can be predicted with a high degree of confidence.

It is with ways of devising such a strategy and monitoring its implementation that we shall be concerned in the next two chapters.

NOTES TO CHAPTER 9

1. An exposition of the different objectives and approaches appears in Greiner and Barnes (1970). The volume and variety of writings on organisational change has already been noted in chapter 1.
2. This is the typical assumption of the dominant school of planned organisational change. See for example Bennis (1966), the core papers in Bennis, Benne and Chin (1969), and Thomas and Bennis (1972), and the many papers on organisation development that have appeared in journals like the *Journal of Applied Behavioural Science* during the early 'seventies .

3. See, for example, Likert (1961) pages 3 and 6 and *passim*; Likert (1967) figure 8.1 and *passim* chapters 2, 5, 8. For an earlier statement, see also Likert (1958).

4. See, for example, Argyris (1964), pages 123 – 145; Argyris (1970), page 47ff.

5. McGregor (1960, 1967) is less interested in organisational effectiveness than in effective management of people.

6. See, for example, Herzberg (1966), especially chapter 6.

7. See, for example, Trist and Bamforth (1951); Trist *et al* (1963) chapter 3; Rice (1958, 1963); Emery and Trist (1960).

8. We have discussed the problems associated with goals in chapter 2.

9. Op. cit. chapter 6.

10. Ibid. chapter 12.

11. Op. cit. page 18. See also Lawrence and Lorsch (1967) page 17ff.

12. Rice (1958) page 32, page 227ff; Rice (1963), page 185ff; Miller and Rice (1967) chapter 3; Emery and Trist (1960), page 94.

13. This is similar to the definition of efficiency by Katz and Kahn (1966) in terms of output–input ratio, but with the additional requirement that the allocation of resources between activities should be right.

14. Merton's (1957) comments on overconformity in bureaucracy can be interpreted largely as pursuit by individuals and departments of support activities to the detriment of the organisation's focal activities and overall effectiveness.

10 Strategy Formulation: An Approach to Departmental Improvement

So long as a change-promoting team confines its activities to analysing the patterns of relationships that exist within a department and building a conceptual model of them, there is very little risk involved, and there is no commitment on anyone's part to further courses of action. It is only at the stage where a strategy is to be implemented, and changes are to be introduced, that a programme of departmental improvement becomes effective and thereby involves taking risks. A sound strategy for departmental improvement is important for the sake of the organisation and its success, and for the sake of credibility of those involved. If avoidable failures occur, the whole change programme is likely to suffer.

This chapter is concerned with a way in which the understanding gained through systems analysis can be used to devise a strategy for reaching an improved situation. The strategy should be consonant with the theory and method. It must fit into the procedure as a logical consequence of open sociotechnical systems analysis and model building for if a programme of improvement is to be based on the concepts of the open socio-technical systems approach, it is crucial that when the changes are introduced, there is no reversion to more orthodox confrontation methods, or to industrial engineering methods which may define single targets for improvement. Unless the sophisticated tools of analysis are matched by sophisticated modes of action, much of the advantage of socio-technical understanding will be lost.

Let us however begin by examining the characteristics of orthodox programmes of improvement. In most industrial organisations, line managers are accustomed to measuring performance, and therefore improvements, in fairly clear, precise, often quantitative terms. They are accustomed to working to fairly short time scales, and most innovations must prove themselves after a fairly limited trial period and do so against some straightforward measurable criteria. The kind of improvements usually encountered include such things as technical (process) innovations, new handling techniques or methods of quality control, new manning arrangements or principles of work allocation, new methods of payment or campaigns to reduce materials wastage, warehousing costs or machine downtime. Generally only one problem is identified at a time, and efforts are concentrated on those improvements which will reduce variable costs or raise efficiencies in the one area. A 'target' or 'goal' may be set, and success is achieved, and recognition given, when the quantified goal is reached.

So orthodox programmes of improvement tend to be concerned with unidimensional changes that are measurable and occur over a fairly short time-span. Having set the objective at the start, they examine in detail various means of attaining that objective, the relative efficiency of each and the technical, economic, behavioural and other constraints on each, until finally what appears to be the most efficient means of reaching the objective is found. That means is then pursued, and the results monitored, the monitoring process being designed to measure progress towards the defined goal, and that only.

There are some characteristics of these programmes which reduce their effectiveness. Little attempt is made to build upon the achievement by generating some learning process or some further improvement from it; and often the effects (adverse or beneficial) on wider aspects of organisational performance are ignored as irrelevant, at least by those who do the measurement and give the recognition. If the systems view is accepted, we cannot accept such an approach. In systems terms, 'better' performance requires us to examine overall activity and to obtain a better total fit of organisational characteristics together, and with the environment. Pursuit of a single end may even reduce the possibility of this.

What distinguishes our approach from, say, an industrial engineering approach can be summarised in a series of statements

(1) that an improved situation must arise out of and be constrained by the way the system is at present working;

(2) that the improved situation that is finally reached must be dependent also on what happens in the course of the change process itself;

(3) that, consequently, it is impossible to set any precise initial targets or objectives in the usual sense of those words.

Indeed it is not possible to say much at all about the nature of improvement until fairly detailed analysis has been made of the way the organisation is working at present, how costs are made up, how well the market is satisfied, what are the characteristics of the various control systems, what conflicts they create and how these are resolved, what socio-technical systems exist in the organisation, what latent functions, hitherto unperceived, may be being performed by some areas of apparent inefficiency, what parts of the environment most influence the system, and so on. A systems understanding of the organisation in this sense allows us to do two things

(1)   to define an area (or a number of fairly extensive areas) within which performance can be said to be potentially better than present performance. This we have discussed in chapter 9; and

(2)   to begin to examine what effects would be caused by changes of different kinds made to the system.

Our criteria of organisational performance can give some idea of the region or regions which would constitute improvements over the present situation, if they were attainable. But we cannot establish what precise end situation within one of these regions an organisation should aim at. This can only be done by analysing the interactions likely to occur during the process of change, and by looking at a number of alternative strategies for change, using some clearly defined decision criteria to determine the choice of strategy. Once a likely strategy is chosen, then by monitoring the changes as they are introduced and adapting or modifying the strategy according to the information being received in the monitoring process, progress towards the region of improvement is obtained. Not only the strategy but the potential goal is likely to change as the strategy develops and better understanding of the dynamics of the system is achieved through the monitoring process.[1]

The aim of this chapter is to show in detail the implications of these ideas for choosing a progressive series of changes—ideas that provide a means whereby we can begin to introduce a sequence of improvements in performance which do not result in too many unexpected adverse reactions or an increase in conflict or dissatisfaction. This is not a chapter dealing with advice on how to consult and communicate with the shopfloor, how to persuade departmental foremen or managers to take the ideas on board, how to manœuvre one's way through the intrigues of organisational politics, how to involve trade union officers, or such practical problems. Important as these are, they all involve some other aspects of the implementation process. However, we do suggest that by planning progressive improvements on the basis of an adequate model managers are likely in fact to meet fewer difficulties in the processes of consultation, involvement, or obtaining approvals and resources, because their perspectives are likely to be nearer to those of others affected. The demonstration that follows does not lead to any measures that are radically new or exciting in themselves or that will effect dramatic overnight improvements in performance. Rather, like socio-technical analysis itself, these ideas lead to a slow, fairly painstaking step-by-step sequence toward improvement. The difference with other problem-solving techniques is, we would claim, its consistency and its basis in a more adequate theory.

THE MEANING OF STRATEGY

Formulation of a strategy for change can be seen as a specific stage in equence that includes investigation, analysis of facts, model-building, roposal formulation and implementation of improvements. It is the stage hich follows on after model-building and after such testing, statistical or therwise, as appropriate of the plausibility of relationships in the model. t is an essential step, so long as specific improvements are to arise out of the vestigation.

here are a number of aspects to a strategy

(1) Definition and proper agreement as to what kind of situation will chieve greater effectiveness, better performance of the organisation in elation to its environment. As we have suggested there will be a number of hese 'improved situations', or alternative ends, among which a choice will ave eventually to be made. But the definition of ends must be considered longside the means available. Which end is chosen will depend not only n the magnitude of the estimated improvement in performance, but also n the likely consequences—adverse or beneficial—of trying to reach that tuation. There will be costs and difficulties, as well as benefits, associated ith any suggested change.

(2) Decisions about the means of getting from the present to a given new tuation: the 'best' way of getting from A to B. Again, there will almost ertainly be a number of alternative routes from A to any given B. Not only ae end, but the means of reaching it has to be chosen using the same kind f argument. The means must be selected in relation to the understanding f the present system which has come from socio-technical analysis, and in elation to the consequences throughout the system which are likely to be et in motion immediately changes of a particular type are introduced.

(3) Because knowledge of the system and of the way it will react to hange can never be perfect and because there are always other internal nd external influences on the system outside management control, the rategy developed must have a high degree of flexibility built into it, and ose implementing it must be highly sensitive to what is happening lsewhere in the system, no matter how refined the socio-technical model, r how much statistical or other confirmation it has been given.

(4) Because of this, the choice of individual steps in the strategy, their quence and timing, become of great importance. Usually it would not be ise to make the change to the defined situation in one large stride. Better move one step at a time, and use each step as a means of confirmation nd verification of the likely consequences, and to use the progress made at ach step as a building block which will allow the next, bigger, step to be troduced. It may be advantageous to reach the final goal by a slow and undabout route if by that means the goal can be reached without a great eal of disturbance to the social fabric or to the needs and expectations of ose who are members of the system.

Although these four aspects can be distinguished conceptually, in ractice they are interdependent. Means and ends interact with each

other, and each must be examined in the light of the other. In particula
because of the dynamics of change, the choice of a particular means m
either open up new possible goals or close the options for others.
deciding on the end (the improved situation) we want to reach, we ha
inevitably to consider the means available to get there, and tl
consequences which will begin to occur immediately one starts putti
these means into effect. Both the route and eventual goal will be affected l
constraints on the sequence of moves, and on the timing available. A
once having started down a particular route, the consequences of havi
taken the first steps may be to make the preferred end unattainable, c
conversely to open up new possibilities to more preferred ends, or to ma
one want to change the route itself.

THE SOCIO-TECHNICAL MODEL AS AN AID TO STRATEG FORMULATION

The model of the sociotechnical system has obvious value in providi
better understanding on the way a system is working at present, and of tl
sort of consequences likely to arise if specific changes are made in parts
the system: say a change in the way people are paid, in manning levels,
control mechanisms, in production planning mechanisms, etc. To consid
a proposed change and then look at its likely consequence in this way
really a passive use of the socio-technical model.

We want, however, to make more positive use of the model—to use it
suggest what moves should be made, to suggest an appropriate sequen
for these moves, and to suggest how they be introduced so as to reach tl
final improved situation with the fewest adverse effects.

Inevitably, there must be some element of uncertainty in the choice o
strategy in a complex system. However, we can reduce the amount
arbitrariness and increase our confidence in the strategy. Let us now look
some of the preliminary thinking needed before we can consider the fi
steps towards improvement.

The Existence of Constraints
People outside the department—whether in the company, the division
works, or the change programme itself may impose constraints on tl
direction of departmental improvement, in the form of expectations whi
have to be fulfilled or which those involved in the change believe th
cannot challenge. Current economic conditions affecting other areas m
force the company to emphasise short-term costs for the time being, in sp
of some demonstrated requirements of the system. There may be
expectation by individuals elsewhere in the company that the project w
result in a particular form of change: say, better working conditions
enriched jobs, or higher labour productivity. There will always be tl
constraint that a department is part of a wider system—the factory—a

e factory may be part of a wider group, with other works sharing the
me labour market and the same overall philosophy of controls.
onstraints such as these have to be taken into consideration, and the
olution has to lie within them, so long as the team is not able to induce
thers in the company to change them. So a first step is to define the
onstraints within which the solution, and the means to it, must lie. Such
onstraints must not of course be confused with cherished ideas (whether of
eam members or of senior managers) or other obstacles which can if
ecessary be overcome after some effort.

ost Sensitivity

o define improved performance requires knowledge of the make up of
osts in the area being considered. The investigators must analyse the costs
ttributable to the various activities going to make each unit of
roduct—materials, labour, supervision, maintenance, losses of materials
nd products through wastage and rejects, wear and tear of and capital
harges on plant and buildings, design activities, the cost of the personnel,
echnical and other services actually given to the department, and so on. A
ost breakdown will show how the productive activities of the department
re using resources, and indicates some areas where potential savings are so
mall that it would not be worth spending a great deal of effort to produce
hem. By itself it cannot do much more than this. In combination with
ther aspects of strategy it can do a lot to define the nature of the
mprovement to be aimed at.

Costs per unit of product are not the only dimensions of improvement.
Ve also look for better performance in terms of adaptation to the needs of
he environment—the ability to develop and grow in the longer term in a
hanging environment, an improved fit between the activities of the
lepartment and the long-term needs of the organisation. So the cost
ensitivity index is just a partial indicator of performance, to be borne in
nind during the process of devising strategy.

It is also a reminder that the cost elements in any system (for instance
vage costs, engineering maintenance costs, wastage of materials, costs of
abour turnover) are interdependent. To reduce labour turnover it may be
ecessary to raise wage costs, while at the same time wastage might fall. So
he index cannot be used with mathematical precision. However, it gives
he investigators more information about the system and its use of
esources, and allows them to form some ideas of the relative importance of
lifferent activities, and rather less certainly to give some idea what kind of
changes would be likely to meet the cost criteria for improvement.

Manipulability

Manipulability may be defined as the ease with which in a particular
system a particular change seems likely to be made: what constraints from
within the system there are on change. There are various dimensions to this
index

(1) how costly will it be to introduce a particular improvement;
(2) how much resistance from within will be found in introducing i
(3) how complicated are the consequences likely to be of introducin the new situation, or moving towards it;
(4) how difficult would it be technically or physically to introduce tha situation.

The different aspects of manipulability must be distinguished. Fc instance, to improve maintenance standards may be costly while y having few adverse consequences throughout the rest of the systen reduction in costs of power or raw materials may have neither complicate nor costly effects, but may be technically impossible. A change in hours c work may have virtually no direct costs, and may technically be benefici but may create much resistance and have many very difficult conse quences. The various possibilities for change are not independent of eac other. If one element in the system is changed, the degree of manipulabilit of other elements may well be increased or decreased in consequence.

Nevertheless, subjectively (and only subjectively) it may be possible t rank elements in the system in a series indicating the degree c manipulability, or conversely the difficulty and complexity of introducin them. Since this is largely an intuitive process the index can be devise quickly and without a great deal of labour, and can give the investigator useful preliminary feel about possibilities for change. However, we sugges this is all it can do, and examination of the socio-technical mode preferably using the framework outlined in chapter 8, will be necessar before detailed consideration of a strategy is possible.

The Nature of Improvement in Performance

To devise an appropriate strategy for improvement requires agreement o the criteria for assessing performance and agreement on what woulc constitute an improvement. Analysis would be needed of the focal tasks o the system, and how support activities were contributing to the efficiency of these tasks; whether the greater deficiencies were in costs or ir adaptation to market needs; how efficiency in resource utilisation and allocation might be assessed; what kinds of situations would constitute improvements in performance on these criteria; and what kind of genera picture the team would expect to see after the changes had been made.

Later stages in strategy formulation would then need to keep this enc situation (or one or two well-defined alternative end situations) in view, sc that the individual stages in the strategy could be related to the eventual achievement of the end.

Adaptation of the Generalised Socio-technical Model

The generalised framework described in chapter 8 can guide an in-vestigation through the likely patterns of influence and consequence in the system and can provide outlines as to where to look for the starting point

nd the subsequent steps in the strategy. The end point will often entail
ome change in behavioural performance or in cost and technical
erformance. But since managers cannot operate directly on these it will
ave to be reached by influencing them indirectly through other classes of
ariable.

We suggested in chapter 8 that variables in some boxes usually
nteracted in a complex way with many other variables. To start a process
f improvement by changing some of these is likely to lead to immediate
ifficulties. The initial move would usually be a change in a variable with
wer and simpler interactions with the rest of the system, the consequences
f which would be easier to predict. Such areas may include: market
emand, or the mechanisms which mediate between the organisation and
e market (which in a subsystem might mean a successor department);
hysical resource inputs; and the designed technical variables such as
yout, designed work allocation procedures, designated stock levels,
uality control criteria, conditions of work, or the training scheme,
ecisions on which can be made directly by management. If, as a bonus, a
ange in some of these variables influences performance directly, without
ausing too many other complications, we may consider those as
articularly attractive possible starting points.

Suppose, then, we make a change in some resource input or designed
chnical variable so as to create either some minor improvement in
erformance, or more freedom of movement in some of the more difficult
reas, we shall by this means have opened up some new options on the basis
f which a step-by-step path, or network of paths, can be devised, to enable
s progressively to move into more complex areas and from there to help
ttain more significant improvements in performance. As change pro-
eds, the model can be continuously tested by monitoring the reactions
gainst expectations, and additional confidence created in the effectiveness
f the steps being taken.

MMARY

Ve have outlined a procedure for formulating an initial strategy for
nprovement—a strategy whose implementation should be subject to a
onitoring process, and must be flexible enough to be modified with
xperience of the reactions of the system under change. The procedure
ay be summarised as follows

(1) Identify the constraints which are imposed on ends and means by
resent-day company policy, by the works or market situation or by the
rogramme itself—constraints imposed from outside or for reasons not
oncerned directly with behaviour within it. Consider what effects these
ave both on the end situation likely to be attained and on the means
vailable.

(2) Analyse the breakdown of costs—that is, all the elements which ?
to make up the total cost per unit of the product—and hence obtain
measure of cost sensitivity. This measure may be useful as giving a cle
idea of resources employed as well as being one element in the definition
performance. It can also provide a preliminary idea of what changes mig
be worthwhile in terms of the cost savings they are likely to achieve.

(3) Examine each element of cost in terms of the various criteria
manipulability of the system and quickly rank them according to som
notional view of how amenable each is to change.

(4) Define fairly clearly the criteria of improved performance in ter
of the definition in chapter 9.

(5) Now begins the process of deciding on the first step in the strategy f
change. This should be a move which can be introduced without causir
too many upsets in the whole system, which is not too costly, which w
itself result in some small improvement or help to make subsequent mov
more acceptable. It is likely that this first step will be a change in one of t
market demand, physical resource input, or technical design variables
the system. Preferably it will be one which leads directly to some increas
freedom of movement (say a potentially improved effort–reward relatio
some potential reduction in conflict or some immediate small cost savin;
or to attitudinal and behavioural changes such as would prepare the w;
for further changes. One possible way in which this latter can be achieve
is to involve those concerned in planning and designing this first move
the strategy, if that appears appropriate.

(6) After the first step has been achieved, the change it has made m;
have opened up some further possibilities for improvement. The success
the first step can then be used as a stepping stone towards further move
each one being monitored so as to test the socio-technical model and asse
the effects of successive steps on the system. But the real purpose of ea<
successive step is the contribution it will make to attainment of the fin
improved situation.

To set the whole procedure out in general terms fails to give the fu
flavour of the difficulties and problems of strategy formulation ar
implementation. Each tactical step in the strategy will depend on t
particular circumstances of that production situation. Moreover, ea<
subsequent step, though it must fall within this general framework, will l
influenced by the results of the monitoring process. It is very difficult
demonstrate the practicability of this process and the difficulty reflects t
whole difficulty of the sociotechnical approach: detailed rules ar
procedures have inevitably to be contingent upon particular situation

However, in part IV examples are given of possible applications of th
strategy to the cases analysed in part II (though necessarily without bene
of feedback from the monitoring process). In each case, the strategy follov
closely the steps we have outlined, so far as these steps are appropriate
the particular situations. The strategy outlined in these examples may l

garded as the initial proposals for implementation—proposals which
ust be flexible and continuously open to modification on the results of
perience during implementation.

NOTES TO CHAPTER 10

1. The ideas in this chapter were, we had believed, developed independently on
the programme, in relation to circumstances arising on its different projects,
and without conscious influence from other work. We have, however, since
been struck by the similarity in concepts and terminology between these ideas
and the writings of Lindblom on strategy. What unconscious or forgotten,
direct or indirect, processes of transfer may have been responsible we cannot
begin to speculate. See for example Lindblom (1959, 1964) and Braybrooke
and Lindblom (1963). However, while Lindblom's objective is to describe
the decision processes he believes may occur in government and society, our
main orientation in this chapter is to put these processes forward as developed
tools for use by managers.

11 The Evaluation of Success in Change

We have said in chapter 10 that in more orthodox innovations, the evaluation of success, like the defined objective of an innovation, tends to be unidimensional: the evaluation criterion will often be simply how nearly the project has come to meeting the single objective set for it at the beginning. There is little ability to distinguish between the monitoring of the change process and the evaluation of success. The latter is assumed to be increased to the extent that the former is successful.

Evaluation in systems terms must obviously differ from this. To be consistent with the systems philosophy, it has to be multidimensional. We must never assume that a measurable improvement in one direction is an indication of an overall improvement. We have to demonstrate that it is not offset, or more than offset, by consequential adverse changes elsewhere in the system or in the relations between the system and its environment. Preferably also the evaluation mechanism should be based on some theory which explains why movements in different directions do occur in different parts of the system.

The systems approach allows us, however, to make a distinction between evaluation criteria which claim to measure changes in organisational performance on an 'objective' basis and to be independent of any preconceptions involved in a particular change strategy; and a process of monitoring in which the assumptions about relationships that lie behind the change strategy are also the assumptions of the evaluation process.

 We first look at the more independent method of evaluation. This would necessarily be multidimensional, but would be divorced from any monitoring or feedback process by which the strategy for change was being tested and confirmed or modified. It should be possible to collect information about a large number of performance variables over a reasonable period of time and assess the state of satisfaction of the labour market, product market, and other areas of the environment, the efficiency of the transformation process, etc. There are at least twenty or thirty variables, most of which are available as a matter of routine in many industrial organisations, which can be used in combination as indices of environmental satisfaction or of economic efficiency. A list of possible indicators is given in table 11.1 classified according to the criteria they are most likely to measure.

The variables suggested in table 11.1 are pertinent to our own declared

TABLE 11.1

ome Likely Variables in an Independent Multidimensional Evaluation System of
Organisational Performance

. *Labour market and input market criteria of performance*

Rates of labour turnover
Index of labour stability
Rates of voluntary absence and sickness absence
Accident rates
Average earnings compared with index of local earnings levels
Overtime hours as percentage of total hours worked
Overtime pay as percentage of total pay
Reported trends in quality of recruits or difficulty of recruitment
Number and duration of disputes about pay
Number and duration of other disputes by cause
Problems encountered with materials suppliers
    trends in availability of material
    delivery dates
    specification problems
    costs as compared with alternatives

2. *Product market criteria of performance*

Changes in share of product market for various products
Percentage of delivery dates not being met
Trends in delivery time being offered
Variations in finished stock levels, related to various in order levels
Rise or fall in surplus capacity or in capacity overload
Index of customer complaints, or other indices of customer satisfaction
Trend in total value of sales (related to charge in economic conditions)
Successful introduction of new products into range
Ratios of unit costs to selling price

3. *'Efficiency' (closed system) criteria of performance*

Ratios of total costs, labour costs, materials costs and capital costs to volume of
    production
Indices of work content per unit of output and per man hour
Index of production per employee for constant capital employed
Percentage of materials scrapped or wasted
Percentages of components or products rejected or scrapped
Ratio of value of plant to volume of production
Trends in machine downtimes
Trends in manpower utilisation
Variations in total stock levels and in intermediate stock levels from a defined optimum

4 *Input/output criteria of performance*

Ratios of sales volumes to
    wage and salary bill
    direct labour costs
    total materials costs
    fixed capital charges
    maintenance costs
Unit costs as ratio of selling price

definition of organisational performance. They are, perhaps, remarkabl for excluding indicators of social and psychological need satisfactio management style, subordinate attitudes or motivation. Some other well known multidimensional indices of performance[1] are based as exclusivel on the latter as ours are on measurable technical, environmental an economic criteria and perhaps we should comment on the difference. It i not that we discount the importance of satisfaction or motivation. How w regard it in the context of organisations is clear throughout this book. W have chosen not to include in our index any criteria related to styl attitudes or interpersonal relationships, decision processes or informatio flows, since we are aiming to measure performance on the rationa dimensions of efficiency and environmental fit discussed in chapter 9, an we must always doubt the inevitability of a direct positive relationshi between styles of management (where these are not obviously based on th needs of the particular situation and arise out of a diagnosis of those needs or personal satisfaction on one hand and 'rational' performance on th other. These variables would at best be intervening variables in terms o our definition of performance, and their consequences could only b assessed in relation to what is known about the workings of th socio-technical system, the states of satisfaction existing and needs of th system for particular modes of operation.

Table 11.1 includes indices of final performance. However, a mech anism for evaluation based on these principles creates in practice a numbe of problems. Firstly, those who are evaluating have to bear in mind th question of environmental change occurring at the same time as programme of improvement is being implemented. Concurrent change would affect organisational performance (as they would also affec attitudes and satisfactions) and a mechanism for independent evaluatio requires some experimental controls to be established:[2] (a) performanc in the area being evaluated would have to be monitored over considerable period *before* the implementation of the improvements begar the direction of existing trends established, and the effects of implemen tation measured in terms of the deviation away from existing trends; an (b) to take into account changes occurring in the product market o labour market or in general economic conditions, or concurrent technica or organisational innovations, simultaneous evaluation would be neede as a control in a parallel department affected by the same environmenta changes, but where no implementation of the strategy for improvemen was in operation.

There is a more intractable problem, inherent in attempts to assess th significance of movements in a large number of variables. In any change situation some indices will necessarily be showing apparently advers trends while others are showing improvements, and an overall index o improvement would almost certainly be misleading, unless its in terpretation were based upon an understanding of the causes of thes movements, and in particular upon a satisfactory model of the whol

ystem, produced at the beginning of the evaluation process to explain why
differential movements would occur and what their significance is in terms
of overall performance.[3]

Now, this is interesting. What it implies is that where the indices in the
multidimensional measuring instrument are moving in different directions, performance can only be evaluated if a systems model of the
production area concerned is available. From such a model it would be
possible to predict that differential movements would occur at particular
stages, and satisfactory explanations of differential trends could be made
before the event. Clearly, no one model of relationships between variables
will apply to all situations. Relationships in a systems model differ very
greatly from one situation to another. Hence, if this independent view of
evaluation is to hold, it will be necessary either to be satisfied with an
assessment of performance which consists simply of a graphical or tabular
presentation of differential movements in twenty or thirty different
statistics, and use intuition to interpret them; or to be drawn inexorably
towards an index of evaluation which is designed to fit one industrial
situation only: the situation where improvements are being implemented
and where the evaluation is taking place.

Moreover, one necessary feature of a systems model is that during the
change process all the relationships in the model will by definition be
changing, and the model which is used for the evaluation must continually
be modified to correspond to these changes in relationships. *Ergo*, the
model which is being used for evaluation must also be made to fit the
specific change strategy which is being introduced. It is no longer really
independent, and the more satisfactorily this form of evaluation is
developed as a practical and theoretically valid tool for evaluation, the less
the differentiation between it and the second method of monitoring a
strategy as it is implemented.

Let us therefore look at this second method. As we have said, it makes no
claim to be independent of strategy. It would directly measure success in
diverting the organisation away from its original tendency, and towards
the area of improved performance which had been defined for it. The
evaluation system itself would be based openly on contingency theory and
each evaluation exercise would be tailormade to fit the particular area
being evaluated, the particular strategy which had been devised for that
area and the particular stage in the strategy which had been reached. It
would measure the success with which each step in the strategy was tackled
and resolved, and it would do this by means of a comparison between the
actual performance of the system and what had been predicted for it at that
stage. Individual variables in the evaluation system would be related back
to the original socio-technical model which had been developed, and which
showed the interactions of the variables with each other, and predicted
changes in the relationships as implementation proceeded. In this case, the
evaluation criteria and the feedback process which we suggested in the last
chapter was needed to monitor and help modify strategy as it proceeded,

might well be the same thing.[4] At least they would have a very larg
overlap.

This kind of mechanism for evaluation is, of course, open to dangers, an
in particular the danger that the criteria of evaluation and the strategy fo
change are made to support each other, that the tendency of the evaluatio
mechanism may be to justify the strategy in all circumstances. There is als
a problem of being led back into the controversy about quantification
Should not a valid evaluation mechanism be quantified in some way? An
since we say it should be in the form of a systems model which include
elements of social relations in the socio-technical system, is it possible t
find means of measuring the relationships which are at the basis of this kin
of model?[5]

There are four ways of answering these doubts. As we have implied b
the fact that we have written this book, we believe a systems view c
organisational behaviour provides a more satisfactory understanding an
a more complete picture of real organisational situations than othe
approaches; certainly better than many approaches associated with clea
measurement of performance. If systems thinking gives us a bette
understanding and a more reliable predictor without necessarily warrant
ing or even allowing measurement, then we should tend to use it for tha
reason.

Secondly, we have seen that a satisfactory independent evaluatio
mechanism based on systems concepts is not really possible. It must com
to be based on the same model of the organisation as was used for th
formulation of strategy, and it must develop over time as the systen
changes. An evaluation mechanism which is consonant with the concept
used in the programme of change is necessarily subordinated to th
assumptions and preconceptions of the change programme itself.

Thirdly, the nature of this research necessitated continuous critica
assessments of results, constant striving to criticise and falsify predictions
continuous confirmation that they are in fact borne out in practice, or i
they are not, continuous enquiry as to why this is so, and a readines
continually to think out afresh the nature of the system, and what is th
appropriate strategy, as feedback information is obtained. By keeping i
close touch with the operation of the system, finding as many externa
checks as possible on progress, and in particular being continuousl
involved with the people in the system, those involved in implementin
changes are able to avoid some of the dangers of providing self-fulfillin
hypotheses. They seek continually to test the relationships in th
socio-technical model, continually to practise scepticism and doubt. If thi
is done effectively, confidence in the validity of the monitoring system wi
develop.

The fourth argument relates back to our discussion about verification c
the relationships in the socio-technical model in chapter 7. If, for som
reason, quantitative confirmation of a model is wanted rather than, or as
complement to, experimental confirmation, then it may be possible to us

atistical techniques to test many of the relationships in the system, irectly or indirectly, so long as data are available in the appropriate form ver a long enough period, and so long as relationships remain fairly onstant. However, we would argue in the case of evaluation that atistical confirmation is rather a poor substitute for the confirmation vailable from the feedback when one begins to implement change. A ersistent demand for a statistical method of evaluation by a team of anagers or their seniors, in preference to taking the first steps in a strategy r a change and monitoring them, could be an indication of anxiety and of wish to delay the change process, more than of a desire for scientific alidation. It could itself be an indication of the state of some of the lationships in the system, which are likely to act as constraints on the rategy for change.

What we have been trying to do then is, having induced a controlled rocess of change into an area, to use the changes induced as experimental evices to help confirm the relationships in the hypothetical model of the rea, and to build on this confirmation to allow us to proceed more and ore confidently with the change strategy. So long as we have defined roperly the end situation, so that it is within an area of improvement over ne present, and so long as the predicted effects of each step in the change rategy are borne out by the monitoring process, the model can be said to e confirmed, and the strategy to be heading the organisation on the road improvement. If some predictions are not borne out, then that is an pportunity for further learning about the system, and for modification nd further testing of the model. The new learning can then be used in eciding on the next step in a revised strategy, and monitoring of predicted utcomes, based on the revised model, will continue.

Although we do not give examples here of the use of this monitoring and valuation device, its potential utility is evident from some of the ggestions for improvement made in part IV.

OTES TO CHAPTER II

1. The most popular is Likert's (1967) profile. See also Blake, Mouton, Barnes and Greiner (1964), Litwin and Stringer (1968), Golombiewski *et al.* (1971) for other examples among the many in this area.

2. Some part of the controversy about controls is reported in Burgoyne and Cooper (1975), page 58, which refers particularly to evaluation of management development activities.

3. This problem with multidimensional evaluation mechanisms is not often discussed, but it is inevitable, and may be one reason why the development of sophisticated many-sided measures has been neglected. Seashore *et al.* (1960) discuss some problems of multidimensional assessment of job performance in the absence of a satisfactory model of interrelations.

4. Burgoyne and Cooper (1975), page 54, make some lucid comments on the content of, and necessary channels for, the two aspects of feedback which they

categorise as (a) information to check, test and improve assumptions, and (b) information on what is now going on. The former is the more crucial for us.

5. The desire for measurement is a value position and it is liable to be adopted by those for whom a simple indication or confirmation of progress is more important than understanding about the complexity and problems of progress. For this reason it can have dangers. See the sharp comment by Becker (1970) on this kind of attitude.

PART IV

Particular Strategies for Improvement

2 Improvement in the Finishing Shop

We have been discussing some theoretical ideas about how patterns of events in industrial organisations are determined, what is the nature of organisational performance and how it can be defined, how it is possible to devise new means of improving performance and monitoring and evaluating the improvement. Theoretical discussions can add to academic understanding of organisational behaviour, and they can perhaps show more clearly the limitations of various approaches to explanation and to improvement, some of which we have criticised in chapters 9 and 10. However, general models and developments in theory are only of real practical value when the usefulness of the ideas can be demonstrated in application to specific industrial situations in all the complexity of the real world.

We attempt such demonstrations in the next three chapters, in relation to the three cases discussed in part II. The demonstrations cannot be entirely convincing for reasons we discuss further in chapter 15, where we shall relate the strategies proposed to some actual experiences in the programme of organisational change. However, we believe they show the value of making the sort of careful analysis suggested in chapter 10, within the general socio-technical framework set out in the two earlier chapters of part III. Too frequently policies for improvement or for survival, whether in individual units or in the overall organisation, are based on insufficient analysis of the situation, inadequate definition of what kind of improvement is wanted, and lack of strategic planning in the implementation of the changes. In these chapters we are dealing with departments all of which were believed to have problems that had proved intractable to any attempts at change. In each case possibilities seem to have been opened up for continuous improvement.

Let us first consider the possibilities of improvement in the performance of the Finishing Shop. The long-term trend in demand in the Finishing Shop was downward and within the foreseeable future was expected to reach a low and fairly stable replacement level, perhaps fifty per cent below the present level. Meanwhile, seasonal fluctuations in demand were likely to continue. The shop had had a history of redundancies and layoffs going back over many years, and was seen as a problem area virtually incapable of dramatic improvement.

At the time of the investigation management had two main goals for the

Finishing Shop. In the short-term they wished to obtain an increase in output of between twenty and thirty per cent for each grinder, and to regain conrol, as they saw it, of work-studied job values, as one means of lowering labour costs generally. They also wished to maintain or improve discipline and so control the amount of unofficial time-wasting and other practices of which they disapproved. In the longer run there was a desire to discover alternative means of finishing the bulk of these components, and leave only a small amount of work to be done by the present methods.

The socio-technical systems analysis on the other hand had disclosed the following more subtle features of the shop

(1) The technical design, workflow and control procedures, manning levels, official training procedures, supervisory structure and pay system had all been carefully designed in relation to a clear view of technical needs.

(2) However, the main conveyor had become the focal point of attitudes and conflicts between one grinder and another, and between the grinders and two of the other occupations. The process could only be kept going so long as both chargehands and grinders 'manipulated' the designed procedures to some extent. The consequent role behaviour of chargehands had led to a management perception that supervision was ineffective.

(3) Because of the constraints on supervisors' behaviour, they had never been able to operate effectively the well-designed training scheme, and consequently standards of skill were low and very variable.

(4) Excessive recirculation of components for reprocessing was due partly to variable skill standards. The less skilled men skimped their work in trying to keep up with the better skilled, and this practice was reinforced by the payment system, which encouraged men to work as fast as possible, by the conveyor system and by variable surface quality of raw components.

(5) Frequent machine breakdowns interfered with the ability of men to earn their expected bonus level. They were caused by insufficient preventive engineering maintenance and by the increasing size and weight of components as the market changed. Further, the pay system induced men to rush work through the conveyor in the early part of the day and it increased the amount of recirculation. Both of these practices tended to overload the equipment and increase the likelihood of breakdown. The more time supervisors had to spend on emergency repairs, the less time they had to either control recirculation or to improve operative skills.

(6) The bonus rates were set separately for each occupation, according to theoretical work content. They did not take into consideration the dependent nature of the various stages in the process. Thus the grinders, by controlling their own output and earnings, necessarily determined the earnings of every other occupation and, because of inconsistent work values, caused day-to-day fluctuations in them. These facts, and the perceived inequities in average bonus earnings, increased potential

conflicts in the shop, and to resolve these there was some unofficial modification of the work allocation system and a certain amount of helping out between operators.

(7) The two conveyor systems built a good deal of mechanical rigidity into the work of the shop. Supervisors tried to overcome the worst effects of this by working during tea and meal breaks. The rigid manning ratios between various occupations had added to these rigidities and exacerbated the possibility of conflict between groups. The grinders not only determined the pay of other occupations, but by their decisions whether or not to take a day's absence they could determine the work level of other occupations and could cause redeployment of men to other departments at reduced rates of pay. Many aspects of behaviour officially unauthorised and frowned on by management were in fact attempts to make it tolerable to live with all these potential causes of conflict.

Let us now go through the steps suggested in chapter 10 and consider a strategy for improving this situation. First, two early findings may be set out separately, since they rely little on socio-technical analysis and have few related effects on the rest of the system. First, production scheduling in the Finishing Shop, and the variable workload of the shop, were clearly related to the patterns of manufacture of the raw components, stockholding policies (both for intermediate stocks and for finished stocks), the costs of stockholding and fluctuating customer order levels. An orthodox operations research study of these relationships might achieve immediate changes and help avoid severe fluctuations in labour requirements and consequent cyclical redundancies and changing of shift patterns.

Secondly, straightforward economic and technical arguments showed that there would almost certainly be no 'disappearance' of the Finishing Shop and its processes in the next few years, given foreseeable market trends. Even if other processes were developed it would be uneconomic for more than about a third of the output of the shop ever to be transferred on to those processes, and the shop as a whole must continue to operate, though doubtless at reduced size.

We can therefore go through the various stages in the formulation of a strategy for improvement with some uncertainties resolved.

The constraints on change

There were a number of external constraints on what other changes it would be possible to effect in the Finishing Shop. In the first place, the shop was fairly specific to one particular product and had to live with the long-term decline in demand and wide fluctuations in the customer's call-off rates. Among other things this would inhibit any large capital expenditure and keep management's attention firmly fixed on costs. The shop was one small department in a much larger works, and the factory environment would impose further constraints on change, notably on any radical change in payment system or average earnings. Further, senior management held a number of strong preconceptions, particularly about what the main aim of improvement should be: to obtain a large increase in labour productivity and savings in labour costs. In fact this seemed reasonable in the long-term, but senior managers' concern about the day-to-day problems in the shop made them rather reluctant to contemplate a long-term strategy to this end. Finally, the perceptions held by members of the investigating team must influence what could be achieved. Some members of the team had strong views that shopfloor involvement and enrichment of jobs must be one result of change, and the strategy had to take these wishes into account.

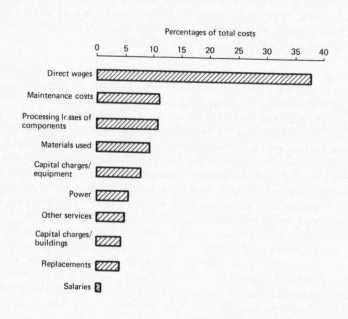

FIGURE 12.1   Cost structure in the Finishing Shop

Cost sensitivity

The approximate breakdown of the costs of finishing a component is shown in figure 12.1. Labour costs are by far the most important element, with maintenance costs and the cost of rejects the other major elements. To reduce labour costs by twenty per cent, as senior management desired, would be three or four times as beneficial in terms of total cost saving as the same proportional reduction in maintenance costs or in the number of components rejected, and very much more beneficial than a twenty per cent reduction in the minor materials used. However all the elements involved in cost are interdependent and a reduction in either labour costs or maintenance costs might only be obtainable at the expense of considerable increases in, for example, reject rates.

Manipulability

Some of the fairly important elements of cost were obviously of low manipulability in the sense in which the term is defined in chapter 10. For example, capital charges could hardly be reduced because the capital investment on which they were based had already been made. In the case of minor materials, it seemed unlikely that management could economise further except at the expense of some frustration and inefficiency on the part of grinders and polishing machine operators. It appeared unlikely that the physical amount of maintenance done in the department could be reduced. Whether the same service could have been provided at less cost by the engineering department (or a better service provided for the same cost) would have entailed a detailed examination of the engineering department as a support activity to the rest of the works. Indeed, it might conceivably be necessary to increase maintenance costs as a means of obtaining overall cost reduction in the Finishing Shop.

Thus, the only two components of cost which were apparently open to easy manipulation were the wastage or reject rate of components, and the labour cost of finishing a component. Labour costs, although manipulable in the sense that theoretically it was possible for a grinder to grind considerably more components each shift, had low manipulability in the sense that the consequences on relationships within the socio-technical system of obtaining an immediate large reduction in labour costs might be serious and unpredictable.

So far we have considered some preliminary steps in the formulation of a Finishing Shop strategy. These have clarified to some extent the nature of the problems to be dealt with. The strategy itself requires further consideration of the socio-technical model, and the likely consequences of change on it. First, the system must be examined to decide what kind of situation would constitute an improvement on the present, and for this we continue to use the scheme proposed in chapter 10.

THE NATURE OF AN IMPROVED SITUATION

The focal tasks of the shop and its associated warehouse were: to grind and polish components to meet the specifications required by the product market, in quantities and at the times demanded by the customer. Performance may be defined as satisfaction of the market over the long period at as low an overall cost as possible. There were few complaints about the quality of work produced in the Finishing Shop, or about delivery dates, despite the marked fluctuations in demand. However, the cost (in terms of the amount of resources used in satisfying the market) was obviously capable of improvement. One cause of high costs was the way management had reacted to market fluctuations by imposing workload fluctuations on the shop, and the suggested re-examination of production plans and warehousing policy might help resolve this.

Further examination of how total cost per component could be reduced without affecting satisfaction of the product market led to a picture of the improved situation somewhat as follows: a revised pay system and wages structure which would encourage high productivity, labour stability and low absence; a workforce with high and constant levels of skill, achieved through more effective training; reduction or elimination of the present causes of tension and conflict, possibly through redesign of the physical layout, a restructuring of job patterns and better maintenance; a change in supervisory structure and possibly of control systems, to obtain a better match with technological, task and social requirements in the shop; and a reduction of wastage and rejects. The problem in devising adequate strategy would be in discovering a way to combine all these changes together.

A STEP-BY-STEP STRATEGY FOR CHANGE IN THE FINISHING SHOP

We have suggested in chapter 10 that, once having clarified the kind of change to be aimed at, by examining the constraints under which the team must operate and gaining a picture of the nature of improvement, then a programme of change should ideally proceed step by step, starting in a more predictable area with preliminary steps that could help open up a pathway towards the final situation. In the Finishing Shop there was limited choice of an initial step. Given its position as one link in a manufacturing chain, there was little possibility of influencing market demand greatly without considerable complications in other parts of the chain. To change some aspects of the technology would have entailed considerable capital expenditure, which, as we have already suggested, seemed to be ruled out in the immediate future. Training procedures, manning arrangements and work allocation procedures had complex interactions with things like plant capacity, payment system and the attitudes existing in the department so that to have operated immediately on these would have had unpredictable consequences.

The one possible area of improvement that did not have many interacting complications was the reject level. Improvement in this would produce immediate though moderate improvement in costs, the effort–reward relationship for shopfloor workers would be improved, and (especially if reduction in rejects was accompanied by a reduction in the number of components recirculating for reprocessing) attitudes both of management and shopfloor might begin to change. Both the level of rejects and the rate of recirculation had identifiable causes which included: the variable quality of raw components coming from the manufacturing area, the variation in grinders' skill, the imprecisely defined inspection standards, and the payment system. The level of rejects appeared to be the more straightforward of the two problems.

(1) The first step proposed was therefore to set up a joint investigation, involving the departmental manager, supervisors and representatives of the grinders and other employees, to find ways of reducing both the level of rejects and the rate of recirculation. The terms of reference would allow the inquiry to cover the quality of incoming raw components, the standards of skill and the effectiveness of training, inspection standards and the match of these standards to customer requirements. If this inquiry was successful, it might lead directly to cost savings of perhaps £4000 or £5000 per year. More important, any success achieved in reducing reject levels or recirculation rates would ease the congestion which occurred in the shop and help reduce friction. Perhaps most important for succeeding steps was that involvement of the grinders in a constructive enquiry in cooperation with management on a problem that was of common concern could begin to change the mutually suspicious attitudes between management and the shopfloor.

(2) If the simultaneous operations research study of stocking policy and production scheduling had resulted in the proposals expected, job insecurity and fear of periodic redundancy would at the same time have been reduced.

(3) Almost certainly, one result of the joint inquiry would be proposals to improve standards of training. Better training, resulting in improved and more constant skill standards, would further reduce the causes of conflict in the shop. However, it would probably lead to higher average hourly productivity and, given the operation of the payment system, would result in yet more idle time for the grinders. It would involve some costs, and these would have to be seen as an investment, laying the foundation for further improvement.

(4) If higher total output per grinder (as distinct from hourly output) was to be possible a reduction in the rate of breakdown would be necessary. Reconsideration of maintenance policy would therefore be an essential next step. Again, additional maintenance costs must be seen as an investment opening the way for more efficient plant utilisation in future. A reduction in the rate of breakdown would further reduce some of the conflict situations in the shop and help stabilise earnings. It would loosen the constraints on supervisory behaviour and permit chargehands to pay more attention to training and workflow.

(5) At this stage, net cost savings would have been negligible, but some flexibility might have been created in the system, both through changing attitudes and through greater effective capacity of equipment. Only when additional capacity had been created could output be raised. At this point therefore (and purely as a tactical step, not an end in itself) it was proposed to lift the ceiling (the cash maximum) off the potential earnings of grinders and give them an incentive to increase daily output, as well as the facility to

do so. Rather than simply removing the ceiling, however, it was suggested that this should be negotiated against their agreement to revise some of the work-studied job values that were recognised to be slack. Removal of the earnings ceiling would not increase costs of processing, and if renegotiation of job values was effected it could improve costs and increase the sense of fairness in the shop. Grinders did not in fact like working with slack job values and expressed some frustration at the continual need to resist change in what they saw as an inefficient and unfair pay system.

(6) To increase grinders' maximum earnings without a simultaneous rise in the earnings of polishers and conveyor men would be to court disaster. Therefore, any savings obtained from higher grinder productivity must temporarily be sacrificed to obtain greater equity as between grinders, polishers and conveyor men and other occupations. One suggestion at this interim stage was a common rate of pay for conveyor men, polishers and packers and a common incentive bonus, possibly based on the throughput of finished components through the shop. To the extent that higher grinder output was forthcoming, too, so it might be necessary temporarily to increase the number of conveyor men and polishers.

(7) So far, the whole sequential series of steps were to be interim changes, mainly designed to produce a situation where rapid improvement in overall efficiency would be possible. However, one further difficulty is evident. Market demand was already met with the existing number of grinders, even given the original low grinder productivity. Improvement in grinder productivity could be used temporarily to build up finished stocks, as part of the parallel strategy of cushioning the shop from short-term fluctuations in call-off rates. However, given market stability, there must eventually be fewer grinders, and it would have to be recognised that some reduction in total numbers would eventually have to be made whether this was by occupational restructuring, natural wastage, or negotiated agreement on redundancy and redeployment. At this stage, no move was suggested other than that the problem should be recognised and discussed. The ability to use the improvements to build up stocks would be welcome at this time.

(8) A change in authority structure, to make inspectors and packers responsible to the Finishing Shop manager and supervisors was advisable if the shop was to operate as a flexible production unit. To have made this change earlier in the strategy would have brought into the open the conflicts caused by the differentials in earnings and conditions between inspectors and packers on one hand and grinders, polishers and conveyor men on the other. However, once pay differentials were reduced and the tensions due to excessive rejects and recirculation lessened, a change in the authority structure would be possible.

(9) Once the five occupations in the shop had been brought together greater flexibility could be introduced, and it was suggested that as a first stage, and with full involvement of those concerned, the strict manning rules between occupations should be eliminated and there should be a

eduction in the occupational distinctions between conveyor men, packers
nd polishers. Rather than leaving the rigidities in the conveyor system to
be relieved by unofficial and inefficient helping out by the grinders, a
group of seven or eight men could together load the conveyor, operate the
polishing machines and undertake final packing, and be allocated between
these jobs as occasion demanded. Further, since the grinders' skill entailed
nowledge of inspection criteria, flexibility between grinders and in-
pectors might be possible. Given this situation, the roles of chargehands
would obviously be changed, and skill in labour allocation and workflow
ontrol according to conditions might have to be developed. These
proposals would change both working relationships and status re-
ationships in the shop. However, enough was known of the socio-technical
ystem to make it fairly clear that the changes would be acceptable.
nvolvement in these changes would itself help to improve relationships,
nd self-allocation to the jobs as occasion demanded could well eventually
esult. There might be some breakdown of the distinction between high
tatus grinders and inspectors on one hand and low status occupations on
he other.

(10) This stage would probably be reached some six to eight months
fter the beginning of the first step. Although none of the steps so far taken
s in itself in any way unorthodox or outside the experience of many
managers, one distinctive feature of this approach is that each step has
een part of a consistent strategy. In no single step was there any idea of
etting a target for measurable improvement and putting in hand the
rocedures necessary to obtain that improvement. Each step was to have
he objective of easing the total situation in the Finishing Shop to the extent
f allowing the process of improvement progressively to continue. It would
e important to monitor the effect of each step as it was introduced, and to
nsure that any unexpected consequences were noted and lessons learnt
om them. The situation now reached was still an interim state, but
onsiderable changes and improvements would already have been effected
a the patterns of activity. At this stage, it was suggested that a period of
onsolidation take place, and no further changes be introduced for a time,
vhile the new situation was assessed and performance monitored. At the
ame time, it would be necessary to consider what might be occurring in
he environment to affect the success of any future changes. If the existing
tuation had improved performance and changed attitudes and patterns
f behaviour in the shop, any future steps could be rather more radical, and
o would have to be prepared carefully, on the basis of the more complete
nderstanding now available of the way the system was working.

(11) The final step it was possible to foresee would be simultaneous
estructuring of the whole payment system and occupational structure in
he shop, and a reassessment of its future labour requirements. It should
ow be possible to do this in discussion with and involvement of everyone
a the shop, and it might be possible as a result to abolish the occupational
istinctions and greatly simplify the pay system. One pay system that

might emerge from these discussions would be one or perhaps two basic rates and a throughput bonus common to the whole shop or to each shift. A new look might also be taken at the way work was put through the shop. It was, however, impossible to predict precisely what form this restructuring of pay and occupations would take. Some members of the investigating team had hoped from the start that it might go as far as a fundamental change in methods of work, equipment used, concepts of responsibility and means of motivation generally. However, as a result of the monitoring process which would have accompanied all the previous steps, understanding of the socio-technical system and its possibilities for change would have developed, and the moves eventually undertaken could proceed with confidence, and with the involvement of everyone concerned in them. At the time of the original investigation radical restructuring would have been an extremely high risk undertaking and would probably have resulted in adverse reactions and resistance on the part of everyone concerned.

A step-by-step strategy that proceeded in the way described would gradually have opened up the way for some of the larger moves to be implemented easily and to be welcomed by all concerned in them, from managers to the more unskilled workers. Once the ground had been prepared by the earlier stages in the strategy it might well be advisable to make these more radical moves all together, to achieve a complete restructuring of the expectations of people in the department and establish a new set of values and relationships more congruent with each other and with the purposes of the shop. The aim would be that a new pattern of relationships would be formally designed into the system, rather than resulting from informal manipulation of a system designed for quite different purposes. Manipulation is not necessarily a bad thing, and is frequently inevitable given the nature of the formal design. However, the performance that results from it is likely to be below either designed performance or potential performance, and the situation probably less satisfying to those involved in it. The hope would be that as a result of this programme of change the designed, the potential and the actual performance would be much closer to each other, and that mechanisms would exist to ensure that they remained close.

This, then, was a possible strategy resulting from the socio-technical analysis and model-building exercise. As we have suggested, it is valuable to go through the possible steps in detail for a number of reasons. The exercise will show the nature of the initial moves that are available to begin the process of improvement; to go through it will demonstrate clearly the kind of thinking that should be behind any programme of implementation, and bring to light a number of likely dangers; and discussion of the programme between managers and others concerned will be an effective way of involving them and helping them take the whole thinking on board.

In practice, as we shall show in chapter 15, events are unlikely to follow

he processes outlined in this initial framework. The actual progress of
mplementation must be influenced by the wishes and the ideas of those
esponsible for implementation, and by the feedback being obtained from
he monitoring process. Success, however, seems to depend on a carefully
lesigned strategy having been worked out and applied.

13 Improvement in the Press Room

As we have shown in chapter 7, the situation in the Press Room was ver
different from that in the Finishing Shop, and few of the same problem
were seen by management to be important. Working conditions wer
recognised to be poor, but labour turnover and absence had been reduce
to low levels in the last two years by the actions of the senior foremar
Output per man was satisfactory and few disputes or grievances now cam
to the notice of the departmental manager. The main difficulty was tha
total production was stagnant in a buoyant product market situation. Th
industrial engineers believed that equipment was not used to its fu
capacity, but there appeared to be difficulties in greater usage of th
capacity. One origin of the enquiry had been the establishment by senic
management of an enquiry into means of improving working conditions, t
encourage easier recruitment and retention in an attempt to increas
output.

The features of the shop that emerged as important from the socic
technical investigations included the following

(1) Poor working conditions, together with full employment in th
locality had restricted the supply of labour, and one requirement was th
assurance of high and stable earnings. Those now employed in th
department were mainly anxious for relatively high earnings and som
men travelled from a neighbouring town to work there.

(2) The crucial elements in the pay packet were bonus and overtim
earnings, and it was important for retention of people in the departmen
that men could achieve the earnings they expected in relation to the effo
they were willing to put in for them. However, not everyone in th
department had the same needs or the same attitudes to the effort−rewar
bargain.

(3) With the varied product mix, work-studied values often did nc
correspond to the operator's perception of work content and the re
lationship between effort and reward was seen to be different for differen
products. Stability in earnings could only be achieved through varyin
effort. This was compounded by other conditions in the department.

(4) The quality of the raw materials coming into the departmen
varied. Poor quality of material could increase the amount of rejects an
wastage, and it was believed by operators that some grades of materia

permitted more rapid output than others. The effect of variations in material quality was seen to be different for different sizes of product. The importance of quality variations on the behaviour of operators was influenced by the operation of the wage payment system. The perceived raw materials properties were believed to effect operators' ability to earn their target amount of bonus, and the variation in raw material had come to be seen by both operators and supervisors as an important constraint in the shop which had to be improved.

(5) In designing his production schedule, the senior foreman used a complicated model which took into account quality variations of raw material and earnings expectations of the employees. In this way, he had increased satisfaction among his subordinates, but had compounded the inadequacy of production by producing an inappropriate mix of products for the warehouse.

(6) Patterns of work dictated that the labour force should be divided into small teams, and designed work allocation procedures generally specified teams of three men. However, with three people working together on a press, it was difficult for all three to be continuously employed, even though the press was operating continuously. Although work-study values took this into account, levels of earnings then fell below the men's expectations in terms of the effort involved. Further, it had become difficult to form teams of individuals with well-matched earnings expectations, and the ensuing conflicts had been one of the causes of past high rates of labour turnover. High rates of absence and turnover had in the past led to increased recruitment, and hence to a high proportion of trainees in the labour force. These trainees were a highly unstable group and when deployed among established teams, they tended to increase intra-team difficulties by reducing the earnings potential of the whole team. Rates of separation among more established employees therefore rose as a direct result of increased rates of recruitment.

(7) To overcome these conflicts within teams and to keep the level of earnings high, the senior foreman had reduced team size, often from three men to two, and by doing so had increased satisfaction with the effort–reward ratio, reduced labour turnover, but simultaneously created some underutilisation of the presses. This had, in turn, encouraged a fairly high level of overtime working, satisfactory to a few of the workers. However, because it was voluntary, overtime was ineffective in balancing the needs of production to the numbers employed.

(8) Finally, the senior foreman had reduced the effect of bonus fluctuations by paying the operators on 'average' rates in certain circumstances where officially he should have paid them on the normal job values. Expectations of high and stable earnings had become established among the operators who put additional pressure on the supervisor to maintain this situation, and by the time of the investigation he was in a trap to the extent that he had no means of radically changing his behaviour. The supervisor had begun to put emphasis on the problems caused by

variations in raw material quality, because this was one factor outside hi
own control creating dissatisfaction among subordinates and limiting hi
ability to change the situation.

We will now examine the possibilities for improving performance in th
Press Room, using the same procedure as for the Finishing Shop.

The Constraints on Change

The Press Room had to take advantage of the expanding product marke
for its one product range if the future of the product range was to be assure
in competitive conditions. Therefore, an assurance of increasing outpu
seemed to be essential. Unlike the Finishing Shop, there was a manage
ment expectation that capital expenditure should be made in the Pres
Room and some of this devoted to improving working conditions
Advantage could be taken of this. However, it would be necessary t
ensure that the people working in the department remained as satisfied an
as productive as at present, and it would also be necessary to satisfy some
the needs of managers and supervisors, particularly the senior foreman
who had attained a position of considerable prestige, power and indee
respect in the department. If the effectiveness of the senior foreman was t
be maintained, the high degree of motivation which his high status an
control over sources of power had produced would have to be maintained
probably by the substitution of new responsibilities for some of those h
now undertook.

Cost Sensitivity

An approximate cost breakdown for the Press Room is shown in figur
13.1. In this case, the raw materials comprised nearly forty per cent of th

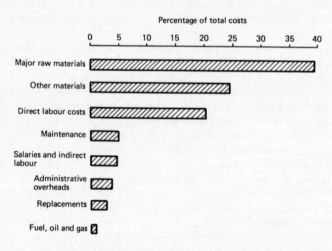

FIGURE 13.1   Cost structure in the Press Room

osts reported for the department, and other minor materials a further wenty-four per cent. Labour costs comprised about a fifth of the total, and naintenance costs about five per cent.

Manipulability

t appeared that between thrity-five and forty per cent of the major raw naterial disappeared in one way or another in the course of processing. Although fairly high wastage was inevitable, more efficient usage of both najor and minor materials would create relatively few consequences lsewhere in the system, and materials costs were therefore not only the nost sensitive to cost savings but fairly easily manipulable. It appeared at rst sight, therefore, that improvement in the Press Room could be a more traightforward process than in the Finishing Shop. In the latter, probably nore common case, the more sensitive elements of cost were among the east easily manipulable.

Thus, the two or three preliminary stages in this assessment seem to show fairly clear picture of the position and the possible areas of freedom in the 'ress Room. Again, before we can begin to devise a strategy for mprovement we must examine carefully what would constitute improve- nent in this department.

HE NATURE OF AN IMPROVED SITUATION

'he focal activity of the Press Room was the conversion of raw materials nto sections in the mix of sizes and types and in the quantities demanded y the warehouse and eventually by the product market, and at times emanded by them. Performance, therefore, was to be judged on two imensions: the satisfaction of the warehouse and product market and the fficiency with which the Press Room used resources in this process. Now it clear that the two situations, in the Finishing Shop and the Press Room espectively, are different. Whereas the Finishing Shop was satisfying narket requirements in quantity, mix and delivery dates, but at excessive ost, the Press Room had a highly productive and stable labour force, roducing efficiently (though with rather high rates of materials wastage nd underutilisation of equipment), but was unable to satisfy the xpanding market requirements in either volume, or mix of production. mprovement in this department would therefore probably lead in the irection of better quantitative and qualitative satisfaction of potential aarket demand, possibly of modifications in stocking policy, and better atisfaction of warehouse requirements (including satisfaction of needs of ie socio-technical system in the warehouse) while at the same time costs er unit of output, utilisation of plant and equipment, satisfaction of the eòple employed, rates of wastage, etc. would be maintained at least at ieir present levels.

Although theoretical studies indicated that the equipment already in the Press Room was capable of the increased output required, a question which must be asked was whether organisational structures and procedures would allow better utilisation to take place. Expansion of production would necessarily raise the question of team size and deployment, as well as questions about the appropriate wage payment system.

A STEP-BY-STEP STRATEGY FOR CHANGE IN THE PRESS ROOM

It appears that there are fewer constraints on the initial steps that could be taken in the Press Room than in the Finishing Shop. There was a wide immediate choice, partly because there were fewer constraints on incurring capital expenditure. However, one advantage of the rather tight conflict situation in the Finishing Shop was that once some freedom of movement had been achieved, the goodwill created could be built on in the formulation of further moves. One danger in the Press Room situation is that the good attitudes and satisfied expectations might be adversely affected by the early steps in the strategy.

The following were the steps suggested

(1) Two possible openings would be likely to help in later stages: improvement of the poor working conditions and reduction of the variations in quality of raw materials. We will look at these in turn.

(2) Improvement of working conditions would cause few unforeseen consequences, but the effect of improved working conditions on performance would not be great, and would probably be limited to easier retention of newly recruited labour and better attitudes to work in the Press Room. Management was already committed to capital expenditure on dust extraction and since the expenditure was to be undertaken in any case, maximum advantage might be gained by involving the shopfloor in more detailed inquiry into just how conditions in the department were perceived by those employed there and how they affected social structure and relationships and attitudes to employment in the shop. Better appreciation of the place of working conditions in behaviour might possibly lead to a different direction of expenditure from what had at first been contemplated. Involvement in this inquiry would help ensure that any improvement made did increase satisfaction and eventually performance. However, to improve working conditions would involve capital costs and have no immediate short-term effects on satisfaction of the market. This would be a facilitating move only.

(3) Variability in the quality of raw materials affected productivity and the reject rate, caused bonus fluctuations and was an important cause of the senior foreman's modifications to the production schedule. More important, it was the operators' perception of variable quality rather than technically determinable variations that affected productive behaviour

n inquiry into the relationship between raw material quality, wastage of
material and rejects would produce more information, but it would again
have to involve the shopfloor if it was to disclose the real effects of material
quality on wastage, given the actual methods employed, rather than the
effect of fluctuating quality on designed methods using theoretical curing
times. A joint inquiry could examine how far variations in material quality
as measured by laboratory analysis corresponded to variations seen as
significant by the people actually handling the materials. The inquiry
might result in falling wastage rates simply as a result of interest roused and
information received by the operators; and it would probably produce a lot
of further information about the working of the system, some of which
might be used in influencing the policy of the supplying department and its
production methods. Not only would the Press Room management
probably gain information about influences on behaviour in the shop and
the effects of materials on it, but both operators and managers would gain a
clearer view of the relationship between objective criteria of quality and
subjective perceptions about it. This would help establish some commonly
agreed grounds on which to base subsequent proposals. The likely increase
in output would be small but other benefits would have accrued.

(4) The studies of working conditions and raw material quality are both
preliminary steps: changes leading to fairly minor improvements, but also
because of the possibility of involving those concerned) yielding valuable
information to help plan further and more difficult steps. Indeed, the next
stages would necessarily have to enter more complex areas where change
would produce a greater number of consequences. More consideration
would have to be given to these, in the light of the dialogue already
established. The two requirements would be (i) to reduce the fluctuations
in earnings and introduce greater stability in the perceived effort–reward
relationship without the supervisors having to resort to manipulation; and
ii) to reduce the imbalance between the capacity of a piece of plant and
the necessary patterns of work of a team of given size. In this case the
change in earnings seemed likely to create the fewer difficulties.

(5) The existing payment system gave individuals, acting as members
of teams, some opportunity to decide their own effort–reward bargain,
though in attempting to do this conflicts could be caused within teams.
Moreover, deficiencies in work measurement had created fluctuations in
the effort–reward relation as between different products and different
presses. The requirements from a pay system for the Press Room seemed to
be an assurance of high stable earnings in a context which encouraged high
productivity and cooperation between members of the team. One adverse
effect of the present system was the considerable fall-off in effort and
therefore output when earnings expectations could not be met. It appeared
from examination that technical and labour market requirements might
best be met by a system combining a fairly high stable element with a
bonus based on total weekly production, either in the shop as a whole or on
each press, so that while earnings were still related to output, the

frustrations caused by random fluctuations would be eliminated.

However, to change the pay system alone would simply transfer th
symptoms of dissatisfaction away from pay and make technical and othe
difficulties more pressing. It would bring into the open the problems c
imbalance between technical design and manning procedures. Moreove
if a pay system succeeded in satisfying operator needs without manipu
ation, the role of the supervisor would become far less important. It wou
be necessary to redefine supervisory responsibilities to give the foremen
responsible and well-integrated role in the system.

(6) To improve technical design (capacity and layout of equipmen
work allocation rules etc.) is a more difficult problem, the implications c
which would need to be clarified before proceeding to the next sequenti
step. It is impossible to separate out technical decisions from their soci
implications. So long as the concept was retained of small teams eac
engaged in the whole operation from pleating to sawing, press capaci
would create working difficulties within teams, whatever the team size. S
long as the small team concept remained, therefore, the choice had .to b
between designed underutilisation of equipment or designed underem
ployment of people, and this could only be ameliorated to a minor exte
by the acquisition of specific new pieces of plant such as supplementa
sawing or pleating equipment. Although a change in the system of pa
would alleviate the problems in three-man teams to some extent, th
inherent difficulties in matching skills and personalities in three-ma
cooperating teams would remain.

(7) An alternative solution would be to change the concept of sma
cooperating teams and divide the Press Room into larger groups, eac
working on one operation such as pleating, pressing, or sawing, and eac
group having its own partial production schedule. Such a division wou
create a completely new socio-technical system and its effects would ne
careful analysis. It would require intermediate buffer stocks to be he
between each process so that full advantage could be taken of the increase
flexibility. This solution is somewhat similar to the occupational brea
down in the Finishing Shop which had caused many problems ther
partly due to the natural tendency towards decreasing flexibility. O
foreseeable difficulty was that to employ men permanently on a
unpopular occupation like sawing, where dust made conditions ve
unpleasant, would have somewhat the same effect as with the polishers
conveyor men in the Finishing Shop—a perception that the conditio
were inequitable and a consequent increase in rates of labour turnove
Moreover, small cooperating groups are likely to satisfy social ar
psychological needs better than horizontal groups, and this system, despi
a predictable reversion to manipulation and unofficial helping out, wou
lead to increased rates of turnover and absence, and other manifestations
dissatisfaction.

(8) The present system as managed by the senior foreman ha
produced a productive and well-motivated department, and the

onditions would be worth preserving. To keep them it would probably lso be necessary to retain the small cooperating team concept, and it night be necessary for management to accept that, despite the apparent nefficiency, more capacity must be acquired, and this type of plant would lways remain underutilised. The alternatives of underemployment of eople in three-man teams or of larger non-cooperating groups, whatever he pay system, could lead to demotivation and to production difficulties vhich would support the senior foreman's statement that larger numbers ed to lower output.

(9) However, we have assumed that the system must be designed by nanagement alone, in the light of what is now known of behavioural atterns and their causes. There are other technically feasible solutions uch as an increase in labour flexibility between teams, or more omplicated methods of deployment between operations, none of which ould be introduced unilaterally by management without adverse con- equences. If there were close consultation with those involved, it might vell be possible to find solutions socially more satisfactory and capable of naking better use of equipment, than any management could introduce nilaterally. What team arrangements and plant arrangements might atisfy these criteria cannot be decided before the event. New solutions vould create new relationships and new problems, which can only be nown to those experiencing them. They might range from two-man teams ssisted by a pool of spare men, to rather larger teams each operating two ress lines, to self-allocation of men to teams according to the nature of the roduction schedule, or to some changed responsibilities such as quality nspection by team members or responsibility for determining the length of un between cleaning down and changeover, or responsibility for making he actual changeovers. Self-inspection, for example, by changing the alance of work, might help redress the discrepancy between machine apacity and potential labour productivity.

(10) This is the third area where involvement of the shopfloor has been uggested in this strategy. The advantages to be gained in getting nformation and involvement of those actually doing the job, discussing roblems with them, giving them access to information on what concerns hem, or securing their cooperation in the decision-making process, were in ach case either real advantages in devising better solutions, or pre- equisites to changes. Shopfloor involvement is not an inevitable part of lepartmental improvement, but there will be cases such as the Press Room vhere involvement in redesign by those doing the job has obvious benefits. Ve should not turn our backs on it for purely doctrinaire reasons, or ecause it does not fit in with the existing culture of the works or the firm. Neither, of course, should we advocate it simply because it may be ashionable.

(11) The changes suggested for the department would progressively trip the senior foreman of the more important aspects of his present role, specially the patronage system he had devised to satisfy needs left

unsatisfied by the formal controls. This source of status and power and supervisory satisfaction would have to be replaced with some other role still functional to departmental needs. Greater operator responsibilit whether for product flow or for quality would on the face of it further erod the foreman's status. Further, the supervisory strength in the departme might well be reduced: the department would be unlikely to require thre shift foremen and two day foremen, with real supervisory responsibilitie In compensation, therefore, the senior foreman's responsibilities might changed either by giving him greater managerial responsibilities with the Press Room, or by widening his responsibilities into fields lik production planning, raw materials control, or even warehouse super vision in a newly integrated department which combined both section The solution would only become clear as the new design of the Press Roo took shape, but it would have to be borne in mind throughout the proce of change and improvement.

As with a strategy for the Finishing Shop, so with the Press Room, it ha been necessary to give a great deal of consideration to devising a plan tha would encourage permanent, self-sustaining changes to occur to set th department on a course of improvement. However, these again could be n more than an initial set of proposals, open to modification when put int practice. The actual course of events in the Press Room is discussed in th final chapter.

14 Improvement in the Lower Foundry

The patterns of behaviour in the Lower Foundry and the problems perceived by management to exist there were not predominantly related to features of the socio-technical system of work at shopfloor level. In the other two departments much that was characteristic in behaviour and much of what were perceived by managers and supervisors to be problems could (in the language of chapter 8) be traced to conflicts that occurred, and interactions that took place, because of the inefficiencies of technical design and mediating mechanisms, and particularly because of the poor match between task constraints on behaviour and the constraints of payment, manning systems and other controls. Sources of difficulty for men working on the plant were by no means absent in the Lower Foundry, but they were already fairly well understood by the foundry manager, who was trying to improve the situation. It was not so necessary to resolve differences in perception between managers and men actually working on the plant. However, the foundry manager was unable to effect some of the improvements he would like to have made because of technical and marketing factors, combined with the operation of controls and of policies laid down outside the foundry.

We may summarise the findings from the Lower Foundry study in a few paragraphs.

(1) The Lower Foundry supplied three main product markets, all quite different from each other, the one feature common to all products being the high technical content and consequent technical difficulty of manufacture. The market for cups was however now almost entirely an export market, and success of grilles depended upon the creation through marketing effort of a market for a product quite new to this country, while boxes were being sold to a small declining traditional domestic market. The current volume of production in the Lower Foundry was insufficient to make the most economic use of its technical capacity. Marketing effort was equally diverse. The main effort towards expansion was in the grille market, where considerable promotion activities had taken place but contingency plans for other markets would be necessary should the hoped-for expansion not occur. No great effort was being made to develop new products, either for related or for new markets, and the tradition of concentrating on products with a high technical content had not been seriously questioned.

(2) There was obviously some mismatch between the existing technical facilities and the requirements of the product range. The one large and complex furnace had tended to dominate the production facilities and had created orientations towards melting technology as being the overriding consideration. On the whole, the product markets were seen as restrictions on the ability of management to use plant at its optimum efficiency. The economic requirements of furnace technology included a high and steady throughput of metal, and to achieve this the three main products were produced simultaneously at as high a production volume as could be sustained by the existing markets. There was little opportunity for introducing fundamentally greater flexibility into production patterns, in order, for instance, to retain a stable labour force. Labour had been treated as the one flexible resource, with frequent redeployment, some redundancies, and high and variables rates of overtime.

(3) There was inherent difficulty in the manufacture of the highly technical products; low yields with high rates of rejects and metal losses were inevitable, especially given the large number of newly developed designs and the variety of types produced, with correspondingly short production runs. Underusage of production facilities helped to raise costs and the need to use a common alloy for all product lines meant that raw materials were unduly expensive. Given the tight specification of product characteristics, the rather outdated equipment was inadequate, and the inadequacies were compounded by a rather poor maintenance service. Further, dilatory provision of pressing tools created delays in meeting delivery dates, increased rates of reject and reduced the bonus earnings of those working on the plant.

(4) The reasons for poor maintenance and inadequate provision of tools were related to factors in the environment outside the Lower Foundry. The Board had long expressed some reluctance to invest highly in its operations when the returns relative to investment elsewhere were believed to be low. Concern expressed by the Board about the factory's contribution to profits had been interpreted by senior factory managers as directives to increase the contribution in the fairly short-term. Cost reduction exercises had followed and had affected overall long-term efficiency.

(5) Priority given to the needs of the Upper Foundry had left the Lower Foundry seriously under supplied with engineering and other services. The department had for a decade been treated as a poor relation of the Upper Foundry, in a factory which itself had had a difficult history. It had a legacy of relative neglect, leading to the outdated equipment, and an image, of which it was conscious, that its labour and its supervision were second rate as compared with other parts of the factory. Past neglect meant that a considerable amount of capital investment would probably be necessary before it could be brought back to a highly efficient department with a growing reputation.

(6) One present characteristic of the Lower Foundry was the instability of its workforce, caused partly by growing employment opportunities in

he local labour market, partly by the poor reputation of the factory and he foundry for redundancy and redeployment, partly by the poor working onditions and the knowledge that earnings fluctuated violently. In-tability meant that skill levels were too low on average for the equirements of production. However, despite the technical problems aused by labour instability those now entering the factory seemed to be vell suited to the conditions currently being offered. Since their attach-ment was so loose, redundancy and redeployment could be effected vithout a great deal of hardship, relying largely on natural wastage. The ery high rates of overtime offered suited those who were looking for high arnings, regardless of hours worked. The foundry was attracting the men t deserved.

(7) Pressures on the foundry manager reduced his ability to improve the ituation. The controls on him and the criteria by which he was being ppraised were short-term and based on rates of machine downtime, reject ates, manning levels and so on. The experimental situation and the atterns of production in the department as well as poor equipment and ngineering services, on the other hand, reduced his ability to attain high fficiencies of this kind. Of this conflict the foundry manager was aware, nd although he had started to reorganise the department with the aim of mproving long-term performance, the low technical efficiencies the lepartment was currently producing put considerable pressure on him to nake them look as good as possible. Further, he was conscious of the need o satisfy the earnings requirements of his subordinates, and for this they ad to maximise output and minimise rejects. One consequence was a onflict between the foundry manager and the departments he was upplying who were continually being pressed to accept production which lid not entirely pass their quality control criteria. To force borderline roduction through the inspection process was the way the foundry nanager had found to minimise the effects on himself and on his ubordinates of his technical inability to meet the criteria on which he was eing assessed.

That was the situation. There are complications in using the suggested rocedure for examining the possibilities for change. Success in the Lower 'oundry brings in more external considerations than the other cases.

The Constraints on Change

The constraints on the foundry manager from outside were hindering him rom improving performance and it would be necessary for those mplementing the programme of change to probe against these constraints n an attempt to discover which of them could be removed. If none of the onstraints proved capable of change, then there would be little hope of adical improvement in performance. Indeed, this was one case where it night be necessary to examine many of the variables which managers requently take as immutable and see how they could be influenced.

Nevertheless, there were some fairly clear limitations on what could be

done. It would, for instance, be impossible in the short-term to contemplate changing the dominance of the one large furnace. Further, until
the Foundry had demonstrated that it was capable of becoming a
profitable production unit, high capital expenditure on replacement of
outdated plant would be ruled out, and the Foundry must do a good deal
towards improving its economic performance before it could be re-
equipped really to meet its needs. Given the inherent difficulty in
manufacturing highly technical products the inadequacies of the existing
plant would be a continuing source of inefficiency.

Change in product mix or markets was not currently being actively
considered, though it might be possible to change this situation and
secure new marketing and technical development effort. The local labour
market on the other hand was unlikely to change in the short-term. Unless
unemployment rose, recruitment difficulties would certainly continue.
The reputation of the factory could not be radically improved in the short-
term.

Many of the present constraints were imposed by the rest of the factory,
including the low priority given to engineering and other services, the lack
of authority given to the foundry manager and the controls to which he was
subject. These would be constraints on change unless the implementation
programme could help to change the perspectives of people outside the
Lower Foundry. Similarly, the constraints imposed by the company
centre, reinterpreted as they were by the division and factory management, could be probed by the team.

Given involvement of managers outside the foundry it might be possible
to turn some of the constraints into opportunities. One of the terms of
reference of the change programme itself was to look at company-imposed
constraints on managers, and to consider the effects of these. There were
thus opportunities in the situation that could be turned to good account.

Cost Sensitivity

The breakdown of total costs in the Lower Foundry is as shown in figure
14.1. The cost of raw materials provided by the melting department,
constituting about forty-five percent of total costs generated by the
foundry, was the most important item. The cost of the molten metal has
been divided into two parts: the cost of the raw materials from which the
molten alloy was formed, and the cost of the melting process itself. The
metal content of rejects or waste material could usually be recovered and
any savings effected in the rate of rejects could only be offset against the
process costs of melting, which in fact constituted over 70 per cent of the
molten alloy cost.

Of other items of cost, the most important were direct wages, power,
maintenance costs and the costs of tools and mould parts provided to the
department. As would be expected, power was twice as big a constituent of
the costs of cups and grilles (fourteen per cent) as of the boxes produced on
the side presses. On the other hand, the cost of tools constituted nearly one-

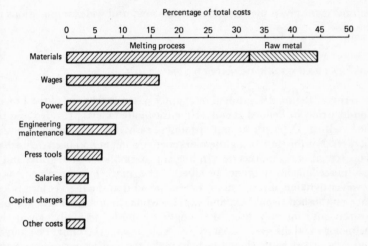

FIGURE 14.1   Cost structure in the Lower Foundry

:ighth of the costs of manufacture of a box, compared with under five per :ent of the costs of a cup. Maintenance costs varied between three main)roduct lines, being almost twice as important for the production of grilles ıs of boxes, partly because of the maintenance of the recently developed ıealing process, and possibly because production of grilles was given higher)riority in maintenance than the two static or declining products.

One point to be considered was that costs in these high technology narkets, though naturally important, may not have been critical to the uccess of marketing effort.

Manipulability
Γhe make-up of costs was not very different from that of the Press Room, ınd the rate of rejects was high, ranging from about twenty-five per cent in he case of boxes to as much as forty per cent for the other two products. As vith the Press Room, therefore, a reduction in the rate of rejects would nake considerable savings in the cost of the component, both in costs of netal used and in power. However, because of inherent technical lifficulties it was not likely to be easy to attack rates of rejects, and onsiderable compensatory costs, in labour, maintenance and tools)rovision, could well be incurred in an attack on the reject rate. Wage costs ınd the costs of maintenance and tools provision, all seemed to have been)runed to the maximum extent already, and were probably not manipul-ıble items in this sense. Thus, consideration of manipulability showed elatively few opportunities for direct improvement in any major item of ost.

Again, these preliminary stages have to clarify the situation somewhat. Iowever, it will be necessary to examine carefully what would constitute improvement given the technical background and wider implications of this case.

In terms of the model outlined in chapter 9, the focal tasks of the Lower Foundry may be defined as converting the molten metal provided to it by the Melting Department into products satisfying its chosen product markets. For the time being the market environment had been defined as those sectors of the market demanding cup assemblies, boxes, grilles and a few miscellaneous jobbing products. The market environment was however dynamic in two senses. It was hoped that the market for grilles, once established, would expand rapidly while the market for boxes and possibly also for cup assemblies might diminish. Secondly, given the technology and the spare capacity available new markets might be sought and new products developed to help make the conversion process more efficient.

There seemed to be an imbalance between the resources devoted to the focal activities and those devoted to the support activities necessary to carry out these focal tasks efficiently. Our suggestion has been that insufficient resources were devoted to engineering support services like maintenance and tools provision. Support activities were provided by other departments in the factory and it was to some extent the policies laid down for the foundry by senior management which had produced this apparent imbalance.

The short-run constraints imposed by company, division and factory on the operation of both the focal tasks and support tasks for the foundry may also have been inhibiting the department from performing efficiently over the long-term, and possibly detracting from its ability to satisfy market needs. The short-run constraints were due to the perception of senior management that viability of the foundry (as well as other areas of the factory) was threatened. The short-run constraints were in danger of creating a vicious circle and reducing long-term viability still more.

Since currently, even with fairly low efficiencies of production, there was considerable underutilisation of capacity, a worthwhile improvement in the economic performance of the foundry seemed to require an expansion in the markets it served—either for its present range of products or for new products suited to its production facilities. A successful attack on the efficiency of the manufacturing process would be dependent upon the solution of the marketing problem. There was inherent technical difficulty in manufacture, and the possibilities for improvement of production efficiency given the product mix were not of enormous significance. Nevertheless, the rate of rejects was high even for established lines, and the amount of metal lost during the casting process because of technical faults was also high—up to twenty per cent of the metal drawn from the furnace ever reached the tempering or annealing process. More adequate plant, better-maintained plant, an adequate supply of accurate and undamaged tools and better trained and longer service operators and temperers might all have helped to improve these figures.

Thus we see the improved situation in the Lower Foundry as entailing a larger, and probably wider market for its products, based, at least in the short- and medium-term, on the same alloy type as its present range. Accompanying this would be moves towards a technically more efficient foundry, better maintained and supplied with engineering and technical services. Given the make up of manufacturing costs, and assuming market expansion was achieved, there would be an economic case for additional capital expenditure even in the short-term, provided it resulted in a moderate increase in technical efficiencies. Further, an improved situation would be likely to include a better fit between the production needs of the foundry and the kind of people who were attracted into it. This in turn would require the foundry to offer conditions of employment likely to attract men from the locality who would stay and progress in the foundry into more highly skilled occupations. It would eventually lead to a situation where the men working on the plant would take greater responsibility for production efficiencies.

STRATEGY FOR CHANGE IN THE LOWER FOUNDRY

This section will differ from the equivalent paragraphs in chapters 12 and 13 in that the actual sequential steps taken by those implementing the strategy would depend on their success from time to time in probing and removing certain of the constraints imposed on the operation of the foundry from outside.

Indeed, the essential first stage in a strategy for change might be the establishment of an effective dialogue between senior management of the factory and those charged with implementing the programme, so that the situation in the foundry might be discussed on the basis of the new data forthcoming from the inquiry and of the models that had been proposed. In this way the team would be able to formulate stages in its strategy as they found constraints being relaxed by management (or as they discovered perceived constraints to be non-existent) or as new opportunities opened up through discussion.

Nevertheless, expansion of the product market seems to be the key to improvement, and to take precedence over most other changes that might be contemplated. Now, the marketing problem was not a straightforward one that could be tackled through orthodox market research. Existing markets were highly technical, and despite the obvious primacy of the divisional marketing department's role in policies for further market expansion an inquiry into either expansion of present product lines, or extension into other highly technical markets ought to involve both the technical management of the cup assembly plant and the foundry management, in order that the technical problems and potentialities of the foundry and the expertise of the assembly plant should be taken into consideration. Proposals to expand into high-volume production of less technical products might also involve the foundry management in helping to guide policies in directions appropriate to the facilities of the foundry. The first proposal therefore would be for an urgent interdepartmental study of market possibilities using existing skills and technical facilities. Indeed, one outcome of the inquiry might be to change the emphasis given to the marketing of highly technical lines like cup assemblies and any allied products that it was economic to develop and give the technical and market-orientated management of the cup assembly plant more responsibility for developing markets suited to its business. Technical links between the plant management, marketing specialists and the market might be strengthened.

This initial strategy would be contingent upon the ability of the implementing team to persuade senior managers of the technical skill involved in marketing some of the products of the Lower Foundry, and perhaps to change slightly the production orientations of those managers.

If the marketing inquiry showed success, it would do a great deal to reassure senior managers about the potential viability of the Lower Foundry. If through market expansion the foundry was able to work to full capacity, then some labour problems, particularly problems of redeployment, would be ameliorated. However, it could exacerbate the technical problems in the foundry. Market expansion would entail a considerable amount more experimental development work, with its disruptive effect on production runs, reject rates and bonus earnings. New products and new varieties would require efficient provision of tools by the engineering department and this would initially entail high costs. Therefore although an expanding market would be a prerequisite for long-term viability, it would have to be accompanied by a solution to many of the technical difficulties in the foundry.

Further moves to improve the efficiency of production in this direction seemed to require three things: improved engineering maintenance of key pieces of equipment, readier provision of casting and pressing tools by the engineering department, and a more stable and better trained labour force. Better routine maintenance would be more costly, and in addition any programme of planned preventive maintenance, for instance, would involve considerable initial effort in making up a backlog. It would entail additional manpower in the engineering department. Similarly, prompter provision of tools would result in higher costs for the foundry and an expansion of the highly skilled labour force of the toolroom.

However, a further look into cost sensitivity puts this in perspective. If by increasing the efficiency of maintenance services and supply of tools to the auto lines the rate of rejects could be cut from forty per cent to, say, twenty-five per cent and the rate of metal lost during casting from twenty per cent

say, fifteen per cent, then the cost savings in the foundry and the melting
ocess together would more than compensate for even a fifty per cent rise
engineering costs. Further, because of the high cost of materials and the
gh value of products, capital charges were a very small element in cost.
me capital investment in new equipment, if it resulted in increased
elds of good products from an equivalent weight of metal, could well be
own to be economic on these narrow grounds, as well as being essential
· expansion. Given the ability to incur these costs (and assuming skilled
gineering labour was available in the neighbourhood) better engineer-
g facilities would create few complications for the foundry management.
On the other hand, to obtain greater stability amongst those employed
the department so that greater skills could be acquired, would be a
atter of some difficulty, and it is beneficial to look at the question of
eater technical efficiency as a whole, in systems terms, rather than
king at the several aspects of it separately. For instance, if greater costs
engineering services were to be incurred the foundry manager would
ed to develop and use different skills in the management of a more
mplex department where the balance between added costs and added
ectiveness would have to be constantly monitored. A department that
d better plant, was better maintained, and produced better efficiencies,
uld require better skilled employees, but it would also have beneficial
ects on the behaviour of the people currently involved in the process.
owever, there were a large number of factors creating labour instability,
cluding fluctuations in bonus earnings (which would be exacerbated by
creased development work) the effects of redeployment, and the existing
or reputation of the foundry, which it would probably take considerable
ne to rectify.
As one way of accelerating change, the possibility might be tested of
volving those now working in the foundry in a study of ways of improving
e employment situation. If this involvement could take place, further
oves towards more efficient operation might be considered, such as
creasing the responsibility given to skilled men for production efficiencies
the possibility of further reducing redeployment and giving assurances
no forced redundancy.
On the other hand, involvement would almost certainly result in
quests for improved working conditions and better welfare and other
cilities, requiring some additional capital expenditure not directly
lated to increased production. It would be necessary to demonstrate to
e company that this expenditure had indirect advantages for de-
artmental performance measurable in monetary terms. Involvement,
wever, would be doubtfully acceptable in the existing climate. Perhaps
main advantage would be a more rapidly rehabilitated reputation for
e foundry in the local labour market, and a useful lever enabling
anagement to break out of the regressive spiral.
Although it has been impossible in this case to map out a clear sequence
small steps in a strategy for improvement, what we have suggested is that

changes in both market composition and technical efficiency must ▌
pursued more or less concurrently, to the extent that it was possible
persuade senior levels of management to relax constraints and provid
facilities. If market expansion took place in the absence of technic
improvement, difficulties in satisfying the market could be envisaged. If o
the other hand, technical improvements were effected at present rates
production then the excess capacity in the department would result in st
greater problems of redeployment and an acceleration of decline throug
the regressive spiral.

One further change, foreseen as part of an improved situation in t▌
foundry, would probably follow the other two. This was to chang
departmental responsibilities somewhat so that the foundry might eve
tually become a centre responsible for producing efficiently to clear
defined quality standards and willing to guarantee, with the help of t▌
quality control department, the standard of the components it produced
the warehouse and assembly plant. We suggested in chapter 6 that such
concept failed to match the control systems currently imposed o
departmental managers in the factory. It would assume that the found
could be treated as a unit and evaluated according to its overall ability
satisfy the needs of the areas it supplied at reasonable cost. In the course
the implementation programme, and in the dialogue hopefully establishe
with senior management, the latter might be influenced to the extent th
the nature of controls would change and the foundry management perhaj
be trained to make the kind of decisions necessary for success in the
circumstances.

A concept of the foundry in these terms would have to be accompanie
by a change in management orientations in the factory away fro
preoccupation with melting and foundry technology (important thoug
these would remain) and towards the view of the factory as a syste
designed primarily to satisfy a market environment. Finally, if great
economic success was achieved as a result of the strategy, then it might l
possible eventually to consider the appropriateness of the technic
facilities, particularly melting facilities, for the nature of the business t▌
foundry was engaged in. A perception of the foundry as an expanding ar
potentially successful business enterprise with a profitable future wou
enable the management to consider the economics of a number
alternative technical arrangements, more suited to the multiple produc
of the area. It is perhaps a paradox that only at the end of this strategy ca
we begin to think about the appropriate shape of the total faciliti
required for the performance of the department to be maximised.

Clearly, however, unless support could be gained from senior manag
ment in the factory from the start, and unless they could be persuaded
provide the material and other resources to set the foundry on the initi
stages towards success, then improvement could well be impossible. It w;
not in this case within the power of the foundry management itself to pu
itself out of the regressive spiral.

PART V

The Wider Context of Change

5 Departmental Improvement and Organisational Change: In Practice

Let us look again at the main themes of this book. They include a description of some means to analyse and explain the behaviour that takes place in a production department, to assess performance there and to improve departmental performance. We believe the state of departmental performance is of interest for a programme of organisational change since there is a clear connection between improvements made in performance at the workface and the direction of overall processes of change in the wider organisation: changes in structure and relationships, or in control systems and decision-making processes. Our concentration on smaller and more particular areas arises from our initial view that organisational change would only be effective and lasting if it were based on improved satisfaction of the identified needs of the units where the focal activities of the organisation take place. If we could identify and bring into the open the requirements for success at the workface, and if we could then demonstrate means of improving the performance of individual units clearly to higher levels in the authority structure of the organisation, then, our initial thinking assumed, the latter would begin, either spontaneously or under pressure from middle managers involved, to provide the facilities and support needed for improved departmental effectiveness. As a result the style of management and the overall culture of the organisation might begin gradually to change and become better suited to the conditions required for higher overall performance. Various mechanisms could then be called into play to stimulate this.

We want in this chapter to comment on these relationships between departmental understanding and the involvement of junior and middle managers on one hand, and the behaviour of the wider organisation on the other. We will deal with this in the context of experiences with our three cases, and in relation to the strategies we have proposed to help improve the situation in those three cases.

The programmes suggested in part IV for departmental improvement are the programmes of the change team, and at this early stage they were strongly influenced by the academic members attached to the change

team. They are based on the ideas described in part III, and it is th
general ideas incorporated in each strategy that are important rather tha
the strategy itself. There is no assumption that any of the three is the on
effective strategy for improvement in that situation. Moreover they on
describe the initial stage of strategy formulation. They omit the who
dynamic process of stage-by-stage implementation, monitoring an
modification of the strategy as a result of experience.

We envisaged that the strategy would normally be implemented l
local managers, in cooperation with supervisors, shop stewards an
workers in that area, together with specialist advisers from function
departments. For the sake of the wider programme it would be mo
important that this team of people should be committed to a strategy
their own devising which they felt they owned and were responsible fo
than for the programme to follow exactly paths laid down by outsiders.
the programme were to produce a self-perpetuating change in modes
behaviour and approach to problems, then we believed that the decisio
on what was to be done in particular production areas must be made l
those who would take final responsibility for their success or failure, an
that these people must be convinced of the rightness of the proposals an
become committed to them before implementation started. Not on
would their own change of approach and understanding then become sel
sustaining, but others would see the change, and they would be motivate
towards convincing others of the rightness of the new approach. Furthe
by their involvement in the monitoring process and by criticising ar
modifying the tactical steps as improvement occurred, their understandir
of and feel for the process would be reinforced and they would becom
more able and practised in the new approach.

So our outline strategies in part IV can be seen as suggestions to start c
the process of implementing changes, and to illustrate the kind of thinkir
and the kind of steps that the change team would encourage tho
concerned to consider. The actual sequence of events would be unlikely
follow the course outlined exactly. The strategies do however illustra
how the systems framework can be used and it is important that sufficie
understanding and care be put into devising the steps of the strategy ar
sufficient monitoring and testing done during implementation, if it is not
fail. A mistaken move can set back the whole process of department
change irretrievably, and may consequently put the wider programme
some jeopardy. The advantages of involvement and responsibility by loc
managers and supervisors concerned must therefore be set against tl
attendant risks that a less suitable series of steps might be selecte
monitoring be less sensitive than it should be, and breakdowns occur.

Our hope was, as we have said, that if this process were successful, tl
local managers would be motivated to press for wider changes to enab
them to operate more successfully. Their enthusiasm, and the recogniti
of their success, would be our best advocates for change at the higher leve
of the organisation.

With these considerations in mind, let us look at what actually happened in our three cases. These are three early cases out of the large number investigated and we have shown in chapter 7 how they differed as cases for analysis. One reason for reporting these particular cases is that between them they may illustrate a need to reconsider the validity of our theory of outward spread of ideas and the mechanisms we proposed for organisational change. The outcomes illustrate a number of dangers and problems for those involved in the change process.

The simplest outcome is what happened in fact in the Lower Foundry. About the time the enquiry was ending, but before any move had been made towards implementing any consequential changes, the General Board of the company decided, on advice from the division, to stop manufacture of cups and grilles completely, to close the Lower Foundry on the grounds that it was an uneconomic operation, and to merge the cup assembly plant with one of its foreign competitors, who soon closed the British assembly plant down. The works and divisional management did not feel able to support any representations or counter-arguments made by the change team after the decision had been taken, and no strategy for improvement was ever tested in practice. Instead, the change team was able to observe from a distance the ensuing process of redundancy among staff and management and learn from the observation of this process some further facts about organisations and organisational behaviour. The investigation had helped establish the methods of inquiry and helped the team to acquire certain expertise and understanding, but its impact outside the team was virtually nil, and there were of course a few suspicions elsewhere in the company that the inquiry was itself partly responsible for the closure.

In the Press Room, for reasons which we hope will be analysed in more detail elsewhere, the investigating team (of which the local manager and supervisor and supporting specialist managers were members) continued to express interest in and agreement with the systems analysis and the model of behaviour it proposed. They had some reservations, due not so much to disagreement about accuracy, or about assessment of consequences, as to different perceptions about the legitimacy of the consequential behaviour patterns and the legitimacy of the actions being suggested to improve the situation. The investigation had, moreover, been set a task by the works manager, and had a timetable for achievement. Members of the project team perceived themselves to be under pressure to make proposals and recommendations on time, particularly those for capital expenditure. The works manager was conscious of the urgency of meeting the market situation. He had not been involved in the discussions leading up to the proposed entry of the change programme into his works, and did not know a great deal about its objectives. Although he had welcomed the attachment of members of the change team to his existing project team, he saw them as likely to make an expert contribution to the work of the team, rather than to be the stimulus towards more general

change in the way his works would be managed. He did not therefor
change, or expect to have changed, the terms of reference for the project c
his methods of control of it.

For reasons of this kind the project team decided not to use a strategy fc
implementation that arose wholly out of the system analysis, but to go for
somewhat modified mechanical and industrial engineering approacl
This involved a number of proposals for technical innovation, consistin
mainly of the provision of dust extraction and better ventilation equip
ment, additional sawing and pleating equipment and some automati
conveyors, mainly designed to improve working conditions and increas
the capacity of the plant around the presshead. The specialist mechanic;
engineers on the team undertook the design and reported back to the tea»
with their proposals, costed in the usual way.

At the same time, inquiries were made into the possibility of improvin
raw material quality, in cooperation with the manufacturing an
technical departments and for this inquiry operators were required t
complete forms identifying the batch of raw materials they were using an
describing its characteristics in relation to the products they wer
producing, as an aid to redefinition of quality by the technical departmer
and eventually to discuss with the producing department ways (
improving average quality. The reason for these forms was explained to th
operators though they were not involved in their design, nor in decidin
the kind of data required.

When outline capital proposals were complete, a fairly large con
munications exercise was initiated by the project team in which th
departmental manager was closely involved. Meetings were held at th
start or the end of shifts to explain to those concerned what the proposa
were and ask for comments and suggestions on the plans for new layou
and equipment. Comments received were then discussed by members (
the team but were found to be rather unhelpful.

As was explained to the men in the information sessions, it was envisage
that new manning levels and new pay systems would be introduced, bt
details would have to await the advice of the industrial engineers after th
equipment was designed in detail. These would be implemented when th
equipment was installed. However, the Works Manager was insisting th;
something must be done quickly to expand output and a recruiting driv
took place to re-man the department temporarily with three-man team
The senior foreman continued to argue against the interim recruitmer
policy and in order to overcome his perceived obstructionism, r(
sponsibility for hiring and firing was taken away from him and given to th
subordinate day foreman.

Subsequently it was noticed that rates of labour turnover, absence, id
time and lateness were increasing, and means of tackling these problen
were vigorously sought. The project team took the opportunity presente
by a newly negotiated central wage agreement to recommend an interi
system of pay for the Press Room giving a considerably higher wage for th

work they were doing with fewer causes for fluctuation. Once this was introduced, the department manager tightened discipline: men were suspended or dismissed for absence and other breaches of discipline, and standards of recruitment raised, until the manager felt he had got rid of the poor quality labour in the department.

Meanwhile, production began to rise to meet the demands of the market and the effect of this was reinforced by a change in warehousing policy and more discrimination in marketing policy. Finally, the new equipment was installed and new manning arrangements were completed. Despite commissioning problems little difficulty has subsequently been reported in meeting market requirements. It is not possible to discover how the costs, in monetary terms or in terms of employee satisfaction, of the increase in production compare with the potential costs of implementing a strategy based more clearly on the implications of the systems model. The project team's approach was obviously a good one in orthodox terms. It was seen by the project team and by senior management to have been very successful, to have taken a much broader view of the problem than usual and to have introduced quite a new element into change, in the form of the communications sessions with the men concerned, to which considerable emphasis was given by the project team.

The Press Room, then, resulted in a specific improvement, but the expected learning by local managers and project team members, and the hoped-for spread of change did not occur in the way expected. The management members of the project team expressed interest in many of the concepts arising from the open socio-technical systems framework, but for a number of reasons declined to make full use of them, and so (whatever the eventual success of the project in terms of increased output) they failed to learn much from, or to confirm the usefulness of, the new ideas by going through the whole process of applying them.

Senior management in the works were pleased with the outcome of the project, which met their expectations, and they gave full credit to the contribution of the change team towards its success; but the messages the works manager received from the project team were not new ones. In other words they were not requests for more discretion, were not reports of new understanding of behaviour or new concepts of management, and did not include reports about either experiments actually to involve subordinates, or the growth in skill and understanding of individual managers and supervisors. The behaviour of higher levels of management was therefore not affected as a result of implementation, and there was no reason why management style, or modes of decision-making or authority relations, should change, since apparent success had been achieved within the present modes. Everyone from the works manager to the local departmental manager (but excepting the senior foreman and some members from the central change team) was in a sense confirmed in his existing behaviour patterns, and in his perception of the change programme and the roles of its members as specialists in analysis, by what appeared to be the success of the innovations made.

The change programme did gain approval for what the works manage saw as its peculiar contribution—stimulation of the project team into usin a wide, interdisciplinary approach to the investigation, basing th innovations on a wider range of facts than usual and introducing programme of formal communication to the men before the changes wer introduced. The Press Room experience was good for the standing of th programme in the company, but as there was no accompanying spinoff i terms of changed behaviour, the satisfaction it produced could have bee positively harmful for the spread of its wider aims.

The outcome of change in the Finishing Shop is perhaps mor interesting. This was one of the earliest departments examined by th change team, and for reasons connected with the institution of th programme the local managers and supervisors were not closely involve in the inquiry or model-building exercises. Only at a rather late stage (afte the initial study had been made and ideas about strategy very full discussed) did the company grant permission to involve local managers i the implementation of the ideas. The change team then instituted a fairl well-coordinated programme to involve all those concerned. First they fe back the findings of the inquiry report to local managers, invited thei comments and instituted a long series of discussion meetings with them i which the Finishing Shop model was discussed, together with many nev ideas and concepts from social science texts about the managemer process. In parallel with these discussions, and with the full agreement the local managers, the supervisors and shop stewards in the area met in rather more abbreviated series of meetings with the same basis information and discussed some of the same concepts. Initial enthusias was aroused in both groups about the possibility of introducing a ne system of work and of relationships into the operation of the shop, an about the possible outcomes.

At this time the discussions were always led by members of the centr change team who had undertaken the study. However, no ideas about strategy for change were put to any of the parties, though some of th problems of change in the shop, including pay systems, problems redundancy and capital expenditure, were brought up and discussec Towards the end of the series the suggestion was made to local manage that this must be their programme, and that whatever changes were mad as a result of the discussions they would take responsibility. Immediatel two managers closely concerned with the shop threatened to walk out fror the discussions on the grounds that, like all consultants, the change tean having made their recommendations and committed local managers to new, high risk and possibly ill-thought out policy, got out from under an left the local people exposed to all the ensuing risks. This reactio predictable though it probably should have been, had not in fact bee predicted and it was one of the more striking indications which made th team realise the effects of company culture on the possibilities of chang

'he change team had carefully to re-explain the basis of the programme
nd to give assurances that one of its functions was to continue to lend
apport to the managers with advice and help, and particularly to support
aem in relations with higher levels of management in the works. Finally, a
ather more cautious level of enthusiasm was achieved and the managers
greed to go along with the idea of implementation of improvements which
aey recognised were based on the new understanding they had obtained of
ae needs of the shop.

Next, meetings were held in the local mess room with all the workers in
ae shop. Here initial hostility and scepticism was met, which changed to
auted enthusiasm when the men recognised that for the first time the
aanagers were demonstrating an ability to communicate and apparently
) understand the problems of work in the shop and were prepared to
onsider changes on the basis of this understanding. The men began
uickly to contribute ideas and make explicit their thinking about the
roblems, which in its turn helped to confirm in managers' minds the basic
orrectness of the explanatory model.

From this time on, the managers worked together with the change team
) evolve their own plans for implementation. It soon appeared that they
ad been impressed with the response of the supervisors and shopfloor
epresentatives, and with the willingness of the men to help in solving the
roblems of the shop. They agreed that a programme of implementation
hould involve supervisors and that there should be continuous con-
ultation with shopfloor representatives. Subordinate involvement, then,
carted right at the beginning of the implementation process, and was not
onfined, as in the suggested strategy of chapter 12, to discussion of specific
oints such as quality control and reject rates.

It soon became clear that the men's representatives were concerned
bout engineering faults on the plant and its maintenance provision,
raining, the pay structure, and means of effecting the foreseen reduction in
aumbers. As a result of the discussions it was decided to give first priority to
mprovement of plant, and a fairly prolonged battle was fought with senior
nanagement to get approval for a certain amount of capital expenditure
equired to make the plant more reliable and engineering maintenance
nore effective and more economic. Delays occurring in this almost led to
lemotivation on both sides. The capital expenditure was however finally
pproved. Interim changes were made in the pay of conveyor men and
olishers and at the same time the managers, under some influence from
deas about autonomous work groups, suggested that more flexibility
vould be secured if the grinders had more responsibility to decide their
verall patterns of activity. It was agreed that the production scheduling
or the shop should be put in the hands of the grinders and that they should
e given the necessary information about the requirements of the
ustomer.

Two things limited the potential benefits of autonomous production
cheduling. First, so as not to make the scheduling criteria too complicated

for them, the men were provided only with the requirements of the fina
warehouse over the next two weeks, and allowed only limited choice as t
the best patterns of production to achieve these requirements. Little wa
therefore achieved in the way of lengthening production runs or reducin
the medium-term fluctuations in the load to which the shop was subjec
More important, the production planning manager of the factory had nc
been involved in the decision to hand this responsibility over, and he knev
little of the thinking behind it. It later became apparent that he ha
resented being deprived of a job hitherto perceived to be a highly technica
one, was convinced that the experiment could not succeed, and saw littl
reason to go out of his way to help the shop out of any difficulties that arose
The management team had not paid much attention to the complicate
patterns of communication between customer, warehouse, productio
planner and Finishing Shop which had facilitated flexibility in planning t
meet changing customer needs; the production planner religiously kept t
his old communications channels; the warehouse manager did not realis
the implications of the new productive scheduling system for his ow
liaison with the shop, and on occasion urgent orders from the customer, c
urgent changes in his requirements, failed to be passed on to the grinder
The customer began to make loud complaints for which the grinders too
the blame. Fortunately the continuing discussions during the implemer
tation process helped to identify the customer's problems and the causes fc
this and procedures were modified. The production planner then becam
more involved in the whole implementation process, which was by th
time spreading to neighbouring departments in the works.

Wider revision of the pay structure continued to cause problems. Th
senior management could not contemplate grinders' pay rising further ou
of line with the rest of the works. The discussions, and the change proces
itself, therefore had to continue slowly while means were found of allowin
movement in pay to take place. Problems over future manning leve
however seemed at first to be surprisingly easily disposed off. The men i
the shop had had long experience of periodic redundancy and redeploy
ment and proffered the information that, provided satisfactory monetar
compensation were forthcoming, enough people would be willing to leav
the shop voluntarily to avoid the need for any forced redundancy. Pay
however, was again an obstacle, since official company policies o
redundancy pay were inadequate and senior managers did not feel able t
create a precedent by offering greater monetary inducements either for th
or for men to accept redeployment to rather less well-paid jobs elsewhere i
the factory. Concepts of legitimacy again arose here. The consequences c
the present situation were recognised, but the legitimacy of the grinder
reactions were not, nor was the legitimacy of any policy that coul
compensate them for loss of earnings to which they were not seen to b
entitled.

While these two problems remained in abeyance other moves wer
continuing. More attention was paid to training; the inspectors an

ackers were brought more closely under the control of the chargehands, while retaining their present pay rates; and occupational flexibility was increased. Further, in order to demonstrate their own commitment to the process, and as an earnest of their appreciation for the men's cooperation, the local management team gave a guarantee that until the pay and redundancies problem was solved there would be no further recruitment into the shop. Unfortunately this guarantee coincided more or less exactly with one of the unpredictable fluctuations in the product market, in the form of a rise in demand against the seasonal trend, lasting for several months. Bound by its undertaking, the management of the shop had no option but to increase the overtime hours available very considerably, to the point where for many weeks grinders were earning £8 a week overtime or more (a large sum at the rates ruling at that period).

Finally, pay proposals satisfactory to both junior and senior management were worked out, and a new pay structure put to the men's representatives. The work-studied system of piece rates was to be abolished in favour of an output bonus that would permit an increase of at least £2 a week over present weekly earnings (without overtime), and would give management considerably higher output. However the men rejected with some contempt the idea of giving up their existing £8 a week overtime pay for an extra £2 on weekly pay to produce the same amount, and at this point the whole programme exploded in a dispute in which the management team felt wholly let down by the men's representatives, and the latter felt that the concept of the programme, as they had been led to understand it, had degenerated into a normal bargaining situation with management attempting to gain production at the expense of earnings. Again, contrasting perceptions of the situation became explicit, and as a result feelings ran so high on both sides that they were counselled to allow matters to cool off for some weeks before making further approaches. The local managers, who had withstood considerable force of attack from their superiors about the levels of overtime in the shop, now felt able to recruit additional grinders and bring overtime back to normal.

In the end the discussions were taken up again, but further reorganisation of the shop and further increases in output per man became relatively unimportant. The shop has continued to operate, with better and more cooperative attitudes, and much better understanding between manager and subordinates than previously, but the overall improvement in costs and efficiency had been rather disappointing, as compared with the potential at one time foreseen.

The Finishing Shop outcome illustrates a number of points: the fact that a careful and perhaps conservative strategy, properly devised and monitored, may be necessary if the risk of disillusion and reversion to even worse attitudes is to be prevented; the need to monitor the environment, both in the rest of the organisation (the production planner) and in the product and labour markets; and the possibility that it will be necessary to involve senior levels of management in the whole process of model-

building and understanding from the beginning if they are ever to b
influenced, and if they are to be persuaded to support and provide facilitie
when they are most needed. One question that arises in all three cases (bu
with particular clarity in the Lower Foundry) is whether it is enough eve
to involve senior levels in the works, or whether factory management ma
find themselves inhibited from lending support to new ventures by th
prohibitions on them from divisional and company levels. The process c
procuring departmental improvement is not as simple as our theories a
first suggested. We have in the open socio-technical systems approach
means of obtaining better understanding of what is going on within
department, and we have shown how what is going on might be changed i
a desired direction, and reactions to the change monitored an
controlled—given the right external conditions. But we have apparentl
given insufficient thought to how to influence these external conditions an
ensure they are propitious.

* * * * * * * *

Let us therefore summarise the whole import of this book and see wha
place the processes we have outlined hold in a larger programme c
organisational change. There are three points in particular we would hop
to have demonstrated

(1) The open socio-technical systems approach to investigation is
valuable one and provides insights not otherwise available into th
complicated causal system: the way various factors generate attitudes
conflicts, values and relations between people, and how these influenc
patterns of behaviour and facets of performance in comparatively smal
industrial systems. It provides, we believe, more adequate explanation
than other developed approaches. It certainly seems to indicate that eve
small departments using fairly simple technologies can exhibit com
plexities in their interactions far greater than is normally suspected.

(2) The techniques described in parts III and IV are again derive
from open socio-technical systems ideas. They are potentially useful an
soundly based tools which, given the appropriate supporting mechanisms
can help achieve improvements in departmental performance, and at th
same time advances in local management skill. But the environmenta
circumstances must be such that they can be applied successfully. It ma
often be that some of these circumstances must be created through othe
mechanisms available from the wider change programme.

(3) There is a great deal in our original conception that organis
ational change should be effected via identification of the needs of th
workface, and that these are best identified through detailed investigation
using a socio-technical approach. To bring about organisational chang
there must also be some mechanism for spread of the ideas. The origina
scheme included such a mechanism and we have described it in chapter 1

However, it may be necessary to construct on its foundations a rather more complete set of mechanisms for inducing broader change, such that means other than rational arguments are available to persuade, influence or otherwise operate on the organisational power structure and to change established interdepartmental and interstratum relationships and to influence the perspectives of individual managers or members of established project teams.[1]

There are thus a considerable number of important positive attributes in the overall approach to change we have described—attributes that distinguish the approach from most other organisational change programmes. There are, however, aspects of induced change that we have not dealt with in any detail in this book, and the fact that in the three cases analysed here the implementation as it affected the wider change programme was rather ineffective is an indication that a considerable time went by before we managed even approximately to integrate all these mechanisms into the larger programme.

In the first place the process of implementing departmental improvements using rather unorthodox theories and methods is risky for local managers; its outcome is problematic and there are cases in which the projected improvements never eventuate. When this happens, the hoped-for consequences—self-sustaining behavioural change, reinforcement of learning and spread of ideas throughout the company through example, or via the processes of 'cell division' already touched on—cannot be effective. Local managers need to be strongly supported and protected from these risks. Secondly, it may be difficult to get managers or project teams (more resistant, say, than the Press Room team) to accept that the socio-technical approach has anything to offer that is relevant and not already known; or to get more senior managers to agree to open their areas to detailed investigation, with its attendant risks of uncovering some areas of serious inefficiency or apparent incompetence, or to accept that to pay attention to specific social or psychological problems does not necessarily make the shop floor personnel 'big-headed' or exhibitionist. Members of the change team need counselling skills and the ability to persuade and influence their colleagues when they meet these resistances.[2] Thirdly, it is often difficult to induce any upward spread of change in relationships to take place, even from the most successful departmental improvements, because of features of wider organisational culture. The change team has to find some means of operating in the wider organisation to influence it and to make it more supportive to change. For this it may need to possess and to exploit a source of political power.[3]

An examination of the relation between improvement in individual departments and wider organisational change, and the many lessons for implementation of the change programme which this relation seems to bring out, must be one of the main themes of a later work. At one level some of the experiences we have reported may be perceived as failures. They certainly failed to effect rapid, or wide changes in style and relationships in the factories in question. In two of the cases there was little resultant change in attitude or behaviour even among local managers concerned Experiences such as these should however lead to advances in the conceptual basis of the wider programme since they force us to look again at the extent of our understanding of organisational behaviour and at the adequacy of the original concepts, and to consider what new mechanism are needed to promote wider changes.

The slow rate of progress in wider organisational change seems to be due to a number of circumstances. Cultural change is inevitably slow especially in a stable and well-integrated system that has not hitherto experienced strong pressure to change. There may inevitably be an initia lacuna in the processes of designing a large change programme, in that it i impossible to define clearly the culture of an organisation or it characteristic modes of behaviour and control, before the programme itself has got under way and made some progress. The way the organisation i likely to react to the stimulus of attempts to change it has to be known to those concerned before they can prepare to deal effectively with it.

In its initial conception, therefore, this programme may have lacked the relevant mechanisms for dealing adequately with the power structure of the organisation, or for influencing the perspectives of those whose suppor it needed. We are in a sense in a vicious circle in that if it is to be effectiv the design of a change programme can only take place when the cultur and power system and modes of behaviour of the wider organisation ar fully understood; but that these features cannot be properly understood until some processes of change have been introduced and the reaction observed. An avoidable defect of this programme may have been tha decisions were made to use the fairly sophisticated methods of approac outlined in chapter 1 before a full and critical consideration had been give to the cultural reactions already noted at the pilot stage, and that our idea of implementation and dispersion were not modified soon enough i relation to the message we were being given about that culture. But this i something that comes from hindsight.

There is however an interesting point here about change programmes c this kind. The self-critical point of view just expressed may in fact be a ver arrogant one. What we have been implying is that we, representing th change team and its academic associates, may devise ways to induc change in, say, a works, or part of a works, which goes against the implie wishes of those in control of the works; or in the company as a whole whic goes against the implied wishes of the chief decision-makers or the mos influential controllers of sources of power and influence in th company—implied in so far as present modes of behaviour of those peop are an indication of what they want from their part of the organisatio Despite what they may state, those at senior levels may indicate by thei modes of behaviour that they do not want the culture to change, or do no want new styles of management to prevail or do not even wan improvement in performance. If it comes to a choice they may prefer the present degree of inefficiency, accompanied by present modes of relationships, to high performance at the expense of a change in authority structure and relationships.

So a determined drive by a company change team to make this kind of programme really effective may be a case of the programme taking over and having an existence and a force of its own, distinct from the actual wishes of those who have created it; and of the programme seeking ways to override the culture of the larger organisation despite resistance by those in powerful positions in it. There is a probability if it is really effective that it sets in motion a sequence of changes that are alien to what the creators of the programme intended, and either sweeps them along on an irresistible tide of change or has to be killed before it destroys the relationships they want to preserve. There is however an opposite danger, that if it is ineffective the whole programme will become discredited and treated as of little consequence, to the disadvantage of the members of the programme. Once involved in a programme of change, team members are in a dilemma. It is necessary to be effective, but not so dramatically effective that someone recognises it as having serious potential for harm and takes drastic action to suppress it. But is it possible to moderate effectiveness?

One question should therefore be asked (to which we still have no answer) when considering such cases as the Lower Foundry, the Press Room and the Finishing Shop. This is whether it is possible to gauge the seriousness with which the decision-makers in the company have treated the decision to institute a change programme and what motives they had for instituting it. Alternatively, one might question the understanding they had about the nature of the programme they had agreed to establish and about the calls that programme would make on them for support if it was to be effective in producing changes. These questions have to be examined at length, and our sequel will attempt to make some examination of them on the basis of actual experiences during the course of the programme.

Organisational change, we have confirmed, is enormously complicated and many faceted. The aspects we have dealt with in this book constitute part of the technology of change, but technology is no more the whole of a programme of change than workplace technology is the whole of an industrial organisation. Appropriate technology is important for success, and deserves careful study and design, provided at the same time the design is made to fit with the other requirements of the programme, and that enough attention is paid to the design of these other requirements, and their integration into the whole open system that is constituted by the change programme itself. It is this total system that remains to be analysed in a further work examining the development and history of the wider change programme.

NOTES TO CHAPTER 15

1. Pettigrew (1975a) has recently proposed a model of specialist activity applicable to intervention programmes, that has considerable potential in it representation of some dimensions of the change team's broader problems

2. For a discussion of some of the sources of stress on the members of an internal change team such as this, see Warmington (1975). The situation as seen by a internal specialist had also been discussed by Goldner (1967).

3. This aspect of programmes of induced change has until recently been much neglected in the literature on intervention and it appears not to have bee seen as legitimate to discuss it in public, although all the more successful 'change agents' and interventionists have long realised its importance However, a recent paper by Pettigrew (1975b) has begun to redress th balance.

Bibliographical References

Anthony, R. N. (1965). *Planning and Control Systems: A Framework for Analysis* (Boston: Harvard University Press)

Arenberg, C. M., Barkin, S., Chalmers, W. E., Wilensky, H. L., Worthy, J. C., Dennis, B. D. (eds.) (1957). *Research in Industrial Human Relations* (New York, Harper and Row)

Argyris, C. (1962). *Interpersonal Competence and Organizational Effectiveness* (Homewood, Ill.: Irwin-Dorsey)

Argyris, C. (1964). *Integrating the Individual and the Organization* (New York: Wiley)

Argyris, C. (1967). Today's Problems with Tomorrow's Organisations, *Journal of Management Studies* **4**, (1), 31−55

Argyris, C. (1968). Some Unintended Consequences of Rigorous Research, *Psychological Bulletin* **70**, 185−197

Argyris, C. (1970). *Intervention Theory and Method* (Reading, Mass.: Addison-Wesley)

Arrow, K. J. (1964). Control in Large Organisations, *Management Science* **10**, (3), 397−408

Barth, F. (1966). *Models of Social Organisation* (London: Royal Anthropological Society)

Beckhard, R. (1969). *Organization Development: Strategies and Models* (Reading, Mass.: Addison-Wesley)

Becker, S. W. (1970). The Parable of the Pill, *Administrative Science Quarterly* **15**, 94−96

Beer, S. (1972). *The Brain of the Firm: The Managerial Cybernetics of Organization* (London: Allen Lane)

Bennis, W. G. (1966). *Changing Organizations: Essays on the Development and Evaluation of Human Organisation* (New York: McGraw-Hill)

Bennis, W. G., Benne, K. D., Chin, R. (eds.) (1969). *The Planning of Change* Second Edition (London: Holt, Rinehart and Winston)

Bertalanffy, L. von (1968). *General Systems Theory: Foundations Development, Applications* (New York: Braziller)

Bier, T. E. (1972). Organization Development as a Third-party Influence, *European Training* **1**, 171−175

Blake, R. R., Mouton, J. S. Barnes, L. B., Greiner, L. E. (1964). Breakthrough in Organization Development, *Harvard Business Review* **42**, (6), 133−155

Blau, P. M. (1955). *The Dynamics of Bureaucracy* (Chicago: University of Chicago Press)

Blau, P. M. (1964). *Exchange and Power in Social Life* (New York: Wiley

Blau, P. M. and Scott, W. (1963). *Formal Organisations* (London Routledge and Kegan Paul)

Blauner, R. (1964). *Alienation and Freedom* (Chicago: University of Chicago Press)

Braybrook, D. and Lindblom, C. E. (1963). *A Strategy of Decision* (New York: Free Press)

Brimm, M. (1972). Comment on an article by Beer and Huse in *Journal of Applied Behavioural Science* **8**, (1), 102–107

Buckley, W. (1967). *Sociology and Modern Systems Theory* (Englewood Cliffs N. J.: Prentice-Hall)

Burgoyne, J. G. and Cooper, C. L. (1975). Evaluation Methodology *Journal of Occupational Psychology* **48**, (1), 53–62

Burns, T. (1961). Micropolitics: Mechanisms of Institutional Change *Administrative Science Quarterly* **6**, (3), 257–281

Burns, T. (1966). 'On the Plurality of Social Systems' in J. R. Lawrence (ed.), *Operational Research and the Social Sciences* (London: Tavistock 165–177

Burns, T. (1967). 'The Comparative Study of Organisations' in V. Vroom (ed.), *Methods of Social Research* (Pittsburgh: University of Pittsburgh Press, 113–170)

Burns, T. and Stalker, G. M. (1961). *The Management of Innovation* (London: Tavistock)

Carter, E. E. (1971). The Behavioural Theory of the Firm and Top Level Corporate Decisions, *Administrative Science Quarterly* **16**, 413–428

Charnes, A. and Stedry, A. C. (1966). 'The Attainment of Organization Goals through Appropriate Selection of Subunit Goals' in J. R Lawrence (ed.), *Operational Research and the Social Sciences* (London Tavistock) 147–164

Chin, R. and Benne, K. D. (1969). 'General Strategies for Effecting Changes in Human Systems' in W. G. Bennis, K. D. Benne and R. Chin (eds.), *The Planning of Change* Second Edition (London: Holt, Rinehart and Winston, 32–59

Cooper, W. W., Leavitt, H. L. and Shelley, M. W., (eds.) (1964). *New Perspectives in Organization Research* (New York: Wiley)

Cyert, R. M. and March, J. G. (1963). *A Behavioural Theory of the Firm* (Englewood Cliffs, N. J.: Prentice-Hall)

Dalton, G. W. (1970). 'Influence and Organisational Change' in G. W Dalton, P. R. Lawrence and L. E. Greiner (eds.), *Organizational Change and Development* (Homewood, Ill.: Irwin-Dorsey) 230–258

Dalton, G. W., Lawrence, P. R. and Lorsch, J. (eds.) (1970). *Organizational Structure and Design* (Homewood, Ill.: Irwin-Dorsey)

Dalton, G. W., Lawrence, P. R. and Greiner, L. E. (eds.) (1970) *Organisational Change and Development* (Homewood, Ill.: Irwin-Dorsey

Davis, L. E. and Taylor, J. C. (eds.) (1972). *The Design of Job* (Harmondsworth: Penguin Books)

Dubin, R. (1958). *The World of Work* (Englewood Cliffs, N. J.: Prentice-Hall)

Easton, D. (ed.) (1966). *Varieties of Political Theory* (Englewood Cliffs, N. J.: Prentice-Hall)

Emery, F. E. and Trist, E. L. (1960). 'Socio-Technical Systems' in C. W. Churchman and M. Verhuist (eds.), *Management Science Models and Techniques* (Oxford: Pergamon)

Emery, F. E. and Trist, E. L. (1965). The Causal Texture of Organizational Environments, *Human Relations*, **8**, (1), 21–32

Etzioni, A. (1960). Two Approaches to Organizational Analysis: A Critique and a Suggestion, *Administrative Science Quarterly* **5**, 257–278

Etzioni, A. (1961). *A Comparative Analysis of Complex Organization* (New York: Macmillan)

Etzioni, A. (1964). *Modern Organisations* (Englewood Cliffs, N. J.:Prentice-Hall)

Foster, M. (1972). An Introduction to the Theory and Practice of Action Research in Work Organisation, *Human Relations* **25**, (6), 529–551

Fox, A. (1966). *Industrial Sociology and Industrial Relations* (Royal Commission on Trade Unions . . . Research Paper No. 3) (London: HMSO)

Gagné, R. M. (1965). *The Conditions of Learning* (New York: Holt, Rinehart and Winston)

Galbraith, J. R. (1969). *Organisation Design: An Information Processing View* (Alfred P. Sloane, School of Management Mimeographed)

Galbraith, J. R. (1971). Matrix Organisation Designs, *Business Horizons* **3**, (4), 29–39

Glueck, W. F. (1969). Organizational Change in Business and Government, *Academy of Management Journal* **12**, (4), 439–449

Georgopoulos, B. S. and Tannenbaum, A. S. (1957). A Study of Organizational Effectiveness, *American Sociol. Review*, **22** (3), 534–40

Goldner, F. H. (1967). 'Role Emergence and the Ethics of Ambiguity' in G. Sjöberg, *Ethics, Politics and Social Research* (London: Routledge and Kegan Paul)

Goldner, F. H. (1970). 'The Division of Labour: Process and Power' in M. N. Zald, *Power in Organisations* (Vanderbilt University)

Golombiewski, R. R., Mouzenrider, R., Blumberg, A. Stokes, B. C., Mead, W. R. (1971). Changing Climate in a Complex Organisation, *Academy of Management Journal* **14**, 465–481

Goode, W. J. (1960). A Theory of Role Strain, *American Sociological Review* **25**, 483–496

Gouldner, A. W. (1954). *Patterns of Industrial Bureaucracy* (New York: Free Press)

Gouldner, A. W. (1959). 'Organisational Analysis' in R. K. Merton, L. Broom and L. S. Cottrell (eds.), *Sociology Today* (New York: Basic Books), 400–427

Gowler, D. (1969). The Determinants of the Supply of Labour to the Firm, *Journal of Management Studies* **6**, (1), 73–95

Gowler, D. (1974). Values, Contracts and Job Satisfaction, *Personnel Review* **3**, (4), 4–14

Gowler, D. and Legge, K. (1970). 'The Wage Payment Systems: A Primary Infrastructure' in D. Robinson, (ed.) *Local Labour Markets and Wage Structures* (London: Gower), 168–214

Gowler, D. and Legge, K. (1972). Occupational Role Development Part 1 *Personnel Review* **1**, (2)

Gowler, D. and Legge, K. (1973). 'Perceptions, The Principle of Cumulation and the Supply of Labour' in M. Warner, (ed.) *The Sociology of the Workplace* (London: Allen and Unwin) 116–148

Gowler, D. and Legge, K. (eds.) (1975). *Managerial Stress* (London: Gower Press)

Greiner, L. E. (1967). Patterns of Organization Change, *Harvard Business Review* **45**, (3), 119–130

Greiner, L. E. (1972). Red Flags in Organisation Development, *Business Horizons* **4**, (3), 17–24

Greiner, L. E. and Barnes, L. B. (1970). 'Organization Change and Development' in G. W. Dalton, P. R. Lawrence and L. E. Greiner (eds.) *Organizational Change and Development* (Homewood Ill.: Irwin Dorsey)

Gross, E. (1970). The Definition of Organizational Goals, *British Journal of Sociology* **21**, (1) 227–295

Guest, R. H. (1962). *Organizational Change: The Effect of Successful Leadership* (London: Tavistock)

Herzberg, F. (1966) *Work and the Nature of Man* (World Publishing)

Hickson, D. J., Hinings, C. R., Lee, C. A., Schnek, R. E., and Pennings, J. M. (1971). A Strategic Contingencies Theory of Intraorganisational Power, *Administrative Science Quarterly* **16**, (2), 216–229

Hinings, C. R., Hickson, D. J., Pennings, J. M. and Schnek, R. E. (1974). Structural Conditions of Intraorganizational Power, *Administrative Management* **19**, 22–44

Jones, R. S. (1969). The Control of Complex Work Organisations *Management Decision* **7**, 6–11

Jones, R. S. (1971). The Pathology of Success, *Management Decision* **9** 224–232

Kahn, R. L. (1974). Organizational Development: Some Problems and Proposals, *Journal of Applied Behavioural Science* **10**, (4), 485–502

Kapferer, B. (1972). *Strategy and Transaction in an African Factory*, (Manchester: University Press)

Kaplan, A. (1964). *The Conduct of Inquiry: Methodology for Behavioural Science* (Scranton, Pa.: Chandler)

Katz, D. and Kahn, R. L. (1966). *The Social Psychology of Organisations* (New York: Wiley)

Lawrence, P. R. and Lorsch, J. W. (1967). *Organisation and Environment Managing Differentiation and Integration* (Boston: Harvard University Press)

Lawrence, P. R. and Lorsch, J. W. (1969). *Developing Organisations: Diagnosis and Action* (Reading, Mass.: Addison-Wesley)

Leavitt, H. J. (1962). Unhuman Organisations, *Harvard Business Review*, **40**, 90–98

Leavitt, H. J. (ed.) (1963). *The Social Science of Organizations* (Englewood Cliffs, N. J.: Prentice-Hall)

Leavitt, H. J. (1964). Applied Organisational Change in Industry: Structural, Technical and Human Approaches, in W. W. Cooper, H. L. Leavitt and M. W. Shelley (eds.), *New Perspectives in Organizational Research* (New York: Wiley) 55–71

Legge, K. (1970). The Operation of the Regressive Spiral in the Labour Market, *Journal of Management Studies* **7**, (1), 1–22

Likert, R. (1958). Measuring Organizational Performance, *Harvard Business Review* **36**, (2), 41–50

Likert, R. (1961). *New Patterns of Management* (New York: McGraw-Hill)

Likert, R. (1967). *The Human Organization* (New York: McGraw-Hill)

Lindblom, C. E. (1959). The Science of Muddling Through, *Public Administration Review* XIX (2), 79–88

Lindblom, C. E. (1964). Contexts for Change and Strategy: A Reply, *Public Administration Review* XXIV, (3)

Litwin, G. H. and Stringer, R. A. (1968). *Motivation and Organizational Climate* (Boston: Harvard University Press)

Lorsch, J. W. and Allen, S. E. (1973). *Managing Diversity and Interdependence: An Organisational Study of Multi-divisional Firms* (Boston: Harvard University Press)

Lorsch, J. W. and Lawrence, P. R. (1970). *Studies in Organisation Design* (Homewood, Ill.: Irwin-Dorsey)

Lupton, T. (1963). *On the Shopfloor* (Oxford: Pergamon)

Lupton, T. (1969). Wage Drift, Productivity Drift and Managerial Strategy, *Management Decision,* **7**

Lupton, T. (1971a). *Management and the Social Sciences* (Harmondsworth: Penguin)

Lupton, T. (1971b). Organisation Change: Top-down or Botton-up Management? *Personnel Review* **1**, (1), 22–28

Lupton, T. and Warmington, W. A. (1973). *A System Approach to Determining the Criteria for Successful Change in the Context of a Particular Action Research Programme* Working Paper No. 6 (Manchester Business School)

McGregor, D. (1960). *The Human Side of Enterprise* (New York: McGraw-Hill)

McGregor, D. (1967). *The Professional Manager* (New York: McGraw-Hill)

Mann, F. C. (1957). 'Studying and Creating Change: A Means to Understand Social Organisation' in C. M. Arenberg, *et al.* (eds.) *Research in Industrial Human Relations* (New York: Harper and Row) 146–167

March, J. G. (ed.) (1965). *Handbook of Organizations* (Chicago: Rand

McNally)

March, J. G. (1966). 'The Power of Power' in D. Easton (ed.) *Varieties of Political Theory* (Englewood Cliffs, N. J.: Prentice-Hall) 39–70

March, J. G. and Simon, H. A. (1958). *Organisations* (New York: Wiley)

Mechanic, D. (1962). The Sources of Power of Lower Participants in Complex Organisations, *Administrative Science Quarterly* 7, 349–364

Merton, R. K. (1957). *Social Theory and Social Structure* (Glencoe, Illinois)

Merton, R. K., Broom, L. and Cottrell, L. S. (eds.) (1959). *Sociology Today* (New York: Basic Books)

Miller, E. J. and Rice, A. K. (1967). *Systems of Organisation* (London: Tavistock)

Mills, A. E. (1967). *The Dynamics of Management Control Systems* (London: Business Publications)

Morse, J. J. and Lorsch, J. W. (1970). Beyond Theory Y, *Harvard Business Review* 48, (3), 61–68

Mumford, E. (1972). *Job Satisfaction: A Study of Computer Specialists* (London: Longman)

Myrdal, G. (1958). *Value in Social Theory* (London: Routledge and Kegan Paul)

Myrdal, G. (1969). *Objectivity in Social Research* (London: Duckworth)

Parsons, T. (1960). *Structure and Process in Modern Societies* (New York: Free Press)

Perrow, C. (1961). The Analysis of Goals in Complex Organizations, *American Sociological Review* 26, 854–866

Perrow, C. (1967). A Framework for the Comparative Analysis of Organizations, *American Sociological Review* 32, 194–208

Perrow, C. (1970a). *Organisational Analysis: A Sociological View* (London: Tavistock)

Perrow, C. (1970b). 'Departmental Power and Perspective in Industrial Firms' in M. Zald, (ed.) *Power in Organizations* (Vanderbilt University)

Perrow, C. (1972). *Complex Organisations: A Critical Essay* (Glanville, Ill.: Scott Foresman)

Pettigrew, A. M. (1975a). Strategic Aspects of the Management of Specialist Activity, *Personnel Review* 4, (1), 5–13

Pettigrew, A. M. (1975b). Towards a Political Theory of Organisational Intervention, *Human Relations* 28, (3), 191–205

Pondy, L. R. (1968). Organisational Conflict: Concepts and Models, *Administrative Science Quarterly* 12, 296–320

Pugh, D. S. (1966). Role Activation Conflict: A Study of Industrial Inspection, *American Sociological Review* 31, 835–842

Pugh, D. S., Hickson, D. J., Hinings, C. R., Macdonald, K. M., Turner, C. and Lupton, T. (1963). A Conceptual Scheme for Organisational Analysis, *Administrative Science Quarterly* 8, 269–315

Pugh, D. S., Hickson, D. J., Hinings, C. R. and Turner, C. (1969). The Context of Organisation Structures, *Administrative Science Quarterly* 14, 91–114

Raia, A. P. (1972). Organizational Development: Some Issues and Challenges, *California Management Review* **14**, (4), 13–20

Rapoport, R. N. (1970). Three Dilemmas in Action Research, *Human Relations* **23**, (6), 499–513

Rice, A. K. (1958). *Productivity and Social Organisation: The Ahmedabad Experiment* (London: Tavistock)

Rice, A. K. (1963). *The Enterprise and its Environment* (London: Tavistock)

Robinson, D. (ed.) (1970). *Local Labour Markets and Wage Structures* (London: Gower Press)

Ross, R. (1971). O. D. For whom? Comment on articles by Hornstein *et al.* and Burke, *Journal of Applied Behavioural Science* **7**, (5), 580–585

Roy, D. (1952). Quota Restriction and Gold Bricking in a Machine Shop, *American Journal of Sociology* **57**, 427–442

Roy, D. (1953). Work Satisfaction and Social Reward in Quota Achievement: An Analysis of Piecework Incentive, *American Sociological Review* **18**

Roy, D. (1955). Efficiency and the Fix: Informal Intergroups Relations in a Piecework Machine Shop, *American Journal of Sociology* **60**, 255–266

Schumacher, P. C. (1971). *Man in Relation to His Work* (Mimeoed)

Scott, W. R. (1965). 'Field Methods in the Study of Organisations' in J. G. March', (ed.) *Handbook of Organizations* (Chicago: Rand McNally)

Seashore, S. E., Indik, B. P. and Georgopoulos, B. S. (1960). Relationships and Criteria of Effective Job Performance, *Journal of Applied Psychology* **14**, 195–202

Selznick, P. (1949). *TVA and the Grass Roots* (Berkeley: University of California Press)

Selznick, P. (1957). *Leadership in Administration* (New York: Harper and Row)

Sills, D. L. (1958). *The Volunteers* (New York: Free Press)

Silverman, D. (1970). *The Theory of Organisations* (London: Heinemann)

Simon, H. A. (1964). On the Concept of Organisational Goal, *Administrative Science Quarterly* **9**, 1–22

Sjöberg, G. (ed.) (1967). *Ethics, Politics and Social Research* (London: Routledge and Kegan Paul)

Strother, G. B. (1963). 'Problems in the Development of a Social Science of Organization' in H. J. Leavitt, (ed.), *The Social Science of Organizations* (Englewood Cliffs, N. J., Prentice-Hall) 1–57

Terreberry, S. (1967). The Evolution of Organizational Environments, *Administrative Science Quarterly* **12**, 590–613

Thomas, J. M. and Bennis, W. G. (eds.) (1972). *The Management of Change and Conflict* (Harmondsworth: Penguin Books)

Thompson, J. D. (1967). *Organizations in Action: Social Science Basis of Administrative Theory* (New York: McGraw-Hill)

Thompson, J. D. and McEwen, W. J. (1958). Organizational Goals and Environment: Goal Setting as an Interaction Process, *American Sociological Review* **23**, (1), 23–31

Tichy, N. (1973). An Analysis of Clique Formation and Structure in Organizations, *Administrative Science Quarterly* **18**, (2), 194–208

Trist, E. L. (1968). 'The Professional Facilitation of Planned Change in Organizations' in *Reviews, Abstracts, Working Groups XVI International Congress of Applied Psychology* – reprinted in V. Vroom and Deci *Management and Motivation* (Harmondsworth: Penguin) 349–362

Trist, E. L. and Bamforth, K. W. (1951). Some Social and Psychological Consequences of the Longwall Method of Coal Getting, *Human Relations* **IV**, (1), 8–38

Trist, E. L., Higgins, G. W., Murray, L. and Pollock, A. R. (1963). *Organisational Choice: Capabilities of Groups at the Coalface under Changing Technologies* (London: Tavistock)

Udy, S. (1965). 'The Comparative Analysis of Organisations' in J. G. March (ed.) *Handbook of Organizations* (Chicago: Rand McNally) 678–709

Vroom, V. H. (ed.) (1967). *Methods of Organizational Research* (Pittsburgh: University of Pittsburgh Press)

Walton, R. E. and Warwick, D. P. (1973). The Ethics of Organisational Development, *Journal of Applied Behavioural Science* **9**, (6), 681–698

Warmington, W. A. (1974). Design, Control, Behaviour and Performance, *Personnel Review* **3**, (1)

Warmington, W. A. (1975). 'Stress in the Management of Change' in D. Gowler and K. Legge (eds.), *Managerial Stress* (London: Gower) 133–150

Weisbord, M. R. (1974). The Gap Between OD Practice and Theory—and Publication, *Journal Applied Behavioural Science* **10**, (4), 476–484

Woodward, J. (1958). *Management and Technology* (London: HMSO)

Woodward, J. (1965). *Industrial Organisation: Theory and Practice* (London: Oxford University Press)

Woodward, J. (ed.) (1970) *Industrial Organisation: Behaviour and Control* (London: Oxford University Press)

Yuchtman, E. and Seashore, S. E. (1967). A Systems Resource Approach to Organisational Effectiveness, *American Sociological Review* **52**, (6), 891–903

Zald, M. N. (ed.) (1970). *Power in Organisations* (Vanderbilt University)

Index